AF606038

Approaches to Teaching Faulkner's *As I Lay Dying*

Approaches to Teaching World Literature

For a complete listing of titles,
see the last pages of this book.

Approaches to Teaching Faulkner's *As I Lay Dying*

Edited by

Patrick O'Donnell

and

Lynda Zwinger

The Modern Language Association of America
New York 2011

Library of Congress Cataloging-in-Publication Data

Approaches to teaching Faulkner's As I lay dying /
edited by Patrick O'Donnell and Lynda Zwinger.
p. cm. — (Approaches to teaching world literature, ISSN 1059-1133 ; 115)
Includes bibliographical references and index.
ISBN 978-1-60329-084-5 (cloth : alk. paper) —
ISBN 978-1-60329-085-2 (pbk. : alk. paper)
1. Faulkner, William, 1897–1962. As I lay dying.
2. Faulkner, William, 1897–1962—Study and teaching.
I. O'Donnell, Patrick, 1948– II. Zwinger, Lynda Marie.
PS3511.A86A8625 2011
813'.52—dc22 2011001924

Approaches to Teaching World Literature 115
ISSN 1059-1133

Cover illustration of the paperback edition: *Washstand in the Dog Run and Kitchen of Floyd Burroughs' Cabin, Hale County, Alabama*. Photograph by Walker Evans, 1935 or 1936. Farm Security Administration, Office of War Information Photograph Collection

Published by The Modern Language Association of America
26 Broadway, New York, New York 10004-1789
www.mla.org

CONTENTS

PREFACE

As I Lay Dying, William Faulkner's fifth published novel, is often considered both his most accessible and most enigmatic major work. Perennially taught in high school literature and AP English courses, college courses in twentieth-century American literature, and graduate courses in modernism, *As I Lay Dying* offers the intertwined themes of family, community, death and mourning, the role of the mother, work, and the relation between nature and culture. It also offers opportunities to explore the presence of voice in narrative; the interrelation of the comic and the tragic; the mode of Southern Gothic; how the historical materiality of post–World War I economics affected the dynamics of work and family in the rural South; and how memory is preserved and altered through the rituals of journey, burial, and the return home. The novel inspires numerous approaches to the reading and teaching of its "simple" story, which relates the Bundren family's quest to bury Addie, the matriarch. Even on a literal level, it is an ideal candidate for a volume devoted to approaches to teaching, for Addie was a teacher, and her narrative, related from the grave in the crucial single section devoted to her roughly halfway through the novel, compellingly describes the web of connections between her pupils and her children, maternal authority and educative conduct, family politics and pedagogy.

Faulkner famously claimed that he wrote *As I Lay Dying* in six weeks while working as a guard at the University of Mississippi's power plant. He was exaggerating only a little: as stated in the editor's note in the "Corrected Text" edition of the novel (the edition used for this volume), "the dates on the manuscript indicate that [Faulkner completed] the holograph version in about eight weeks, between October 25 and December 29, 1929" (264). To use a phrase of one of Faulkner's most highly regarded biographers, Jay Parini, the compressed time frame of the novel's writing is one indication of Faulkner's "maniacal intensity" during this phase of his career (142). Within a period of four years, from 1929 to 1932, Faulkner published *Sartoris* (1929), *The Sound and the Fury* (1929), *As I Lay Dying* (1930), *Sanctuary* (1931), and *Light in August* (1932). In 1936 he published *Absalom, Absalom!*, considered by many to be his masterwork. Collectively, these novels establish the world of Yoknapatawpha, the fictional county Faulkner created that was home to dozens of characters and stories. It is a landscape like that of Lafayette County and Oxford, Mississippi, where Faulkner spent most of his life. The imaginary county of Yoknapatawpha and the city of Jefferson exist in such a way as to permit exploration of the multiple connections among the hard conditions, racial and sexual binaries, historical repressions, genealogical complexities, and mythological ascents to which one has access in the layered and evocative language of Faulkner's novels.

In *As I Lay Dying*, Faulkner added to this rapidly evolving authorial realm the narrative of the Bundrens, a family of poor farmers on its way to bury Addie in Jefferson, according to the terms of her will. It is the story of a cortege beset by natural disaster and human madness, and each member of the small, nomadic, not quite self-contained unit acts out his or her frustrations and desires and, in effect, constructs an identity that emerges only in relation to the death of the mother. Told in fifty-nine chapters and through the voices of fifteen dramatis personae, *As I Lay Dying* is a remarkable tour de force that negotiates numerous questions central to Faulkner's work as a whole: What is the self in relation to work, family, and class and how is it constellated with other selves? Who parents desire, and how is it born? What is the relation between the land and the people who inhabit it? How does language articulate identity, and where does language fall short of doing so? These questions are posed through the specific language and deeply contextualized settings of Faulkner's novels—in the case of *As I Lay Dying*, through the interactions of idiosyncratic characters whose lives, at least in part, depend on witnessing and completing Addie's proper burial.

The journey depicted in *As I Lay Dying* is a quest involving manifold intentions and agendas; much of the novel's enigmatic character as well as its attractiveness to both teachers and readers is its capacity for multiple interpretations that represent and encourage the reader's intentional participation in the Bundrens' odyssey. The range of interpretation is represented by the array of approaches included in this volume, introduced at the beginning of part 2. Yet the multiple interpretations that the novel enables are accompanied by its meticulous delineation of the historical and socioeconomic contexts of the world the Bundrens inhabit. One might consider the technique of the novel as a kind of mythological realism: the Bundrens are exposed to events rendered in biblical proportions—fire, flood, the rituals of burial—at the same time that they traverse a specific landscape clearly located in the poor, rural South of the early twentieth century. They are white farmers eking out an existence on a small plot of mediocre land. Though there is some variation in opinion over the matter (Donald M. Kartiganer and John T. Matthews in this volume view Anse as a landowner, while Deborah Clarke makes a case for Anse as a tenant farmer), many readers of the novel agree that the Bundrens own the land they farm; they are poor by today's standards, but they have the wherewithal to survive and more. As Kartiganer points out:

> [C]learly by Faulkner's design, Anse owns his own farm (putting him in a category of thirty percent of the farm population of 1930 Mississippi), as does his neighbor Tull. . . . Consequently, there is no reference in the novel to the harsh circumstances of tenant farming that Faulkner vividly describes in "Barn Burning" and *The Hamlet*. In short, concerning the Bundrens' financial standing, there is a complexity equal to what we find in the relation between the Bundrens' alleged purpose in undertaking the journey and their ulterior motives.

Part of this complexity is revealed in the individual agendas of the family members participating in the funereal journey that will take them to the county seat. Cash wants a phonograph player, Anse wants new false teeth, Vardaman looks forward to the toy he has been promised, Dewey Dell seeks an abortion. Collectively, the Bundrens have bourgeois aspirations—and the means to fulfill their modest consumerist desires. At the same time, they are portrayed as part of the amorphous group of poor rural whites that includes struggling landowners, tenant farmers, sharecroppers, merchants barely surviving on the local trade, and itinerants.

What this assemblage does not include are African Americans and Native Americans—two groups that receive considerable attention elsewhere in Faulkner's fiction, especially in the other Yoknapatawpha novels. There the indigenous population of his articulated county and those originally forcibly transported as slaves play key roles—sometimes *the* key roles—in the dramatization of the sociohistorical order. Save for one minor scene, remarkable for its knee-jerk racism (and revealingly explicated by Cheryl Lester and Cedric Gael Bryant in their essays in this volume), race and racialized figures are largely absent from the novel. Part of the explanation is that, perhaps more than any other novel by Faulkner, *As I Lay Dying* is focused on a small group of figures—the immediate members of the Bundren family, a few neighbors, and people the family encounters on the road to Jefferson. Limited in time and space, the novel takes place over a matter of days—unlike *Absalom, Absalom!*, for example, which recounts the story of the Sutpens over four generations, or *The Sound and the Fury*, in which the growth and maturation of the Compson children are portrayed through flashbacks and memories. In telling these other stories and histories, Faulkner depicts the complex, tragic interactions between whites and blacks that are at the core of the past in the South.

Presenting a singular sequence of events compressed in time, *As I Lay Dying* is the most dramatic of all of Faulkner's novels. (It has been adapted for the stage by Frank Galati of the Steppenwolf Theatre in Chicago, and, as the adaptation suggests, it bears useful comparison with a one-act play—a chorus of voices interweaving during the slow journey to Jefferson.) The Bundrens' interactions with the world around them are so turned inward psychologically that their world—unlike the larger, complex, racialized social order that Faulkner's fiction so often portrays—consists almost entirely of their struggles to endure and their dreams of satisfying fundamental desires.

Yet one might view Faulkner's portrayal of this self-involved existence (but what form of life clawing for bare survival is not self-involved?) as a commentary on race relations. The Bundrens do not, and cannot, see those with whom they share far more of a historical plight than they do with the white aristocracy of Yoknapatawpha. Ironically, in the hierarchies of Faulkner's fictional landscape, poor whites who do see and encounter blacks consider them rivals for scarce resources, inferiors to them on the social ladder (in the same way they are inferior to rich landowners), or, as in the aforementioned scene, figures to be disdained. Limited by the blinders of Addie's will, the Bundrens see only what is in their immediate field of vision. What lies outside their scope is, in many respects, most of the social world that Faulkner depicts in his other major works.

Certainly, one of Faulkner's chief concerns throughout his fiction is the role of women in the striated society of the South as it evolves from a plantation culture into industrial modernity. Caddy in *The Sound and the Fury*, Temple Drake in *Sanctuary*, Rosa Coldfield in *Absalom, Absalom!*, Eula Varner in *The Hamlet*, Lena Grove in *Light in August*—all are complex characters negotiating gender roles in a world still largely bound over to patriarchy. Addie Bundren may be the one most torn by contradiction. She is only a voice speaking from the grave, in a monologue that takes up but a single chapter in the novel, yet she is the magnetic north of the family's journey, the obsessive subject of concern in the other fifty-eight chapters that memorialize her life.

Mother, wife, teacher, adulteress: Addie exists in a genealogy of American female protagonists, from Nathaniel Hawthorne's Hester Prynne (with whom she is often compared) to Toni Morrison's Sethe, who together symbolize marginalization within patriarchal culture and a vital, if dangerous, rejection of it. Just as Addie in life gave purpose and direction to her progeny—even if, in the case of Darl, as a form of negation—so in death she is the catalyst for a journey through which her husband and children redefine themselves. It is her iron yet self-sacrificial will, bearing mortal consequences, that acquires so much power that it directs life from the place of death.

Several of the essays in this volume speak to the complexities of Addie's character as both central and transgressive, as both inside and outside the novel's social world. It is interesting that Faulkner places this most potent of his female characters beyond the pale—not unlike the position of Rosa Coldfield in *Absalom, Absalom!* as a critical participant in and witness to the Sutpen history, whose presence is transmitted in a conversation with Quentin Compson shortly before she dies. As the novel's title suggests, Addie, on the border between life and death, her continuance a matter of simultaneously living and dying, gains the authority and capacity to critique a social order that would constrict and condemn her to be merely mother or wife or adulteress by virtue of her centrality as a subject who exists no more.

Like many of Faulkner's novels, *As I Lay Dying* marries his concern over social issues and his avant-garde experiments with narrative form. Indeed, what makes *As I Lay Dying* one of his most-taught works is its capacity to yield important insights about the relation between literary expression and social concern, whether the subject is the plight of poor farmers in the postagrarian South, the status of women in families on the verge of disintegration, or the effects of commodification on the formation of human identity. The multiple narrators of *The Sound and the Fury* (including Benjy's "tale of an idiot"), the palimpsestic collage of *Absalom, Absalom!*, the recapitulation of memory as stream-of-consciousness in *Light in August*, and the assemblage of voices that constitutes

As I Lay Dying represent some of Faulkner's boldest attempts to tell the story of the interaction between identity and history from the inside, through processes of interiority rather than recollection of event. In *As I Lay Dying* Faulkner uses fifteen distinct voices to generate a form of intersubjectivity that shows how social interaction is composed of delimited individual perspectives. Each voice is idiosyncratic yet mirrors the world taking shape as the novel progresses; collectively, the voices constitute not a chorus so much as a heteroglossiac assemblage in which the formation and deformation of various communities—those of family, class, and region—are main thematic concerns. By bringing together experiments with voice and an interest in the impact of modernization on the economy, class struggles, and gender roles in the South, Faulkner manifests the importance of the modernist experiment with narrative form and strategy in showing the degree to which the literary and the social are inseparable.

The fourteen essays in this volume examine *As I Lay Dying* from many perspectives. The result is a community of interpretation; in each case, interpretation—perspective—is a means of creatively discussing how this most teachable of Faulkner's novels can be brought to students in ways that change and enlarge their ways of seeing and reading. The essays are presented in part 2; in part 1 we highlight materials from the vast amount of resources available on Faulkner's work that are informative for the reading and teaching of *As I Lay Dying*. Our goal throughout is to bring the hermeneutic and the pedagogical into close contact in ways that encourage and inspire the teaching of the novel.

PO and LZ

Part One

MATERIALS

Publication History and Editions

The edition of *As I Lay Dying* used for this volume is the "Corrected Text," as established by the renowned Faulkner scholar and editor Noel Polk in 1985. It is published in hardcover by the Library of America under the title *Novels, 1930–35* and in paperback by Vintage Books, a division of Random House. Using Faulkner's typescript setting copy and comparing it with the holograph manuscript and carbon typescript of the novel, Polk produced the "Corrected Text" edition; he emended the text "to account for [Faulkner's] revisions in proof, his indisputable typing errors, and certain other mistakes and inconsistencies that clearly demand correction" (263). *As I Lay Dying* was originally published in 1930 by Harrison Smith and Jonathan Cape. The text remained essentially the same until 1964, when Random House published the first corrected edition based on the original manuscript and typescript. The 1985 "Corrected Text" effectively replaced the 1964 edition and is currently the most widely available authoritative edition of the novel.

Biographical Materials

The most comprehensive and detailed discussion of Faulkner's life is Joseph Blotner's two-volume *Faulkner: A Biography*, which was published in 1974; ten years later Blotner published a revised, one-volume edition. He meticulously records myriad details about Faulkner's life and work, and while his biography tends to gloss over some of the more controversial aspects of Faulkner's life, it remains the best informational resource on the subject. David Minter's *William Faulkner: His Life and Work* is a rich assessment of the relation between Faulkner's life and his art; Minter compellingly portrays the evolution of artistic consciousness in the life of a writer torn between a desire for privacy—even, at times, anonymity—and a competing need for public recognition. Richard J. Gray's *The Life of William Faulkner: A Critical Biography* emphasizes the social and cultural contexts that surrounded Faulkner's development as a writer. Judith Bryant Wittenberg's *Faulkner: The Transfiguration of Biography* explores the relation between theme and place in Faulkner's life and writing, while Gary Lee Stonum's *Faulkner's Career: An Internal Literary History* focuses on Faulkner's self-conscious development as a writer whose progression across a career reveals both patterns and inconsistencies in his thought. Jay Parini's *One Matchless Time: A Life of William Faulkner* offers a view of Faulkner's life by a contemporary poet, novelist, editor, and biographer that is admirably attentive to matters of artistic temperament, the intricacies of family relations, and the complexity of Faulkner's vision. Most recently, in *Becoming Faulkner: The Art and Life of William Faulkner*, Philip Weinstein evocatively traces the evolution of Faulkner's interiority and authorial identity as narratives that emerge alongside his novels. For Weinstein, "Faulkner" is a fictional construct that navigates the complex relation between the facticity of life and the strategies of art.

There are numerous memoirs about Faulkner that provide personal accounts of his struggles as a writer. John Faulkner's *My Brother Bill: An Affectionate Reminiscence* portrays from the perspective of his third-youngest brother the local characters, friends, and family with whom Faulkner grew up. *The Falkners of Mississippi: A Memoir*, by Murry C. Falkner, William's second-oldest brother, is an intimate family history that uses the original spelling of the family name—to which the novelist added the "u," perhaps as a way of distinguishing himself from his ancestors. Faulkner's beloved first-born nephew, Jim Faulkner, published family anecdotes in *Across the Creek: Faulkner Family Stories*. In *Count No 'Count: Flashbacks to Faulkner*, Ben Wasson, Faulkner's fellow student at the University of Mississippi and his first literary agent, offers a complex portrait of the young Faulkner as, at once, ambitious and lazy, gentlemanly and drunk (the Count No 'Count of the title refers to the sobriquet conferred on Faulkner by locals for his aristocratic behavior and dress). In 1932 Faulkner began working in Hollywood as a scriptwriter, and he continued to write scripts over the next fifteen years; in 1935 he commenced an affair with the director Howard Hawks's script assistant, Meta Carpenter. Carpenter Wilde's memoir of their relationship is recounted in *A Loving Gentleman: The Love Story of William Faulkner and Meta Carpenter*. Finally, Susan Snell's *Phil Stone of Oxford: A Vicarious Life* provides a biographical account of Faulkner's best friend and lifelong adviser, who nurtured the young novelist's literary ambitions and took on the complex role of mentor, brother in arms, and rival.

Textual Aids and Resources

A useful, if only partially developed, resource for the study of William Faulkner's fiction is the Web site *William Faulkner on the Web*, created by John B. Padgett and hosted by the University of Mississippi. The site contains an abundance of information, including biographical, bibliographical, and critical resources; maps of the city of Oxford and Lafayette County depicting sites relevant to Faulkner's life and work; information about Faulkner's screenplays and film adaptations of Faulkner's fiction; genealogical charts of the families that inhabit Yoknapatawpha County; and a character glossary and time line.

Numerous useful handbooks and guides to Faulkner's fiction have been published over the years, including Margaret Patricia Ford and Suzanne Kincaid's *Who's Who in Faulkner*; Michel Gresset's *A Faulkner Chronology*; and the most comprehensive resource available, *A William Faulkner Encyclopedia*, edited by Robert W. Hamblin and Charles A. Peek. The *Faulkner Journal*, which began publication in 1985, provides some of the best recent critical, historical, and biographical work on Faulkner. Another Web site is the *Teaching Faulkner* newsletter, published by the Center for Faulkner Studies at Southeast Missouri State University. The University of Mississippi Press publishes lectures from the annual Faulkner and Yoknapatawpha Conference held in Oxford, Mississippi, in July; each volume is devoted to the theme of that year's conference. Garland Press publishes a series of interlinear annotations to all of Faulkner's major novels, including Dianne C. Luce's *As I Lay Dying*. Jack L. Capps's As I Lay Dying*: A Concordance to the Novel* is available from University Microfilms. Major resources for the study of William Faulkner exist in the archives and special collections department of the University of Mississippi libraries; the William Faulkner Collection at the University of Virginia; the Harry Ransom Humanities Research Center at the University of Texas, Austin; and the Brodsky Collection at the Kent Library of Southeast Missouri State University.

Cultural and Aesthetic Contexts

Perhaps the most valuable resource for the study of Faulkner in the context of the region he explored in dozens of novels and hundreds of stories is the massive *Encyclopedia of Southern Culture*, edited by Charles Reagan Wilson and William Ferris. Joel Williamson's *William Faulkner and Southern History* is a comprehensive discussion of Faulkner's life and work in relation to the tortured history of the American South. Two books by Richard Godden, *Fictions of Labor: William Faulkner and the South's Long Revolution* and *William Faulkner: An Economy of Complex Words*, discuss the historical, political, social, and economic contexts that inform Faulkner's fiction. Godden builds on earlier work by Irving Howe, whose *William Faulkner: A Critical Study* was one of the earliest full-length assessments of Faulkner's fiction and is still one of the most important, as well as Myra Jehlen's *Class and Character in Faulkner's South* and *The Achievement of William Faulkner* by Michael Millgate. *Faulkner in Cultural Context*, edited by Donald M. Kartiganer and Ann J. Abadie, is an important collection of essays from the Faulkner and Yoknapatawpha Conference that address Faulkner's writing and the rapidly changing culture of the South. More broadly, *Look Away! The U.S. South in New World Studies*, edited by Jon Smith and Deborah Cohn, provides vibrant discussions for understanding the writing of the American South—including Faulkner's fiction—within a global context.

Richard C. Moreland's *Faulkner and Modernism: Rereading and Rewriting* discusses Faulkner's work within the aesthetic, cultural, and historic contexts of modernism. One of the more controversial discussions of Faulkner's career as related to modernist sensibilities is Lawrence H. Schwartz's *Creating Faulkner's Reputation: The Politics of Modern Literary Criticism.* Schwartz argues that Faulkner's rapidly growing visibility as the predominant modern American novelist from the mid-1940s—a process reified by Malcolm Cowley's assemblage of Faulkner's work in *The Portable Faulkner* (1946)—was, in part, the product of cold war politics and the need for a postwar American mythographer who expressed in his work the liberal consensus. Karl F. Zender's *The Crossing of the Ways: William Faulkner, the South, and the Modern World* examines Faulkner in the light of larger modernist and postmodernist concerns with voice, the banality of evil, human freedom, and the social imaginary. Michel Gresset's *Fascination: Faulkner's Fiction, 1919–1936*, adapted from the French by Thomas West, considers Faulkner's absorption with the gaze as informed by the contexts of Sartrean existentialism and the symbolist movement. Daniel Joseph Singal's *William Faulkner: The Making of a Modernist* discusses the "conflict of cultures" in Faulkner's writing and reveals him to be a transitional figure negotiating Victorian and modern sensibilities. In *Seeing and Being: The Plight of the Participant Observer in Emerson, James, Adams, and Faulkner*, Carolyn Porter considers Faulkner within the American philosophical tradition that weaves together history, the social order, and epistemology. In *Reading Faulkner*, by Wesley Morris and Barbara Alverson Morris, Faulkner's complex love-hate relation with the South is explored; the authors argue that his novels perform a political and social critique of the region and conservative forms of modernity. In *Natural Aristocracy: History, Ideology and the Production of William Faulkner*, Kevin Railey discusses Faulkner in relation to the ideologies of southern aristocratic culture as they have emerged since Thomas Jefferson and suggests that as much as Faulkner represents these ideologies in his fiction, he is also a product of them. One of the volumes from the Faulkner and Yoknapatawpha Conference series, *Faulkner and Postmodernism*, edited by John N. Duvall and Ann J. Abadie, offers eleven essays that place Faulkner within the aesthetic, cultural, and political contexts of postmodernism. Finally, one of the most significant assessments of Faulkner within intertwined cultural and aesthetic contexts is *Faulkner, Mississippi*, by the Martinique novelist and postcolonial theorist Édouard Glissant. The book evocatively initiates a conversation on matters of race, nation, aesthetics, and writing between two writers with strong ties to time and place.

Critical Works

The critical books and essays that have been written about Faulkner would fill several library shelves; add to this the thousands of articles, essays, book chapters, and notes on him, and the space required would expand to a large room. Here we can indicate only some of the major developments and significant works of Faulkner criticism. All the works cited contain substantive, focused discussions of *As I Lay Dying* or more general discussions that significantly illuminate the novel.

A good starting point is *The Cambridge Companion to William Faulkner*, edited by Philip M. Weinstein, which contains nine essays about Faulkner's relation to modernism and postmodernism, Faulkner as a colonial and postcolonial subject, Faulkner and race, Faulkner and the culture industry, and reading Faulkner from a European perspective. Classic general critical assessments of Faulkner include Cleanth Brooks's *The Yoknapatawpha Country*, which charts Faulkner's world from a New Critical perspective, and Olga Vickery's *The Novels of William Faulkner: A Critical Interpretation*, written from a primarily formalist perspective. Donald M. Kartiganer's *The Fragile Thread: The Meaning of Form in Faulkner's Novels* uses more up-to-date critical methodologies to challenge notions of form and its relation to meaning in Faulkner's fiction. Like Brooks, other critics have attempted to understand Faulkner in terms of the imaginative cosmos he created and over which he famously claimed himself to be "sole owner and proprietor." At opposite ends of the arc are Elizabeth M. Kerr's *Yoknapatawpha: Faulkner's "Little Postage Stamp of Native Soil,"* which argues for a labyrinthine but totalistic view of Faulkner's world, and Philip M. Weinstein's *Faulkner's Subject: A Cosmos No One Owns*, which compellingly suggests that Faulkner's cosmos and the identities that inhabit it are partial and deeply intersubjective. The mythological aspects of Faulkner's fiction were discussed early on by Walter Brylowski in his *Faulkner's Olympian Laugh: Myth in the Novels* and by Richard P. Adams in *Faulkner: Myth and Motion*.

Faulkner's style and narrative poetics—experimental at every stage of his writing—have been the subject of much critical commentary, including Panthea Reid Broughton's *William Faulkner: The Abstract and the Actual*, Arthur F. Kinney's *Faulkner's Narrative Poetics: Style as Vision*, and Robert Dale Parker's *Faulkner and the Novelistic Imagination*. Stephen M. Ross's *Faulkner's Inexhaustible Voice: Speech and Writing in Faulkner* offers a discussion of Faulkner's narrative that focuses on Bakhtinian and Derridean conceptualizations of voice and the relation between speech and writing. A critical turning point in Faulkner studies was achieved with the publication in 1982 of *The Play of Faulkner's Language* by John T. Matthews, whose discussion of Faulkner's novels is informed by poststructuralist theories of language that show the degree to which Faulkner's writing combines the work of language and the imaginative rendering of an inexhaustibly complex reality.

Another landmark study in Faulkner criticism is John T. Irwin's *Doubling and Incest / Repetition and Revenge: A Speculative Reading of Faulkner*, which engages in its own form of critical experimentalism in offering a psychoanalytic reading of Faulkner's fiction—in particular, the formal patterns of repetition and family relationships. A number of psychoanalytic and psychological approaches to Faulkner are gathered in *Faulkner and Psychology*, edited by Donald M. Kartiganer and Ann J. Abadie, one of the Faulkner and Yoknapatawpha Conference series. Doreen Fowler's *Faulkner: The Return of the Repressed* provides a Lancanian reading of Faulkner's novels. In *The Ink of Melancholy: Faulkner's Novels from* The Sound and the Fury *to* Light in August, André Bleikasten discusses the major novels from interwoven psychoanalytic, mythic, and linguistic perspectives. Some important feminist readings of Faulkner's novels make use of psychoanalytic approaches as well, including Gail L. Mortimer's *Faulkner's Rhetoric of Loss: A Study in Perception and Meaning*, Minrose C. Gwin's *The Feminine and Faulkner: Reading (beyond) Sexual Difference*, and Deborah Clarke's *Robbing the Mother: Women in Faulkner*. Diane Roberts's *Faulkner and Southern Womanhood* discusses the central issue of gender in Faulkner in the light of Bakhtinian narrative poetics, and John N. Duvall's *Faulkner's Marginal Couple: Invisible, Outlaw, and Unspeakable Communities* focuses on Faulkner's representations of patriarchal ideology in his novels.

Race and class are key issues—perhaps the key issues—in many of Faulkner's novels. Many of the critical studies already mentioned include discussions of race and class, which are, for readers like Eric Sundquist in *Faulkner: The House Divided*, inseparable. Sundquist's study focuses on the racial politics of miscegenation to understand the complex relationships between blacks and whites in the social hierarchies of the South portrayed in Faulkner's novels. One of the most important books on race in Faulkner is Thadious M. Davis's *Faulkner's "Negro": Art and the Southern Context*, which discusses the symbolic and thematic implications of African American identity in the novels. In *Figures of Division: William Faulkner's Major Novels*, James A. Snead explores the racial polarities of Faulkner's fiction. *Faulkner and Race*, edited by Doreen Fowler and Ann J. Abadie, is a collection of fifteen essays emerging from the Faulkner and Yoknapatawpha Conference. In *Nationalism and the Color Line in George W. Cable, Mark Twain, and William Faulkner*, Barbara Ladd deploys a new historicist reading of Faulkner's approach to race and formations of nation in comparison with Twain and Cable. In *What Else but Love? The Ordeal of Race in Faulkner and Morrison*, Philip M. Weinstein compares representations and figurations of race in two authors who are often juxtaposed and who stand, as Nobel laureates (one a high modernist white male writer, the other a postmodernist black female writer), in complex relation to each other. Similarly, *Unflinching Gaze: Morrison and Faulkner Re-envisioned*, edited by Carol A. Kolmerten, Stephen Ross, and Judith Bryant Wittenberg, offers essays that consider the intricate intertextual, historical, and cultural relations between the two writers. In *Producing American Races: Henry James, William Faulkner, Toni Morrison*, Patricia McKee uses Toni Morrison's formulation in *Playing in the Dark*—that white identity depends utterly on the construction of the other in black identity—to discuss race as a discursive formation in James, Faulkner, and Morrison. In *Faulkner on the Color Line: The Later Novels*, Theresa M. Towner moves from Faulkner's major phase to the late novels (which are often given scant attention in the critical literature) to show how Faulkner pursued representations of race and identity across his career.

Warwick Wadlington provides a book-length study of *As I Lay Dying* in As I Lay Dying*: Stories out of Stories*. Wadlington, also the author of *Reading Faulknerian Tragedy*, an excellent historical and critical discussion of the genre of tragedy in Faulkner, provides a summary of the novel's impact and critical reception and considers the novel in the light of economics, family history, and the capacities and limits of representation. In *Recalcitrance, Faulkner, and the Professors: A Critical Fiction*, Austin M. Wright uses *As I Lay Dying* as the central work in a fictionalized palimpsest about contemporary issues surrounding the study of literature, pedagogy, readers, and the academy. Wright's is a provocative, creative, idiosyncratic circumlocution around Faulkner's novel.

Maps and Genealogies

Faulkner attempted to construct a fictional landscape that bore a holographic relation to real topographies, as is evident in the several maps of Yoknapatawpha County he drew during his life, including the map that served as the frontispiece for *Absalom, Absalom!* in 1936. He redrew the map ten years later for *The Portable Faulkner*, edited by Malcolm Cowley. In the 1936 map, Faulkner marked the location of the Bundrens' farm; the Yoknapatawpha River, which the Bundrens cross in flood stage to get to town; Tull's and Armstid's homesteads; and the cemetery in Jefferson where Addie's body is taken to be buried. Interestingly, only the river appears in the more compact 1946 map. *Yoknapatawpha: The Function of Geographical and Historical Facts in William Faulkner's Fictional Picture of the Deep South*, by Gabriele Gutting, provides a meticulous, comprehensive discussion of the relation between Faulkner's maps and his fiction.

The tangled genealogies of the Yoknapatawpha novels have been considered for their illumination of a host of critical issues, from incest to class structure to patriarchy. The genealogies of Faulkner's fictional families first provided in Brooks's *The Yoknapatawpha Country* have often been referred to and revised by later critics. Readers of Faulkner are advised to consider the maps and genealogies as rough guides to his novels.

As I Lay Dying as Play and Opera

The fifteen voices Faulkner dramatizes in *As I Lay Dying* lend themselves to playscript and libretto, so it is no surprise that the novel has been adapted accordingly. In April 1995, the Steppenwolf Theatre in Chicago staged an adaptation of *As I Lay Dying* that was written and directed by Frank Galati. The play was performed on the main stage, which was sparely furnished with impressionistic, two-dimensional sets; the actors were positioned across the stage in such a way as to emphasize the delivery of monologues. A second dramatic adaptation of the novel, *In a Strange Room*, titled after Darl's speech in which he gives voice to his alienation, was adapted and directed by Michael Gardner. It was staged in 2004 at the Brick Theater in New York City. In 2002 *As I Lay Dying* was adapted as a folk opera by Recon Crew, a group of four Nashville musicians commissioned by Opera Memphis to create song cycles of both *As I Lay Dying* and *Light in August* using voice, guitar, mandolin, and harmonica.

Part Two

APPROACHES

Introduction

The journey depicted in *As I Lay Dying* is a quest that involves manifold intentions and agendas. Part of the novel's enigmatic character and its attraction for teachers and readers is its capacity for multiple interpretations, which encourages the reader's intentional participation in the Bundrens' odyssey. The essays in this volume represent a wide range of interpretations, from the historical to the figural, from the symbolic to the social. We have grouped the essays into four areas: contextual approaches to teaching the novel, the novel's engagement with modernism, thematic and theoretical approaches to teaching the novel, and comparative and intertextual approaches to teaching the novel.

The first of the essays that examine the historical, literary, and cultural contexts of *As I Lay Dying* is Barbara Ladd's assessment of Addie's gender identity in the framework of modern social history. For Ladd, the novel offers a means to teach the importance of cultural and historical constructions of gender. Cheryl Lester then discusses how the novel can be taught as providing insights into the contemporary reader's act of contextualizing per se—that is, reading the novel in the present in the light of the past and the novel's representation of the past in the light of the reader's (and the nation's) present. Finally, Sean McCann shows how viewing the novel in the context of social and cultural practices can enrich the understanding of its conflicting perspectives on sex, exchange, and belief.

The second section comprises essays that approach the teaching of the novel as a modernist narrative. E. L. McCallum explores the manifestations of temporality in the novel, through the use of montage, which is usually considered a cinematic technique but here is viewed as deploying specific narrative strategies. Homer B. Pettey discusses how the novel can be taught from an interdisciplinary perspective applicable to courses in general education; specifically, he considers how narrative nonlinearity is revealed by placing the novel alongside works of postimpressionist art and how bringing visual and written discourses into contact allows students to more fully understand modernist aesthetics. Heide Ziegler describes how *As I Lay Dying*'s modernism and its engagement of the modern reader's memory are informed by its classical intertexts. She views the work of the reader as an act of remembering the textual past in the process of navigating the novel's contemporaneity.

The third section offers a series of thematic and theoretical approaches to the teaching of the novel. Focusing on the voice and character of Vardaman, Michael Zeitlin examines how Faulkner portrays human interiority through the mind and voice of a child. In illustrating the relations among gender, discourse, and power in Addie's speech, Anna Wannamaker considers the role of language in *As I Lay Dying* and shows how the novel can be used as an essential work in advanced literature, gender studies, and critical theory courses. Lisa Perdigao discusses the representation of the human body in the novel and how bodies—especially Addie's corpse—serve as metaphors for the text. She elaborates on the novel's "pedagogy of the body" as it illuminates modernist and postmodernist conceptions of corporeal materiality in American literary traditions. Deborah Clarke enumerates economic themes and discusses how the novel can be taught as a reflection on rural poverty. In focusing on various "economics"—monetary, sexual, agricultural—Clarke considers material realities, especially as they are reflected in the portrayals of the novel's female characters. Donald M. Kartiganer discusses the intense, complex family dynamics in *As I Lay Dying*. Key to his approach is an understanding of the extent to which the individuality of Faulkner's highly idiosyncratic characters emerges only in relation to the others of family or community.

The final section of essays addresses the teaching of the novel in comparative and intertextual terms. John T. Matthews offers a comprehensive assessment of *As I Lay Dying* in the context of recent postcolonial criticism, and he suggests ways the novel can be read and taught in the light of modernist social and cultural shifts that approach the postcolonial condition. Cedric Gael Bryant considers *As I Lay Dying* together with Suzan-Lori Parks's *Getting Mother's Body*, tracking an intertextual dynamic that illuminates Faulkner's concern with narrative structure and textual performance. Finally, Mark Frisch discusses how the novel—when taught alongside works of other modernists such as Albert Camus, Franz Kafka, T. S. Eliot, and Juan Rulfo—illuminates transatlantic and cross-hemispheric existential themes that are negotiated differently in varying cultural contexts.

We encourage readers of this volume to discover currents that run through it. To mention but a few: Ziegler's interest in the novel's classical intertexts is similar to concerns of Bryant, who examines the significant samenesses and differences between Faulkner's novel and that of a contemporary African American playwright and novelist, as well as those of Frisch, who discusses the modern intertexts of the novel. Essays by Ladd, Lester, Clarke, and Matthews consider the important role that class plays in the novel. From various perspectives, Wannamaker, McCann, Pettey, and McCallum consider the verbal and visual rhetorics of *As I Lay Dying*. And in this book of multiple voices, the figuring of character is paramount, as is revealed in the essays by Kartiganer, Perdigao, and Zeitlin. The reader will find more correspondences in the diversity of perspectives the novel offers that give insights into how it can be read and taught.

Collectively, the essays in this volume reveal that teaching *As I Lay Dying* is both a challenge and an opportunity to develop an engaged understanding of a work that addresses matters of significant concern to contemporary readers. The essays also show the extent to which pedagogy and interpretation are indispensable to the understanding of literature and its rendering of life.

Addie Bundren, Modernity, and Authorship in *As I Lay Dying*

Barbara Ladd

Who Is Addie Bundren?

Ask this question of students and you will hear that she is the wife of Anse, a subsistence farmer in rural Mississippi, and the mother of five children—but not a very good mother. *What happens to her in the story?* She dies, students will say, and she makes her family take her back to Jefferson, her hometown, to be buried. *Why?* Because she hates her family. A few will note that she is an adulterer who bore a child to the Reverend Whitfield. Many observe that she was once a schoolteacher who liked to whip the children. Although they learn that she is outraged by the shape of her life, they find her most clearly stated reasons for "taking" (170, 171) Anse cold (that he owns a farm and is not in debt), and they find it hard to believe that she could not have lived differently—more freely—had she made different choices. Her monologue is largely a mystery. Whereas students are quick to identify Darl as an "artist figure" (they have skimmed *SparkNotes* or another summary), they have not given much thought to Addie's tormented struggle with the words that would define her: *love*, *fear*, *motherhood*. The most important fact about Addie, for most students, is that she is a bad mother.

Assessments of Addie Bundren have seldom been positive. Convention has it that she is a usurper of patriarchal authority; an instance of the essentialized "feminine"; or fundamentally irrelevant, except as a primum mobile for the harrowing journey the Bundrens undertake to bury her.[1] Too often she has been read according to the conventional presumption that motherhood is the substantive identity of women, and her ambivalence about motherhood evokes a recoil among many readers that is more a response to the sentimental construction of motherhood than to its reality—which Adrienne Rich in *Of Woman Born* and a number of other writers have demystified to some degree.[2]

What few have noted is that *As I Lay Dying* explores some of the most profound implications of the social changes associated with modernity, particularly as they pertain to questions of women's individualization.[3] In Addie Bundren, Faulkner gives us a woman caught between traditional ways of life and modern ones, between Victorian ideals of women as icons of domesticity and more modern ideals of women as desiring subjects.

In *As I Lay Dying*, set in the Progressive Era of the 1920s, Addie is dying of unknown causes in her home at the top of a steep bluff in the northern reaches of Yoknapatawpha County. The action of the novel hinges on a promise she has exacted from her husband to bury her in the town of Jefferson with her people. This is an unusual request but not unheard of. Typically, a married couple would be buried side by side, but the wishes of the dying, however unconventional, are usually taken seriously.

Although she is surrounded by her husband, her children, and her neighbors, Addie Bundren is, in many ways, as much a stranger in this community as she is the familiar wife of Anse Bundren. At the time of her death, she has been married to Anse for thirty years, which puts her in her late forties or early fifties. She had her last child in her forties: Vardaman Bundren is little more than five when Addie dies, "wore . . . out" (41). She is from Jefferson, a town girl in a novel that makes so much of the difference between town and country, a former schoolteacher and an orphan, the last of her family left alive. Her memory of her father is limited to his declaration that "the only reason for living was to get ready to stay dead a long time" (169). Otherwise, there is no mention of Addie's genealogy or early personal history. If her stint as a schoolteacher is typical of her time, she must have been hired when she was in her late teens or early twenties by a community familiar with her, her family, and her needs. The assumption would have been that she would teach for a year or two before marrying. (The overwhelming economic and social imperative of marriage for women of her time and place would have made it hard for her to do anything else.) When Anse comes courting, there is a practical acceptance of necessity by both of them. Anse needs "womenfolk," presumably to give him children to help with the farm and to ensure his patriarchal legacy; Addie is chiefly interested in the fact that Anse has a farm and a house (171). It is a time of relative prosperity for some small farmers, and Anse appeals initially to Addie because of his stability as someone who owns land and is "forehanded" (171). So Addie "takes" Anse Bundren.

Anse is reminiscent of "the forgotten man" described by Walter Hines Page in the preface to *The Rebuilding of Old Commonwealths: Being Essays towards the Training of the Forgotten Man in the Southern States*:

> Old Jeff Meddlin lived in a ramshackle house, ploughed a poor farm, made a cross-mark for his signature, and only twice in his life went out of the county where he was born. He was a man with a strong body and with good sense; but his thought traveled in narrow ways, and dyspepsia wore him out before he grew old. (vii)

Anse's problem with food is toothlessness, not dyspepsia. Maybe he has "good sense" of a sort—he has managed to hold on to his farm and may still be "forehanded." But he and Old Jeff Meddlin are both homebodies—Peabody tells us that Anse has not been to town in twelve years (42). His thought "travel[s] in narrow ways"—mostly in "up-and-down ways"—and he complains about the "long ways" reorientation of the land that follows the coming of the road:

> A-laying there, right up to my door, where every bad luck that comes and goes is bound to find it. I told Addie it want any luck living on a road when it come by here, and she said, for the world like a woman, "Get up and move, then." But I told her it want no luck in it, because the Lord puts roads for travelling: why He laid them down flat on the earth. When he aims for something to be always a-moving, He makes it long ways, like a road or a horse or a wagon, but when He aims for something to stay put, He makes it up-and-down ways, like a tree or a man. (35–36)

The distinction Anse makes between the "up-and-down ways" and the "long ways" points to a central conflict in *As I Lay Dying*: the conflict between a traditional culture concerned with narratives of genealogical descent and the preservation of the private sphere as patriarchal property, on the one hand, and, on the other, modernity, with its intrusions (via roads and taxes) into the private realm and its implications for the lives of women.[4] "She was ever a private woman" (18), Anse says of Addie not long before the trip begins, signaling her sequestering in the domestic sphere. Ironically, Addie will become a very public figure during her journey to her final resting place.[5]

In the early twentieth century, an energetic conversation was under way in the United States about the future of the family—and the nation—in a world in which women were increasingly mobile, educated, and interested in a "life of their own." The fundamental question was whether free women—that is, women free to choose between one kind of life and another—would be good or bad for civilization.[6]

Cultural conservatives called for a return to traditional ways of life. They stressed the centrality of wives and mothers to the family and to the continued moral integrity of the nation. They focused on moral reform and hoped to halt what they perceived as a breakdown of traditional values associated with the increasing autonomy of women. In the words of William A. Link, they hoped "to replenish and revive the traditional order, as they understood it, among parents and children as well as husbands and wives" (112). Typically, their attention centered on men and women in their private lives, and women, long seen as the icons of private life, were singled out to bear the brunt of efforts at moral reform. William Maxwell, an Englishman, opined that "we ordinary men want a woman who is . . . so good that we are never uneasy" (647). By and large, educational practice was to remain devoted to "such facts and notions as would give the girl a conception of herself only as future wife and mother" (Hollingworth 25).

The backlash against the modern woman intensified with the economic fluctuations of the years before the Great Depression and then the Depression itself. Americans sometimes referred approvingly to the return to traditional—that is, premodern—gender roles in Hitler's Germany. (This was early, before the United States had taken the measure of Adolph Hitler or knew widely of the persecution of the Jews.) In the United States, as in Germany, the response was fueled by anxieties about racial purity. Cultural conservatives in the United States were energized by the perceived need to preserve the (white) polity in the face of emigration from eastern and southern Europe, the increased mobility and prosperity of African Americans, the trend toward later marriages, and the declining birthrates among white women in some parts of the country (Link 112).

The most conservative regions in the country were, of course, rural areas. Since the mid-nineteenth century, the mental and emotional health of rural women had been of concern to doctors and others closely involved with women. Benjamin Rush, a physician, observed that the rural life often drove women mad (Barker-Benfield 5–6). In "Lucrezia Burns" Hamlin Garland noted that "the wives of the American farmers fill our insane asylums" (102). D. H. Lawrence described the American rural wife as a "poor haggard drudge, like a ghost wailing in the wilderness" (30). During the Progessive Era, reformers began to call for education and social services for these women. According to Walter Hines Page, any observer not blinded by an aristocratic or religious ideology

> will see [rural women] thin and wrinkled in youth from ill prepared food, clad without warmth or grace, living in untidy houses, working from daylight till bed-time at the dull round of weary duties, the slaves of men of equal slovenliness, the mothers of joyless children—all uneducated if not illiterate. Yet even their condition were endurable if there were any hope, but this type of woman is encrusted in a shell of dull content with her lot; she knows no better and can never learn better, nor point her children to a higher life. If she be intensely religious, her religion is only an additional misfortune, for it teaches her, as she understands it, to be content with her lot and all its burdens, since they prepare her for the life to come. Some *men* who are born under these conditions escape from them; a *man* may go away, go where life offers opportunities, but the women are forever helpless. (24–25)

To some degree, the helplessness of women in rural communities was being meliorated by modern conditions even as Page delivered this speech in 1897 to female students at the State Normal and Industrial School for Women in Greensboro, North Carolina.[7] Increasing rates of female literacy and the growth of industry fostered women's independence and, in the process, undermined male authority, effecting significant changes in the family by the early twentieth century.

Since the earliest days of New World settlement, women had been calling, in their letters and diaries, for companionship, entertainment, some relief from drudgery. The building of roads had a major impact on women's lives in suburban and rural areas. Ease of travel meant they could visit friends or spend an occasional day in town, relieving the boredom of days filled with the repetitive duties of home and farm. By the early twentieth century they found that it was increasingly possible to find work outside the home that would enable them to contribute to the support of the family. Part of what they earned was a kind of respect that went well beyond whatever chivalrous sentiments and gestures they had experienced in earlier generations.[8]

The Bankhead-Shackelford Federal Highways Act provided $75 million between 1916 and 1921 for the building of roads in the South (Tindall 15), and if the road-building project lies behind Anse's famous meditation on the road, quoted earlier, it also lies behind Addie's preoccupation with the "long ways": "I would think," she says (with awe), "how terribly doing goes along the earth . . ." (173).

Addie equates "doing" with childbearing. Like so many women throughout history, she longs to control reproduction. Public discourse was vibrant on questions of contraception in the late nineteenth and early twentieth centuries. The American Medical Association, established in 1847 and one of the most powerful, conservative bodies of professional elites in the nation, had always been strongly opposed to contraception and abortion and had moved to regulate birth control and put an end to abortion. Although "recipes" for contraception and for abortion were circulated before the 1870s, in 1873 the flow of information was reduced, as contraceptive devices and information were classified as obscene under the Comstock Act.[9] (This is the context for Dewey Dell's particular difficulty in *As I Lay Dying*: she is forced to deal with medical professionals who, like the druggist, could not, without jeopardizing their businesses, dispense information about abortion or contraception to their customers.) Sending such materials through the mails was prohibited, and the circulation of advice books and pamphlets treating sexuality and birth control fell significantly between 1880 and 1900. Although Connecticut was the only state to make the practice of birth control illegal, in Mississippi in 1885 it was illegal to *talk* about the subject (Brodie 257).

Just as women were beginning to gain some independence, the "professionalization" and "medicalization" of birthing practices by the American Medical Association and the government sought to reaffirm male authority over women's lives. Women fought back. By 1920, advocates for birth control (sometimes referred to as voluntary motherhood) had become vocal under the strategic leadership of Margaret Sanger, who began, not long after her return to the United States in 1917, to challenge obscenity statutes that prevented the circulation of information about birth control through the mail and through physicians.[10] It required decades of legal challenges to the Comstock laws before information about birth control could circulate freely. In 1921 Sanger established the American Birth Control League. Ten years later the Supreme Court ruled in the Stopes case that conversations about birth control were not necessarily obscene, but it was not until 1937 that the American Medical Association officially sanctioned contraceptive advice as a legitimate aspect of medical practice.[11]

The birth control debate is implicit in Addie's story of the deliberate "giving" of children to Anse and suggests that she may have practiced some traditional or folk method of birth control.[12] It is explicit in the story of Dewey Dell who, as an unmarried girl, has received no instruction from her mother or any other woman in the community about birth control—such instruction would typically have come during engagement or after marriage. But in *As I Lay Dying* the issues that confront Addie and Dewey Dell extend beyond the specific issue of birth control into broader debates about the place of women in the polis. Set not long after women were granted the right to vote, *As I Lay Dying* stages the anxieties, conflicts, and complicated negotiations associated with sexuality and gender in a modernizing world.

Although Addie does seem to be a "ghost wailing in the wilderness" and although she may (on some level like Darl) be mad, she is, in other respects, not at all like the "forgotten" woman that Page describes. If Addie is the traditional farmwife in the work she performs, in the psychic hold her fundamentalist god has on her, and in her isolation, she is hardly awaiting a better life in the afterlife. She is not "encrusted" with anything like "dull content with her lot"; she "knows better." She asserts herself even at the moment of her death by "shoving" at Dr. Peabody with her eyes (45). Addie would be an example of the farmwife of Lawrence, Garland, Rush, and Page were it not for her rage and her very modern doubt; but in that rage and doubt, Faulkner created a viable representative of the farmwife of the Progressive Era.

What Does Addie Want?

Earlier in this essay, motivations for marriage were identified as economic necessity and social expectation. But Faulkner gives Addie desires well beyond the conventional ones. "In the early spring it was worst," she recollects. "Sometimes I thought that I could not bear it, lying in bed at night, with the wild geese going north and their honking coming faint and high and wild out of the wild darkness . . ." (170). The migratory flight of birds as Addie describes it refers to the human desire for escape and freedom and points to what is predetermined, unchanging: the reproductive cycle that ties one to repetition and death. Sexual desire is, as we know, one manifestation of desire more broadly conceived, and the above passage demonstrates that Addie's sexual longing, her restlessness, and her will are intermingled forms of desire. It indicates too that Addie is well aware of the dark inevitabilities of reproduction—the fatality of her sexuality—and is angry at what she perceives to be the schoolchildren's lack of awareness of her, a response that underscores her own resistance to the cultural narrative of maternal self-sacrifice. At the spring where she spends her afternoons after classes are over, she "could be quiet and hate them," "the last one . . . with his little dirty snuffling nose" (169). She would beat them, thinking, "Now you are aware of me! Now I am something in your secret and selfish life, who have marked your blood with my own for ever and ever" (170).

Addie's first pregnancy becomes "the answer" to the terror of living (171). It is a new experience, gratifying in that it violates the separateness she despises (and yet loves) in herself. But with the birth of her second child, she feels betrayed, as if reproduction has become a deadening form of repetition and an erasure of her subjectivity, her "I." Her marriage is revealed to her as meaningless, and she ponders darkly on matters of identity and dissolution (the very issues that define the consciousness of her second child, Darl). She is spellbound in forgetfulness:

> Sometimes I would lie by him in the dark, hearing the land that was now of my blood and flesh, and I would think: Anse. Why Anse. Why are you Anse. I would think about his name until after a while I could see the word as a shape, a vessel, and I would watch him liquify and flow into it like cold molasses flowing out of the darkness into the vessel, until the jar stood full and motionless: a significant shape profoundly without life like an empty door frame; and then I would find that I had forgotten the name of the jar. I would think: The shape of my body where I used to be a virgin is in the shape of a   and I couldn't think *Anse*, couldn't remember *Anse*. It was not that I could think of myself as no longer unvirgin, because I was three now. And when I would think *Cash* and *Darl* that way until their names would die and solidify into a shape and then fade away, I would say, All right. It doesn't matter. It doesn't matter what they call them.
>
> . . . I would be I; I would let him be the shape and echo of his word. (173–74)

Unlike conception, this forgetting of names is an intentional and fundamentally creative act of will on Addie's part, testifying to her continuing determination to retrieve her "I," to be one, not three.

The ideology of motherhood is overwhelming in the lives of girls and women. In popular culture the mother is either idealized or demonized. She is the source of love or the cruel withholder of it. She is, when she is good, invariably self-sacrificial when it comes to her children. She is also silenced. Observing that the persona of women writers is usually that of a daughter rather than a mother, Jo Malin asks where we can find "the voice of the mother" (91). In literature mothers are seldom given voices of their own, and if the crisis of subjectivity that accompanies maternity has been recorded in literary texts, it has been recorded so subtly that it has seldom been acknowledged by readers. In many ways, speaking of motherhood outside the register of the sentimental (whether idealization or demonization) remains taboo.[13] *As I Lay Dying* is a brave book.

By no means, however, was Faulkner the first to tackle the subject. When Addie, acknowledging the crisis of subjectivity in the lives of mothers, says, "I was three now" after the birth of Darl, she echoes the melancholy speaker of Elizabeth Madox Roberts's *The Time of Man*, published in 1926, who expresses a similar thought as she ruminates on the birth of a child, her youthful desires, and her own loss of individuality (333). Faulkner's treatment of maternity and subjectivity was also likely influenced by Evelyn Scott's *Escapade,* a fictionalized autobiography from 1923, scandalous for the time because of its graphic depiction of sexual desire and the pain of childbirth and perhaps equally scandalous for its honest, unsentimental portrayal of the impact of maternity (the splitting of the subject) on the woman, who speaks of "the strangeness of finding my body animate in some way unrelated to my will" (25). Scott goes on to provide us with such graphic images of the pain (physical and psychological) of childbirth that scenes were excised before the book's publication. What remains is still harrowing.[14]

A question students ask is why Faulkner would be so concerned with maternity and its relation to voice. The answer is complex and has to do with the impact of modernity on the conditions of authorship in the early twentieth century and, in particular, on the construction of the gender of the author.[15]

Traditionally, the idea of authorship attributed to the author a mastery over language, a capacity to bring words and intentions together in a way that made writing a novel or poem or play a kind of "deed," a "work" accomplished, complete, and inviolate, never exceeding or ignoring the authorial intention.[16] And authorship carried with it an elite status, which meant presumptions of autonomy, self-direction, and proprietorship. The author was a public figure in a culture in which public life was for men only—except for those women who were less than respectable.

Modernity shook the faith in authorial mastery and proprietorship. One of the most important developments was a new theory of language. Ferdinand de Saussure's *Course in General Linguistics* was published in 1913, and although it did not appear in English until 1959, literary modernism responded quickly to Saussure's fundamental insight, built on the long-held idea of the arbitrary relation between sign and signified, that language makes meaning through difference, not sameness, through the interrelations among signs, and is temporal. By "temporal," Saussure means that "the signifier, being auditory, is unfolded solely in time" and "represents a span . . . which is measureable in a single dimension" and is "a line" (648). Therefore, language is associated with polyvalence, indeterminacy, and deferral, not with fixity, determinacy, and presence. "I would think how words go straight up in a thin line, quick and harmless," Addie says, "and how terribly doing goes along the earth, clinging to it, so that after a while the two lines are too far apart for the same person to straddle from one to the other" (173).

Addie Bundren, unlike Anse, does not take the identity of word and deed for granted. She is full of modern doubt. But she does long for it, for presence in language:

> I would lie by [Anse] in the dark, hearing the dark land talking of God's love and His beauty and His sin; hearing the dark voicelessness in which the words are the deeds, and the other words that are not deeds, that are just the gaps in people's lacks, coming down like the cries of the geese out of the wild darkness in the old terrible nights, fumbling at the deeds like orphans to whom are pointed out in a crowd two faces and told, That is your father, your mother. (174)

After her first pregnancy, Addie will not experience anything close to presence, "the answer" to the terror of living, until she enters into her affair with the Reverend Whitfield—and this time "the deed" *is* a matter of a will not only to flout convention with adultery but also to reunite word and deed in what she sees as the ultimate heroic act in a cosmic drama of self-realization; it is a deed that is both a sin in its Godlike hubris and a paradoxical honoring of God in that it is imitative—it is "God who created the sin":

> I believed that I had found it. I believed that the reason was the duty to the alive, to the terrible blood, the red bitter flood boiling through the land. I would think of sin as I would think of the clothes we both wore in the world's face, of the circumspection necessary because he was he and I was I; the sin the more utter and terrible since he was the instrument ordained by God who created the sin, to sanctify that sin He had created. While I waited for him in the woods, waiting for him before he saw me, I would think of him as dressed in sin. I would think of him as thinking of me. . . . I would think of the sin as garments which we would remove in order to shape and coerce the terrible blood to the forlorn echo of the dead word high in the air. (174–75)[17]

The passion—Faulkner said "pride"—of Addie Bundren is hardly sacrifice. It is presence.[18]

The conflict between vertical and horizontal thought, the untroubled vertical perspective of Anse Bundren associated with patriarchal forms of genealogical control (of texts as well as people) and the horizontal movement that Addie is so aware of (precisely because of her own reproductive capacities) is an index of the potential of authorship in modernity, a potentiality embraced by Faulkner in writing *As I Lay Dying* "on the bevel" (82). In short, when Faulkner chooses to represent the signature mark of modernism, a crisis in language (Saussure), in terms of the speaking maternal corpse, that move speaks not only to the restlessness of women, to female desire and will, the demand for birth control, mobility, individuation, but also to issues of authorial desire in modernity.

A more concrete example of the metonymic association between modern women with their demands for birth control and movement and modern authorship is seen in the anxious response of writers to the development of new forms of textual reproduction and distribution. The modern printing press, for example, had become much more efficient and cheaper to use than ever before. Here was a new way to reproduce texts in bulk, and the printing press worked closely with new methods of distribution. But for all the advantages that might ensue, it became considerably harder to protect one's identity as author of a particular text. Writers pursued new copyright laws to protect their interests. Mark Twain—whose works were being pirated and reprinted under his name (or not under his name) all over the world—was much involved in working for the passage of more effective copyright laws to protect his bank account and his stature.[19] Faulkner, conscious of his own genius and legacy and profoundly interested in the authorial performance, was compelled to look for authorship's inaugural gestures and stands and found them in the recurring scene of reproduction, in the contemplation of the conflict between desire and fatality and in the tradition of female abjection.

In "The Work of Art in an Age of Mechanical Reproduction," Walter Benjamin writes that because of new technologies "the distinction between author and public is about to lose its basic character. . . . Literary license is now founded on polytechnic rather than specialized training and thus becomes common property" (232). *Common* property. This was a blow. Where authorship had previously been an elite prerogative, it was no longer so certain. Where authorship had been a masculine prerogative in a world in which women were bound by tradition to the home and family, it was no longer the case, and "[f]or some male intellectuals," John Carey writes, it would be "regrettable" that the democratization of writing "encouraged women" (7–8). The work of D. L. Lemahieu on changes in journalism in the early twentieth century—on the development of "women's pages" and the targeting of women as consumers—confirms, for Carey, that the democratization of writing became for women a means of "awareness, independence, and self-reliance" (8).

The most memorable voice of *As I Lay Dying* remains Addie's. "How terribly doing goes along the earth," Addie says, likening "doing" to childbirth and to the children themselves, with their own doings and their own futures beyond the control of will. Against the background of Anse's vision of genealogy as a matter of descent and ascent, she is speaking of the impossibility of establishing definitive points of origin and destination. On one level, Addie is talking about situational ethics, about the complexities of ethical questions in the real world versus the simple moral ideologies held on to by Anse and others in her community. On another level, Addie's monologue, with its emphasis on the failures of the word, is about unpredictability, about change, transfiguration, forgetting, loss. Through Addie, Faulkner explored a new aesthetic of gender and authorship for modernity.

NOTES

Portions of this essay are adapted from material that appeared in *Resisting History: Gender, Modernity, and Authorship in William Faulkner, Zora Neale Hurston, and Eudora Welty* (Louisiana State UP, 2007) and are published with permission.

[1] For an overview of some of the critical responses to Addie, see Husti. See also Ladd, *Resisting History* 136n27, 139–40n58; Hewson.

[2] See Rich; Hagood observes that women often use the word *pride* in referring to childbirth but "almost never is there expressed a desire for more" children (120). Others who have studied the subject include Cosslett; Hampsten; Hoffert; Leavitt and Walton; Malin; McMillen; Wertz and Wertz 112. I am indebted to Caroline Garnier for introducing me to this body of work through her unpublished dissertation.

[3] See Henninger for a study of the gendered discourse of individualism and the collective in the 1930s; see also Tebbetts for information about the development of ideas of egalitarianism in marriage and women's rights of self-development in the 1920s.

[4] See John T. Matthews 77–78 for a brief commentary on Anse, the state, and patriarchal authority. See also Kartiganer, "The Farm" 281–82, 291, on the vertical as "Being," the horizontal as "Becoming."

[5] For an examination of the movement from the private to the public sphere in the novel, see O'Donnell, "Between the Family."

[6] This perspective was based on long tradition. See Hegel 496–97 and Jean-Jacques Rousseau. For more recent studies of women and civilization, see John Carey 9; Lemahieu 33, 265. For a representative popular-press treatment of the day, see Liddell Hart; see also Jastrow, who argues that the mother's relationship to the child was one of "sympathetic renunciation on behalf of an emotionally cherished 'other'" (385). Such comments appeared frequently in magazines in the 1920s and 1930s.

[7] For treatments of reform work among rural women, see Bailey; Klaus 238–39; Marti.

[8] Good studies on the changing expectations of women in this era include Degler; Freedman; and McGovern.

[9] Gordon, *Woman's Body* 60–71, 167. See also Brodie 281–86 for a good discussion of the impact of the Comstock Act.

[10] See Gordon, "Voluntary Motherhood," and Degler 201, 203, 215.

[11] For a history of Margaret Sanger's struggle to decriminalize contraception, see H. Benjamin.

[12] Gordon discusses folk methods in *Woman's Body* 26–46, 49–71.

[13] For a contemporaneous, and unsentimental, opinion on motherhood, see Hollingworth; also note 2 above.

[14] For discussions of motherhood and identity in Scott's work, see Jenkins; P. Jones.

[15] The gender of the author in British Romanticism is the subject of Catherine Maxwell's *The Female Sublime from Milton to Swinburne*. Faulkner was much influenced by the British Romantics. See also Huyssen vii–viii.

[16] Because many students are convinced of authorial intentionality and are convinced that it is knowable, it is useful to discuss the issue with them. One good source is the entry "Intention" in the *New Princeton Encyclopedia of Poetry and Poetics.*

[17] See Kartiganer, "The Farm" 291–93, for an excellent explication of Addie's understanding of language: "For Addie the purpose of life is indeed to move along the ground, to tip the vertical down to the horizontal, to break from stasis into action, from timeless isolation within the lyric moment to bloody engagement with another person" (291).

[18] See note 2 above for Hagood on farm women and the use of the word *pride* to speak of maternity.

[19] On Mark Twain and copyright, see Michaelson.

"The Past Is Never Dead": Reading *As I Lay Dying* for Our Time

Cheryl Lester

Faulkner's fifth novel, *As I Lay Dying*, continues his literary explorations of life in the post–World War I Jim Crow South, particularly in terms of modernization and increasing mobility. As in *Soldiers' Pay*, *Flags in the Dust*, and *The Sound and the Fury*, Faulkner in *As I Lay Dying* investigates the movement of white laboring-class southerners through a shifting geocultural landscape.[1] The tale of the Bundrens, a poor farming family that travels more than forty miles in a mule-driven wagon to bury Addie Bundren, wife to Anse and mother to four sons and one daughter, offers a window into the experience of millions of families whose transition from farm to town and from subsistence to wage labor was made possible by networks of family, friends, and neighbors. The novel makes only indirect connections between the circumstances of the Bundrens and the acutely racialized construction of life in the segregated South, yet it plainly catapults the family on a course that is not merely idiosyncratic but has broad social significance. By observing that the Bundrens' tragicomic journey depicts shifts that disrupt racialized economic and sociospatial boundaries and menace the social order in the segregated South, I offer a view of *As I Lay Dying* as a situated response to basic transformative processes of modernity.

I teach *As I Lay Dying* as an extended trope or allegory of these complex transformations in the South of the early twentieth century. I attempt to persuade students of the importance of this historical context by examining a pastiche or "blank parody" of the text that shows no regard for its context; linking the mockery of the Bundrens to social hierarchies in the Jim Crow South, the appeal to middle-class readers, and sympathetic elements in the presentation of the Bundrens; connecting stylistic and other formal dimensions of the text with modernist cultural production and the belated modernization of the South; presenting Darl's ambivalent sensitivity to his family and the journey in terms of double consciousness; questioning the salience of segregation and racial discrimination as the Bundrens journey through Jim Crow space; and associating the narrative with enduring social realities, particularly in regard to the racial divide that still perturbs United States' national life.

The Bundrens in Blank Parody

To reflect on the disregard for historical context that characterizes practices of interpretation to which many students are habituated, I show a nine-and-a-half-minute video based on *As I Lay Dying* (Barenblat). Most likely created to fulfill a college assignment, this collaborative multimedia video, formerly available on

YouTube, demonstrates habits of interpretation that Fredric Jameson has analyzed in terms of the cultural logic of late capitalism. The video, which consists of short sketches of a few episodes from the latter sections of *As I Lay Dying*, relies on practices of imitation and pastiche or "blank parody," the "systematic mimicry" of "willful eccentricities" in the novel (Jameson 16, 17). Owing to its superficial engagement with the text at the level of stylistic idiosyncrasies, the video offers a neutral or, one might say, neutered and ineffective, interpretation of *As I Lay Dying*. Jameson writes:

> Pastiche is, like parody, the imitation of a peculiar or unique, idiosyncratic style, the wearing of a linguistic mask, speech in a dead language. But it is a neutral practice of such mimicry, without any of parody's ulterior motives, amputated of the satiric impulse, devoid of laughter and of any conviction that alongside the normal tongue you have momentarily borrowed, some healthy linguistic normality still exists. Pastiche is thus blank parody, a statue with blind eyeballs. (17)

Whereas *As I Lay Dying*, with its multiple narrative voices, might serve as a fitting example of what Jameson calls modern literature's "explosion . . . into a host of distinct private styles and mannerisms," the video serves as a fitting illustration of the deployment of postmodernist codes that Jameson links to the "linguistic fragmentation of social life itself to the point where the norm is eclipsed: reduced to a neutral and reified media speech" (16, 17).

The two student-producers of the *YouTube* video rely on signifying codes from popular mass media, readily recognized by their student peers, to mimic characters, figures, narrative techniques, tropes, and scenes from the novel. For example, to characterize the way chronology connects the action of the novel despite shifts in narrative perspectives and settings, they cite the on-screen digital clock that signifies the passage of real time in the action-drama television series *24*. To convey the salacious proposition that MacGowan makes to Dewey Dell, the student-actor grinds and swivels his hips to a musical soundtrack that features the raunchy opening phrases of Elvis Presley's cover of "Hound Dog." To communicate psychic ambivalence as Darl considers whether to burn the decomposing remains of Addie so that she can "lay down her life" (214–15), the student-actor adopts the voice of Gollum from *The Lord of the Rings*. To signify the burning of Gillespie's barn, the student-producers incorporate shots from a well-known explosion in the film *Speed*. To signify the bluster of Jewel's single-handed decision to retrieve Addie's coffin from the burning barn, the student-actor dresses in a George W. Bush–style Texas cowboy hat and Superman T-shirt.

Making no effort to mask or hide the details of the social reality in which the video was recorded, the students locate the scenes in the kitchen, in the garage, and on the front lawn of an affluent household in a quiet suburban neighborhood. The interiors and exteriors provide anachronistic props and settings for the video's mises-en-scène. A kitchen serves as the drugstore and the kitchen counter as the sales counter that separates the druggist or clerk from the customer. A green plastic receptacle on wheels, a familiar item in suburban trash disposal, serves as Addie's coffin. A two-car garage serves as Gillespie's barn. Yet the settings and props, undigested material evidence of the specific time and place of the video's production, are undeveloped as themes or objects of reflection; they emphasize, if anything, only the detachment from social reality and context that informs this blind parody. Along with the privileges and limitations indicated by the suburban setting, the selection of episodes, the visual and sonic mass-cultural citations, and the choice of costumes, speech, and mannerisms attune the unreflective viewpoint of the video with the chorus of voices in the novel that mock and disdain the Bundrens.[2]

The video does not disclose or produce knowledge about the relationship of the Bundrens to the social realities of the novel. *As I Lay Dying* tracks the Bundrens as they move from an unsustainable premodern agrarian economy, marked by subsistence, frugality, and dilapidation, toward an emergent geocultural landscape, marked by capital, consumption, and mass-produced commodities like automobiles, bicycles, electric toy trains, and graphophones. Blank parody turns a blind eye to the social realities that emerge from the novel and that condition the derision the Bundrens must negotiate as they move from their familiar habitus in the countryside toward town.[3]

Mockery versus Double Consciousness

With regard to social origins, cultural capital, and consumerism, Faulkner was closer to the respectable professionals and clerks of Mottson and Jefferson than to the Bundrens and other country folk who were their objects of suspicion and ridicule. However, by 1915, at around the age of eighteen, Faulkner had gained experience and knowledge—through travel, reading, and military service—that contributed to the development of a critical double consciousness that would set him apart even from those he most closely resembled.[4] Still living in the wake of military defeat and devastation, the abruptly terminated and unresolved period of Reconstruction, and the brutalities of slavery and its aftermath in multiple stages through debt peonage to Jim Crow, Mississippi was especially attuned to the fatality of postwar processes, experiences, and sentiments. In contrast with the more direct opposition expressed by many of Faulkner's contemporaries to the rapid and violent transformation of the South associated with its belated modernization and urbanization, Faulkner placed southern experience within the cosmopolitan and aesthetically sophisticated context of modernity. He had been exposed to the broader context of global transformations during and after World War I through his military service in Canada and, more dramatically, during his 1925 travels abroad, when he visited battlefields and European capitals. He traveled to the Northeast and to Europe and was exposed to systemic changes like those that inspired the modernist and surrealist aesthetic productions of cosmopolitan subjects for whom travel was primarily a means of economic management, cultural consumption, and enlightenment.

Combining white male middle-class privilege in the South with his marginality beyond the South, where as a colonized subject from the periphery he too was vulnerable to ridicule, Faulkner began producing novels that illustrate his dawning awareness of the complex array of forces propelling—and obstructing—change in the South. With his portrait of the Bundrens moving across forbidding cultural and political boundaries, Faulkner put down stakes in a largely unclaimed piece of literary real estate that would develop and circulate representations of the millions of southerners who were migrating from rural hinterlands to urban areas in and beyond the South. His application of state-of-the-art modes of cultural production to a remote, underdeveloped, and racially segregated region like northern Mississippi revealed aspects of modernization that had, in fact, already been experienced, for several centuries, in the polarization of metropolitan and peripheral zones throughout the Atlantic and increasingly global socioeconomic world system. At the same time, modernist aesthetic practices, applied to an underdeveloped and parochial southeastern United States landscape, enabled Faulkner to offer readers an urbane, middle-class perspective on modernization and the South.

The Bundrens and the novel in which they appear are late avatars of transformative pressures that have been explored throughout the social and cultural history of the United States. Although the death of Addie Bundren provokes an immediate problem that the Bundren family has to resolve (albeit with the assistance of their rural community and despite the disdain of the town dwellers they meet along the way), the family's perilous journey from country to town repeats and gives new sense to a formative experience that has structured the lives and mentalities of millions of rural laborers throughout the development of modern social formations. Driven by market forces that relentlessly dissolve early-modern conditions, coercing individuals to leave home to seek new livelihoods in towns or cities, the Bundrens are set loose into the transformative forces of their early-twentieth-century geoculture.

Included among its multiple narratives are the vantage points of various residents of the fictive northern Mississippi towns of Mottson and Jefferson, and *As I Lay Dying* gives ample expression to the disdain that must have greeted country farmers as they were propelled from the hinterlands to small metropoles or large cities. Although families like the Bundrens, Tulls, and Armstids lived at a distance from metropolitan centers, modern processes like mechanization, standardization, routinization, proletarianization, and urbanization encroached on their everyday life. Through commodity chains, such families learned to desire new mass-produced commodities. Because their lives were not integrated with the production or consumption of these commodities and although modern production was bringing about the rapid decline of their way of life, families like the Bundrens faced overwhelming obstacles in obtaining these new consumer items. Their exclusion from the production and ready consumption of such commodities made them vulnerable to ridicule, as was apparent even to the middle-class students whose blind parody of the novel reveals lives that by this time are enmeshed in commodity chains.

Thus it is not difficult to compare *As I Lay Dying* with a series of landmark novels that explore similar processes in the development of the United States, from the period of the Revolution and early republic (e.g., *Arthur Mervyn; or, Memoirs of the Year 1793*, Charles Brockden Brown's radical-democratic portrait of uprooted rural individuals) to naturalism's Zola-inspired critique of emergent corporatism in the era of the Spanish-American War (e.g., *The Jungle*, Upton Sinclair's socialist tragedy, or *The Virginian*, Owen Wister's right-wing classic of rural landgrabs and vigilantism). The relevance of modernist figures, forms, and tropes associated with industrialization, urbanization, and war throughout the Atlantic and global world system is by no means restricted to the system's metropolitan centers (e.g., Berlin, London, Dublin, and New York). All these factors resonate with meaning for peripheral actors and producers, from elite figures such as Faulkner to the different subgroups of rural, laboring whites and blacks represented in Faulkner's novels, because these same forces and phenomena, however differently configured and received, were also transforming peripheral zones and the lives of various status groups throughout the globe.

Historians speak of "the southern great migration" or "the southern diaspora" to describe the mass migration of people from southern farms and hamlets to rapidly growing cities between the 1890s and the 1930s. Broadly speaking, the migration from the South of some twenty million white southerners, nearly eight million black southerners, and one million Latino and Latina southerners over the course of the twentieth century offers a significant context for a novel whose focus is on the circular movement of a poor white southern family between farm and town (Gregory). Louis M. Kyriakoudes describes "the migration from farm to city . . . as one of the defining experiences in the social history of the modern South" and, more broadly, as "a fundamental social process of the modern era" (157–58). Other historians argue that the most significant phenomenon in the social history of the modern South was the mass migration of African American southerners within the South and beyond to cities in the North, Midwest, and West. From 1916 to 1918—during which the college-age Faulkner left Mississippi for the first time (and Darl Bundren was "in France at the war" [254])—nearly half a million African Americans migrated out of the South. By the end of the 1920s, following patterns of family migration, the number had nearly tripled. Although the African American exodus that followed World War II was larger, the mass migration that occurred during and after World War I, to which *As I Lay Dying* offers a critical literary response, was "a demographic watershed, the harbinger of economic, political, and social changes that have transformed the United States" (Sernett 1–7).

Writing about the changes associated with this watershed to cosmopolitan readers in a recognizably cosmopolitan style, with a narrator who is absent and invisible—paring his nails (in the manner famously advocated by Flaubert)—Faulkner surprises readers of *As I Lay Dying* by opening the novel with a scene as narrowly focused and anticosmopolitan as could be imagined. Like a rural version of Walter Benjamin's modern urban flaneur, the semiurbanized Darl is treading through the textual and geocultural landscape so significant to the narrative. Darl's indirect free speech, marked by grammatical infelicity, betrays the author's literary sophistication and the character's humble origins (while suppressing his wartime experience in France and knowledge of modernity):

> Jewel and I come up from the field, following the path in single file. Although I am fifteen feet ahead of him, anyone watching us from the cottonhouse can see Jewel's frayed and broken straw hat a full head above my own. (3)

Flaubert claimed, "Madame Bovary, c'est moi." I propose that Faulkner claims, in the opening pages and in another eighteen of the novel's fifty-nine sections, "Darl, that's me."

From the self-conscious and divided viewpoint of Darl, Faulkner offered middle-class, cosmopolitan readers a complex, critical, and ambivalent view of the Jim Crow South. While Darl's point of view, focused so intently on the immediate surroundings—the path "worn smooth by feet" (3), the cotton field, his diminutive height relative to Jewel, Jewel's straw hat—is markedly narrow, it is also split. Darl, with the reader, gazes back on the scene he both inhabits and sets, as he imagines how it would look to "anyone watching us from the cottonhouse" (3). On the basis of presumptively broader horizons and greater familiarity with modernity, shared perhaps with Darl yet certainly with Faulkner, the reader is cast from the outset as superior and opposed to the cramped and benighted horizons of characters who inhabit an outmoded and disappearing world. Indeed, demonstrating the limited horizons of each character seems to be a principal aim and achievement of the novel's stark shifts from one to another of its more than fifteen points of view. This aesthetic performance also serves to strategically situate Faulkner as a subject whose world will be compatible, in a cognitive and geocultural sense, with the worlds of the middle-class readers to whom his writing appeals.

Thus the Bundrens are presented as subjects beneath the station of the novel's presumptive readers. Jewel's frayed and broken straw hat and patched overalls, like Cora's household economies and Anse's worn-out brogans, distinguish these country folks from the middle-class readers the novel solicits. Their lowly status becomes increasingly acute as the Bundrens move farther from their home. No longer greeted with the neighborly assistance available to them as they traveled through the hinterlands, the Bundrens meet, in the forty-fifth section of the novel, with the hostility, mockery, and disdain of higher-status groups in Mottson. Moseley, who describes himself as "a respectable druggist, that's kept store and raised a family and been a church-member for fifty-six years in this town" (202), gathers from firsthand reports that the arrival of the Bundrens "must have been like a piece of rotten cheese coming into an ant-hill" (203). Grotesquely ill-fitting and hyperbolically out of place, the Bundrens remain marked by and attached to rural life even as they are inexorably drawn or propelled toward modernity, mass-produced goods, wage labor, geographic mobility, and desires for the privilege of higher social status.

Modernism, Modernity, and the Belated Modernization of the South

With *The Sound and the Fury* and *As I Lay Dying*, Faulkner brought to a remote and marginalized region, whose history set it apart from dominant centers of cultural production and national identity, cosmopolitan and state-of-the-art aesthetic techniques of narrative and representation that mapped cultural terrains beyond the nation-state. While writing about an area underdeveloped and stigmatized within dominant United States' culture, a region still grappling with the legacy of the Civil War, emancipation, Reconstruction, and Jim Crow, Faulkner adopted the sophisticated literary techniques of elite European and North American cultural producers, the high modernists of his time, from writers like James Joyce and Virginia Woolf to filmmakers like René Clair, painters like René Magritte, and critical intellectuals like Walter Benjamin and Georges Bataille.

Unlike the rural subjects of *As I Lay Dying*, Faulkner had the education and cultural experience that enabled him to link them with the reverberating effects of modernity described by earlier modernists and surrealists. In effect, he could borrow figures and tropes to capture the startling contradictions in social reality that go hand in hand with modernity and that inform modernist cultural production. Comte de Lautréamont's *witzig*, protosurrealist description (in "Les chants de Maldoror" [234]) of the chance encounter of an umbrella and a sewing machine on a dissecting table, for example, became iconic for the surrealists as a useful condensation of the startling juxtapositions that present themselves as the everyday experience of modernity. Faulkner demonstrates his familiarity with the everyday experience of modernization and with the tropes and signifying practices of modernism when he notes in his preface to *Sanctuary* that *As I Lay Dying* was composed on an upside-down wheelbarrow while he worked the night shift at a coal-fired power plant in Oxford.

The aesthetic innovations of the surrealists and modernists served to capture the dramatic transformations that accompanied the encroaching modernization of the South. Stream-of-consciousness narration as well as multiple and shifting points of view in early-twentieth-century novels by Joyce and Woolf are noteworthy aesthetic precursors to *As I Lay Dying*. Like other works in the canon,

As I Lay Dying adopts surrealist and modernist figurations of disorientation, fragmentation, and partial points of view. Correspondences like these establish the modernist canon as an informing context for *As I Lay Dying*'s response to the upheavals of World War I; technological innovations in warfare, transportation, and communication; and the global destabilization of everyday life driven by both capitalist market forces and capitalist militarism and imperialism.

Seeing key scenes from René Clair's *À nous la liberté* helps students situate objects and events from *As I Lay Dying* in the signifying context of modernity and modernization. The film traces the rags-to-riches-to-rags story of an escaped convict who rises from peddling phonographs on the streets of Paris to become the wealthy owner of a factory that produces them but who then leaves his bourgeois attachments behind for the presumable freedoms of homelessness and itinerancy. As an icon of modernity, the phonograph condenses new cultural and economic flows that connect the Paris of *Entr'acte* or of *À nous la liberté* to the Mississippi of *As I Lay Dying*. Clair's visual critique of commodity fetishism and mass production in the assembly-line manufacturing of the phonograph enables students to connect the circulation of a commodity like the graphophone of *As I Lay Dying* to a cultural context of widely circulating critiques of modernity's industrialization, proletarianization, commodification, bourgeois ideals of selfhood, and so on. In *As I Lay Dying*, the graphophone is not simply a consumer item fervently desired by Cash Bundren and successfully acquired for him as a consequence of his father's abrupt remarriage, it is also a signifier of Faulkner's ambivalent relation to the encroaching modernity associated with new cultural technologies and forms and the industrialization of the South. Clair's film offers visual information about the production of the phonograph and phonographic recordings, a global phenomenon associated with modernity, World War I, and the periodizing concept of modernism that actively exerted force on the agrarian South, whose transformation energized Faulkner's literary production.

Although the traditional, agrarian northern Mississippi setting and the country working people of *As I Lay Dying* may initially strike students as unrelated or only remotely related to the efflorescent modernity of the 1920s in metropolitan capitals across the globe, students can discover, as they attend to small details, the current of modernity overtaking the Bundrens and their traditional way of life. The novel's detailed reports on the family's ten-day procession from the familiar countryside to the unfamiliar and unwelcoming towns of Mottson and Jefferson register the disorientation and shock of the new. Using Addie's death as a pretext for the unlikely journey, the novel follows the pattern of Benjamin's Baudelaire or the subgenre of Anglo-European modernist and surrealist novels that develop the everyday divagations and experiential shocks of city-dwelling flaneurs, such as James Joyce's *Ulysses*, Louis Aragon's *Le paysan de Paris*, André Breton's *Nadja*, and Georges Bataille's *L'histoire de l'oeil*. By threading death and a funeral procession through the narrative structure and geocultural landscape of the novel, Faulkner gives symbolic weight to the epochal transition from the agrarian world of wheelbarrows to the modern, urban world of electric power. In *As I Lay Dying*, the procession—a modernist trope for rapid transformation—invokes widespread criticism and even outrage.

Darl as a Figure of Critical Engagement

As I Lay Dying presents Addie Bundren's death as the salient context for the action of the novel, beginning with Cash's construction of her coffin and the deathbed vigil by Cora Tull and the other neighbor women. Addie may have indeed expressed a wish, following the birth of Darl, to be buried with her kin as a hostile or alienated response to the disappointments of her life with Anse. Having attempted to escape through an extramarital affair from a husband whose marred feet are "badly splayed," whose toothless "mouth collapses in slow repetition," and whose "stubble gives his lower face that appearance that old dogs have," Addie might well want to lie far from him in death (11, 17, 17). While her wishes may provide a pretext for the journey to Jefferson, they are clearly not the only or even the primary reason for the journey.

As Addie lies on her deathbed, Anse warns Darl and Jewel that they will disappoint her if they leave to deliver a load of lumber and she doesn't last until they return. " 'She's counted on it,' pa says. 'She'll want to start right away. I know her. I promised her I'd keep the team here and ready, and she's counting on it' " (17). Yet Darl's telepathic presentation of the deathbed scene challenges the sincerity of Anse's promise to fulfill Addie's wishes. Darl contrasts his father's clumsy, repetitive, and unconvincing gestures of mourning with his concise, economical, and self-serving expression of desire to acquire a set of false teeth:

> Pa stands over the bed, dangle-armed, humped, motionless. He raises his hand to his head, scouring his hair, listening to the saw. He comes nearer and rubs his hand, palm and back, on his thigh and lays it on her face and then on the hump of quilt where her hands are. He touches the quilt as he saw Dewey Dell do, trying to smoothe it up to the chin, but disarranging it instead. He tries to smoothe it again, clumsily, his hand awkward as a claw, smoothing at the wrinkles which he made and which continue to emerge beneath his hand with perverse ubiquity, so that at last he desists, his hand falling to his side and stroking itself again, palm and back, on his thigh. The sound of the saw snores steadily into the room. Pa breathes with a quiet, rasping sound, mouthing the snuff against his gums. "God's will be done," he says. "Now I can get them teeth." (51–52)

Anse directs his complaints, in the first of three chapters written from his point of view, at the road that comes "right up to my door . . . keeping the folks restless and wanting to get up and go somewheres else when [the Lord] aimed for them to stay put like a tree or a stand of corn" (35–36). He resents the taxes he is charged for a road that creates opportunities for his sons and interferes with his claims on their labor. He does not wish to pay the doctor—"I never sent for you. . . . I take you to witness I never sent for you"—and fears he will never "get ahead enough so I could get my mouth fixed where I could eat God's own victuals as a man should" (37). With Addie's death, Anse resolves to "get up and go" (36). Carrying Addie's body to Jefferson to exchange it for a set of false teeth strikes him as an opportunity to participate in practices of consumption readily available to others.

> Nowhere in this sinful world can a honest, hardworking man profit. It takes them that runs the stores in the towns, doing no sweating, living off of them that sweats. It aint the hardworking man, the farmer. Sometimes I wonder why we keep at it. It's because there is a reward for us above, where they cant take their autos and such. . . .
>
> But it's a long wait, seems like. It's bad that a fellow must earn the reward of his right-doing by flouting hisself and his dead. (110–11)

Indeed, Anse's every utterance and act aim deliberately at earning "the reward of his right-doing" here and now "in this sinful world," whatever the cost to others. Although Anse claims, as he imagines that rain will delay Jewel and Darl and hence the family's departure for Jefferson, that he can "see . . . with second-sight," his self-serving focus directs his gaze only toward matters of his own designs (35). Like many other characters in Faulkner, from Jason Compson to Thomas Sutpen, Anse Bundren animates the preconditions of southern economic success, from slavery to "neoplantations" and Jim Crow, whereby white landholders and their households accumulated wealth at the expense of a laboring class of African Americans. Such figures embody attitudes of indifference that make them blind to the environment that they exploit and on which they depend.

By contrast, Darl, whose voice commands nineteen—or almost one-third—of the novel's fifty-nine chapters, is acutely sensitive to the selfishness and self-deception of Anse as well as to the secrets and unexpressed desires of those around him. As a result of this critical sensitivity to others, he is seen—for example, by Cora Tull—as "different from those others" (21). Some "folks say [that Darl] is queer, lazy, pottering about the place no better than Anse" (24). Cora speculates "it was between [Addie] and Darl that the understanding and the true love was" (24). Dewey Dell hates and fears Darl for what "he knew without the words" and acknowledges his farsightedness and sensitivity to the environment, as others do, by referring to "his eyes . . . full of the land dug out of his skull and the holes filled with distance beyond the land" (27). As opposed to the blind parody discussed earlier whose neutrality and lack of purpose Jameson decries, the critical stance figured by Darl involves a sensitivity to others and an assessment of his environment that not only sets him apart but ultimately sets him against his family and vice versa.

Perhaps Darl is "different" or "queer" because, as Faulkner suggests near the end of the novel, almost as an afterthought, he was away "in France at the war" (254). His distance from home and experience in wartime France may serve as a trope for the complex processes that "queered" his point of view, fashioning in him that double consciousness from which he looks critically at himself, his family, country folk, modernity, and the Jim Crow South. In the earlier novels *Soldiers' Pay* and *Sartoris*, Faulkner developed the trope of the returning soldier to establish the emergence of a point of view that is critical of and no longer adapted to southern life and culture. Darl's keen observations of his surroundings, critical point of view, queerness in the eyes of others, oppositional role on the journey, and expulsion from the family may be linked to the knowledge produced by his departure from and return to the South. Darl brings a discomfiting double consciousness to the feelings of resentment, revenge, disappointment, and unsettled scores that govern his father's thoughts and actions. Addie's decomposing body, with its attendant stench and circling buzzards, and Anse's hyperbolic flaws serve as tropes for Darl's double consciousness and heightened sensitivity to the flaws of his southern birthplace. Like Quentin Compson, when his queer behavior leads to his apprehension by minions of the state, Darl responds with a fit of wild laughter, an expression of alienation and criticism that can be seen in Quentin Compson's response at the end of *Absalom, Absalom!*, a prequel to *The Sound and the Fury*. Asked by his Harvard roommate, Shreve, "Why do you hate the South?" Quentin replies, protesting too much, "I don't! I don't hate it!" (303).

Faulkner was not alone in fearing the effects of population shifts, like the southern diaspora, or of developing technologies, like the phonograph, that would increasingly obscure the specificity of particular regions and practices. In 1848, Karl Marx and Friedrich Engels famously observed that, in modernity, "all that is solid melts into air" (83). W. B. Yeats articulated similar concerns in the well-known opening of his famous poem "The Second Coming," which appeared in the *Dial* in 1920. A published poet himself and a reader of the *Dial*, the prominent venue in the United States for modernist poetry of the time, Faulkner would surely have noted a poem with such etymological resonance with his own family name and with the historical dilemma acutely rendered in *As I Lay Dying*:

> Turning and turning in the widening gyre
> The falcon cannot hear the falconer;
> Things fall apart; the centre cannot hold;
> Mere anarchy is loosed upon the world,
>
> . . . .
>
> And what rough beast, its hour come round at last,
> Slouches towards Bethlehem to be born?

Unique to the experience and environment to which Faulkner brought sophisticated modernist techniques of representation was a regime of racial segregation, discrimination, and brutality. While Faulkner's later writings present this regime more centrally and forcefully, the racialized history and life of the modern South is never absent from his early writings.

Racing the Bundrens

With *As I Lay Dying*, Faulkner takes a critical step beyond the southern middle-class milieux of his earlier novels while still situating a portion of the narrative in or around his fictive town of Jefferson. Not until 1942, with *Go Down, Moses*, did he publish a novel that explores the southern plantation and the system of sharecropping, tenant farming, and debt peonage that emerged after emancipation and Reconstruction, along with Jim Crow laws and segregation.

The Bundrens live in an all-white enclave and seem to be indifferent to, if not wholly ignorant of, the circumstances of black southerners. But the closer the family gets to Jefferson, the more an awareness of racial difference creeps into the narrative. Observing the blackness of the soot applied to Jewel's burned back and the blackness of Cash's infected foot and leg, Vardaman says, "Your back looks like a nigger's, Jewel" and observes that Cash's foot and leg "looked like a nigger's" (224). Like the other signifiers—"the drug stores, the clothing stores, the patent medicine and the garages and cafés" (226), "the massed telephone lines . . . and the clock on the courthouse"—the "negro cabins" indicate they are approaching Jefferson (229).

An encounter that nearly explodes in violence reveals that the Bundrens, despite their isolation in Frenchman's Bend, are keenly aware of racial boundaries. As in Mottson, where they are quickly recognized and keenly surveyed as bumbling, ill-equipped country folk with an unacceptable burden in tow, the Bundrens rapidly become objects of speculation:

> Three negroes walk beside the road ahead of us; ten feet ahead of them a white man walks. When we pass the negroes their heads turn suddenly with that expression of shock and instinctive outrage. "Great God," one says; "what they got in that wagon?"
>
> Jewel whirls. "Sons of bitches," he says. As he does so he is abreast of the white man, who has paused. It is as though Jewel had gone blind for the moment, for it is the white man toward whom he whirls. (229)

This single passage, increasingly the object of critical interpretations, dramatizes the racial anxieties that emerge through Vardaman's speech as the Bundrens approach Jefferson. Although most of the narrative proceeds without revealing the Bundrens' knowledge of racial distinctions, these late utterances and incidents reveal that they are aware that there are distinctions to be made between "negroes," or "niggers," and whites. In the passage quoted above, Jewel almost incites a dangerous and violent confrontation by addressing a "white man" with the angry words and attitude of aggression that could have been aimed at the "negroes" without the fear of retaliation.

As the Bundrens and other laboring whites from the countryside move to town, they destabilize the normative social stratifications of a rigorously segregated space. They encounter the dispossessed and disempowered African American laboring families who live in cabins on the outskirts of town—families who, like the Bundrens, come to towns like Jefferson hoping for a share of the profits that accrue to "them that runs the stores." But they assert their racial difference rather than their similarity as members of the laboring class. In the context of rural-to-urban migration, competition between a racially divided underclass finds expression in the white-on-black racial terrorism that marks the Jim Crow years and endures beyond the civil rights era and urban insurrections of the 1960s and 1990s in the structural inequalities and cultural misunderstandings typical of our time.

"The Past Isn't Dead and Buried. In Fact, It Isn't Even Past."

To demonstrate the relevance of *As I Lay Dying*'s allegory of transformation in a racialized historical context, I refer students to this paraphrase of Faulkner, which appeared in a presidential campaign speech delivered by then Senator Barack Obama on 18 March 2008. The speech suggests how a certain construction of the past can serve not merely as an occasion for imitation and pastiche but, more significant, as grounds for understanding and a warrant for social action. Obama gave the speech in response to criticism about the divisive rhetoric of his former pastor, the Reverend Jeremiah Wright. Rather than simply offer excuses or denunciations, Obama took advantage of the controversy to articulate a construction of the past that informs his point of view not only about the Reverend Wright's rhetoric but, more importantly, about the enduring divisiveness of race in American life. As he pointed out, the experience and history that shaped him are not evident in "the snippets of those sermons [by the Reverend Wright] that have run in an endless loop on the television and *YouTube*." Instead, Obama called up often-forgotten complexities from the past to provide a context for understanding and ameliorating conflicts that haunt the American present. He was seeking to change commonly held beliefs about the legacy of slavery and Jim Crow so that more Americans would realize that it is not "dead and buried" and would acknowledge that it still requires redress. Such acknowledgment, he argued, will allow Americans to come together to resolve pressing social problems.

> The fact is that the comments that have been made and the issues that have surfaced over the last few weeks reflect the complexities of race in this country that we've never really worked through—a part of our union that we have yet to perfect. And if we walk away now, if we simply retreat into our respective corners, we will never be able to come together and solve challenges like health care, or education, or the need to find good jobs for every American.
>
> Understanding this reality requires a reminder of how we arrived at this point. As William Faulkner once wrote, "The past isn't dead and buried. In fact, it isn't even past." We do not need to recite here the history of racial injustice in this country. But we do need to remind ourselves that so many of the disparities that exist in the African-American community today can be directly traced to inequalities passed on from an earlier generation that suffered under the brutal legacy of slavery and Jim Crow.

Obama's speech articulates the utopian hope of a more perfect union that could come from acknowledging rather than disavowing the realities of disparate histories, so that people divided by these histories might move toward common ends:

> I chose to run for the presidency at this moment in history because I believe deeply that we cannot solve the challenges of our time unless we solve them together—unless we perfect our union by understanding that we may have different stories, but we hold common hopes; that we may not look the same and we may not have come from the same place, but we all want to move in the same direction—towards a better future for our children and our grandchildren.

Obama's speech paraphrases Faulkner to fashion an inspiring message about the human capacity to overcome differences rooted in a divided past in order to work together for a better future. The message of the speech is that, by recognizing the enduring conflicts of the past, people can move beyond the impasse of irreconcilable differences to fulfill common hopes and reach common ends. President Obama's response to the subsequent firestorm over the arrest of Henry Louis Gates, Jr., in July 2009 in Cambridge, Massachusetts, may suggest how double consciousness continues to inspire and challenge the president.

To Obama's ideal postulate of a collective that might "move in the same direction—towards a better future for our children and grandchildren," *As I Lay Dying* poses a dystopic alternative. It dramatizes the process through which an ignoble patriarch selectively constructs the past and imposes it on the present as a self-serving warrant for collective action. As Anse Bundren's re-presentation of the past achieves legitimacy and succeeds in allocating collective resources toward a particular direction, other experiences of the past and hopes for the future—inarticulate, unspoken, and often unspeakable—are submerged.

When the Bundrens "move in the same direction," it is not on the strength of a common hope for the future, a shared understanding of the past, or even an acknowledgment of their divided experience of the past. Through privileged access to the multiplicity of competing stories, frustrations, and hopes that animate the present in *As I Lay Dying*, students learn not only that a warrant that propels social action may fail to serve or even address the multiple and competing histories, desires, and needs of all members of a collective but also that critical engagement is preferable to blind parody.

NOTES

[1] For a discussion of modernity and black migration in *The Sound and Fury*, see Lester, "Racial Awareness."

[2] Unfortunately, because of a copyright claim by Warner Music Group, this video is no longer posted. But see Barenblat, whose video on Faulkner sufficiently demonstrates the habits of imitation, mockery, and pastiche as well as the unreflected suburban setting that I discuss in connection with the video based on *As I Lay Dying*.

[3] I refer students to Bourdieu's concept of the "habitus" to indicate the idea that distinctions associated with race, class, and gender, for example, are mapped onto social spaces and enforced by the participants who inhabit those spaces and have internalized those distinctions. See particularly the beginning of chapter 3, "The Habitus and the Space of Life-Styles."

[4] I introduce students to the concept of double consciousness that W. E. B. DuBois articulates in the opening pages of *The Souls of Black Folk* and discuss the wide applicability of the African American dilemma of "always looking at one's self through the eyes of others" (5).

Does Anse Bundren Love His Wife? Gifts, Promises, and Obligations in *As I Lay Dying*

Sean McCann

In the fifth of his monologues, Darl Bundren narrates the scene of his mother's death. Although he is not present to witness the event, Darl describes Addie Bundren's last encounters with her sons Cash and Vardaman and the grief that overcomes Vardaman and Addie's daughter, Dewey Dell, when they see that their mother has died. He notes the departure from the room of everyone but his father—Addie's husband, Anse. In the penultimate passage of the chapter, Darl describes Anse's response to his wife's death:

> Pa stands over the bed, dangle-armed, humped, motionless. He raises his hand to his head, scouring his hair, listening to the saw. He comes nearer and rubs his hand, palm and back, on his thigh and lays it on her face and then on the hump of the quilt where her hands are. He touches the quilt as he saw Dewey Dell do, trying to smoothe it up to the chin, but disarranging it instead. He tries to smoothe it again, clumsily, his hand awkward as a claw, smoothing at the wrinkles which he made and which continue to emerge beneath his hand with perverse ubiquity, so that at last he desists, his hand falling to his side and stroking itself again, palm and back, on his thigh. The sound of the saw snores steadily into the room. Pa breathes with a quiet, rasping sound, mouthing the snuff against his gums. "God's will be done," he says. "Now I can get them teeth." (51–52)

How should we understand this passage? The lines that end it are among the most frequently quoted from the novel. Yet perhaps because these words are so memorable, the actions that Anse takes before he finally speaks are almost never noted. What could be the meaning of those actions? Given what we know about the selfishness Anse displays throughout *As I Lay Dying*, we might see his gestures here as theatrical or insincere. Yet Faulkner—or, rather, Darl—takes care to specify that Anse is alone. Anse has no reason to believe he is being observed, and nothing he says or does elsewhere suggests that he wishes to pretend to emotions that he does not genuinely feel. Nor are we given any cause to doubt Darl's vision of events, as we usually are when other characters' observations are revealed to be dubious. There is no reason to think Darl misdescribes the scene of his mother's death and no cause to doubt its likely implication. It is hard to understand Anse's actions at the moment that he touches the hands and face of Addie's corpse except as those of a man who loved his wife.

Indeed, although the possibility is rarely noted, there is nothing in the novel inconsistent with the thought that Anse loved Addie, and there is much that becomes clearer and more resonant if we assume that he did.[1] Addie herself repeatedly draws attention to the possibility, even as she dismisses its value: "Anse or love; love or Anse. . . . Anse, love, what you will" (172). The description of Anse at his wife's bedside seems to acknowledge even as it undercuts the sorrow and tenderness his gestures appear to express. As with so much else he does, Anse is ineffectual in his effort to smooth the blanket covering his wife's body. Still more striking is Darl's account of his father's physical appearance: humped, motionless, with a hand like an awkward claw. When seen in the light of Addie's own simile for the youthful Anse ("he looked already like a tall bird" [170]), the description makes Anse resemble one of the most prominent emblems of Faulkner's novel: a vulture. If he appears to have loved his wife, he also looks in this scene as if he is ready to feed on her.

The idea that loving someone and feeding on them are not opposite but complementary actions is not as exceptional as it may seem at first glance. After all, Faulkner shows us in many ways that loving someone can involve harming them or accepting harm from them. Addie recalls the eyes of the courting Anse "driving . . . at me like two hounds in a strange yard" (171). That is only one moment when Faulkner ties together desire and antagonism, love and need, care and harm. While it is evident that Vardaman, Dewey Dell, Cash, and Jewel loved their mother and mourn her death, they will all be complicit in a journey that subjects her corpse to a degradation that offends their community. Only Darl, who cares least for Addie and who does not even regard her as his mother, resists that abuse.

It is possible that Anse not only loved but also mistreated his wife. He may in this way be typical of the world Faulkner depicts—one possibly extreme version of a more general phenomenon in *As I Lay Dying*: the person who simultaneously cares about, makes use of, and harms the people he or she loves. Indeed, if Anse is, in fact, a buzzard, he's not in that way unique in Faulkner's world. Vernon Tull is also described as an "old turkey-buzzard" (28). Samson confuses the Bundren family with the buzzards that follow them (118). And Faulkner himself remarked in later years that, if he were reincarnated, he'd like to return as a buzzard. "Nothing hates him or envies him or wants him or needs him. He is never bothered or in danger, and he can eat anything" (Faulkner, "Interview" 238).

My students are usually reluctant to see Anse Bundren in such a sympathetic light, and they're doubtful that he actually might have loved his wife. Like most of Faulkner's critics, they're struck by the words Anse speaks at the time of Addie's death and underwhelmed by the actions that precede them. They usually take those words to confirm a message they see implicit in other parts of the book—that Anse is a parasitic monster and deserves to be despised. I remind them, however, that *As I Lay Dying* is a novel whose central technique emphasizes how often even the most confident judgments are partial or mistaken. In that light, I suggest, we should be reluctant to take our initial impression of Anse for granted.

Indeed, Darl's description of his father may be part of a more general pattern suggested by the complex structure of the novel, in which we are presented not merely with varying perceptions of people and events but with conflicting ways of interpreting the motives for their actions. To the extent that *As I Lay Dying* turns on the structure of the Bundren family—and thus ultimately on the relationship between Addie and Anse—it may be that Faulkner gives us not just an account of the characters' conflicting desires or positions but also rival versions of what it means to love and be obligated to another person. On the one hand, in his depiction of Anse, Faulkner hints at the possibility that caring for others and making use of them may not be contradictory but, rather, fully consistent. On the other hand, and more prominently, he encourages us to dismiss this understanding and view love and exploitation as radically opposed ways of relating to others. From this perspective, the lifelong battle between Addie and Anse involves not only a personal conflict or a spiritual difference or even a struggle over gender or power or language; beneath these sources of conflict lies a more fundamental battle between alternative visions of what it means to be bound to another person.

To clarify this issue, I propose to my students that we can understand the conflict between the attitudes of Anse and Addie by seeing it in the context of what the legal scholar William Ian Miller calls "the ideology of the free gift"—a set of ethical attitudes toward giving and obligation that he claims are especially prominent in modern, commercial societies (50). Drawing on Marcel Mauss's seminal study *The Gift* and on the anthropological scholarship that built on Mauss's insights, Miller points out that in traditional societies gifts are understood to be embedded in systems of social exchange that tie actors to strong norms of duty and communal belonging. "In theory," Mauss says, gifts "are voluntary[;] in reality they are given and reciprocated obligatorily" (3). But as Miller and others note, the implications of that observation can be extended and clarified in a manner toward which Mauss himself points without fully elaborating. Mauss's discovery of the social obligations cemented by the circulation of gifts applies in particular to premodern societies that lack disembedded markets. In such societies, every act of donation creates potent moral expectations that, in some appropriate fashion, it will be returned. As Mary Douglas explains in the summary of Mauss's work she provides in the foreword to *The Gift*, "[T]he whole idea of the free gift is based on a misunderstanding. . . . A gift that does nothing to enhance solidarity is a contradiction" (x).

But as subsequent anthropological thinkers drawing on Mauss have noted, implausible as it may seem, the idea of the free gift became increasingly important to the ethical assumptions of modern societies, where, rather than being bound together in one richly contextualized cycle of exchange, social life is disarticulated, and the market, civil society, and the state tend to become increasingly independent realms of activity. In such developed societies, Miller argues, a different understanding of the gift arises. In this modern concept, giving is seen not as typical of economic and social action but rather as exceptional and, as such, ideally free—prompted by no compulsion or obligation and incurring no duty to reciprocate. As the anthropologist Jonathan Parry explains:

> The ideology of a disinterested gift emerges in parallel with an ideology of a purely interested exchange. . . . Those who make free and unconstrained contracts in the market also make free and unconstrained gifts outside it. But those gifts are defined as what market relations are not—altruistic, moral, and loaded with emotion. (458, 466)

If a free gift seems a contradiction in terms for premodern societies, then in modern, commercial societies ideologically the reverse is more nearly the case. A gift that is not given in a spirit of utter freedom, without a sense of duty or the hope of compensation attached, does not count as a true gift at all.

I suggest to my students that these two inconsistent ways of understanding the gift map quite directly onto the rival visions of love implicit in *As I Lay Dying*. The modern understanding of romantic love as passion and the related view of companionate marriage as a freely chosen agreement between autonomous individuals epitomize the logic of the free gift. Love and marriage in this modern view are understood to be ideally free, benevolent, unconstrained by customary obligations, and untainted by interest and ambition. By contrast, more traditional views of marriage, the duties of husbands and wives, and the demands of familial expectation reflect the attitudes about reciprocity and obligation that Mauss believed were expressed in their pure form by tribal societies.

To make these ideas more concrete, I tell my students that Faulkner, who was Mauss's contemporary, was, like Mauss, a member of a generation of modernist intellectuals who were deeply concerned with the way that industrial development had remade society and who often looked to anthropological or quasi-anthropological ideas about primitive cultures to clarify the distinctive features of modern life. Mauss's interest in premodern systems of gift exchange was not merely a product of anthropological curiosity but part of a strong "moral" critique of the individualist biases of "liberal society" (65, 66). "Fortunately, everything is still not wholly categorized in terms of buying and selling," Mauss comments in praise of the "archaic" ideas about giving and obligation he sees underlying the commercial ethos of modern society. "We possess more than a tradesman morality" (65).[2]

Faulkner's attitudes toward the poor white hill farmers, to whom he returned throughout his career, can perhaps be seen in a comparable light. In novels like *The Hamlet* and *Absalom, Absalom!*, Faulkner treated the farmers explicitly in a manner that had become commonplace in American popular culture over the previous several decades: as cultural primitives whose lives were largely alien to the predominant commercial (and interracial) engines of modern American development. Faulkner described the poor white farmers of northern Mississippi's hill country as descendants of the figures William Goodell Frost influentially labeled "our contemporary ancestors" (qtd. in Shapiro xvi). And somewhat like Mauss, Faulkner cast their archaic practices as alternatives to the centers of the nation's wealth and power. They "came from . . . the Tennesee mountains by stages," *The Hamlet* informs us of the people of Frenchman's Bend, and "brought no slaves and no Phyfe and no Chippendale highboys" (5).

Somewhat as Mauss had done, Faulkner drew on the cultural resonance of poor hill farmers to highlight, by contrast, the morally and socially corrosive potential of capitalist development. Throughout his career, Faulkner registered deep concern about the way urbanization and industrial development had transformed the agricultural South virtually overnight. I draw my students' attention to the repeated offhand references to the sale of lumber in *As I Lay Dying* and note that such references are part of a minor but consistent motif in Faulkner's fiction, one that crops up more dramatically in *Light in August* and *Go Down, Moses.* Faulkner was responding to the rapid deforestation of Mississippi that occurred during the first several decades of the twentieth century as the state became a new frontier in the nationally booming timber industry. When Darl tells us that he and Jewel will delay the family's trip to Jefferson by hauling one final load of lumber or when we learn that, to pay off his mortgage, Vernon Tull has chopped down the white oaks marking the ford the Bundrens are to cross, Faulkner points directly to the way the growth of industry and the expansion of national commodity markets were literally changing the landscape of northern Mississippi.

But Faulkner also resembles Mauss in that his treatment of industrial modernization places unusual emphasis on the complexity of uneven development. Numerous critics have emphasized that *As I Lay Dying* takes us on a journey across highly resonant locations in Faulkner's social geography.[3] Traveling with the Bundrens to Jefferson, we move from the hill country of sharecroppers and subsistence farmers to the wealthier towns closer to the delta, from a monoracial community of poor white farmers to the interracial and hierarchical society that is the legacy of Mississippi's plantocracy. That journey all but allegorizes the broader social transformation that also concerned Mauss, taking us from a remote hinterland of the capitalist economy, where the rules of kinship and custom still bind a local community, to an urbanizing commercial society characterized by mobility and anonymity.

Faulkner was one of a cohort of literary intellectuals during the interwar era fascinated by such a journey. Like Mauss, he took an unusually complex view of the process. I draw my students' attention to the distinctiveness of his perspective by noting the ways Faulkner resembled—and how drastically he differed from—his contemporaries among the Agrarians, the southern writers grouped around John Crowe Ransom and Allan Tate who argued in their influential collection of essays *I'll Take My Stand* that the traditional folkways of the rural South were under assault by the forces of economic modernization. The Agrarians viewed hill farmers like the Bundrens as the representatives of an imperiled southern yeomanry and imagined them holding desperately to pockets of rural autonomy in a last-ditch effort to defend a rich "agrarian culture" from the "industrial warfare" of the North (Lytle 229). Likewise, I draw attention to Faulkner's differences with the liberal reformers and political radicals who during the 1930s increasingly shaped the national view of southern poverty and sought through projects of state-led development or political mobilization to bring the region's poor farmers out of confining poverty and isolation. To fully understand *As I Lay Dying*, I suggest, we need to consider that Faulkner accepts neither of these strong views of southern history.

Even as he describes the hill farms and the urbanizing towns of Yoknapatawpha County as two nearly distinct communities, he shows us in the Bundrens and their neighbors a remote farming economy already permeated by global commodity markets and increasingly subject to the growing power of the state and federal governments. Not only do the Bundrens cut timber for sale, they are dependent for their livelihood on cotton—a cash crop whose price fell precipitously throughout the 1920s. Like most readers, my students rarely catch such details on their first view of the novel, so I point out to them that to complete the journey to Jefferson, Anse must take out a mortgage on his cultivator and seeder; that he avoids mortgaging his farm only by trading away Jewel's horse; and that, even with that transaction, the family incurs enormous financial as well as personal costs.[4] The Bundrens, who are small owners in an agricultural sector increasingly dominated by sharecropping, would have labored under the constant threat of losing possession of their land. Their trip to Jefferson must bring them perilously close to peonage.

Thus, where the Agrarians imagined the upland South to be the last preserve of a vibrant and autonomous culture, Faulkner depicts a community already integrated into the nation's commercial and political institutions—and headed on a downward slope toward terrible poverty. Not just Addie's death, which comes tellingly at twilight, or the vividly rendered decay of her corpse but Anse's own apparent sickness and falling wealth, the "shimmering dilapidation" (4) of his cotton house, the futile despair of his neighbors, the washed-out bridge at Tull's, which has been crumbling for twenty-five years—all these details speak of a community in a state of economic decline.

But if Faulkner does not share the Agrarians' romantic view of the southern yeomanry, neither does he imagine the Bundrens being fatefully drawn into the political and economic direction of the nation's industrial economy. Following Ted Atkinson's illuminating discussion of the novel (170–80), I ask my students to compare Faulkner's text with John Steinbeck's *The Grapes of Wrath*, where a similarly situated family of poor white farmers is shown leaving behind their home, their folkways, their deepest convictions—even their family ties—to join a new national compact. What is most striking about the Bundrens in this context, my students observe, is the circularity of their journey and the way, following the expulsion of Darl, they appear to return to the patterns by which they have been living. Despite their small-scale assimilation of consumer commodities like graphophones, false teeth, and bananas, the Bundrens do not make the "dramatic leap" Susan Willis perceives into "a world defined by very different economic and social relations" from those they have known in the past ("Learning" 588). They end up, rather, in a place remarkably similar to where they began.

In contrast to the nostalgia of the Agrarians or the progressivism of liberal thinkers like Steinbeck, Faulkner does not imagine his small farmers poised on the brink of a radically disruptive transition between alternative social orders. Instead, like Mauss, he stresses a complex overlay of the elements of tradition and modernity. His world combines both dirt farms and developing cities, cedar buckets and graphophones, mule carts and automobiles, horse swapping and the sale of industrially manufactured commodities. It might be that Faulkner views his hill farmers in something like the manner that Mauss understands the "archaic" cultural forms he sees surviving beneath the soulless dominance of "liberal society"—as residual elements of a declining cultural order so dwarfed by the economic and symbolic power of a newly urbanized society that, although not entirely lost, they become all but unrecognizable.

What such a description highlights, I suggest to my students, is the resistance Anse Bundren presents to ready interpretation. As Dorothy Hale argues, Anse is distinctive in Faulkner's narrative design in that we are given no ready means of knowing him psychologically. One consequence in this novel dominated by interior monologue is that the ways we might know Anse sociologically, by his history and his actions, tend to be disregarded. It is as though Faulkner solicits our reflexive dismissal of Anse while also planting subtle reminders of the way he might resist our judgments and reveal our prejudices.[5] We are told very little about his past, for example, but we are shown enough to see in his damaged body and his declining wealth a history of hard toil and misfortune. If we have been reading attentively, we know that his feet are badly misshapen from childhood labor, that he was once crushed beneath a load of falling lumber, that he has experienced serious illness and may have suffered a near fatal encounter with heatstroke. We know, too, that he was once industrious and "forehanded" enough to maintain "a good house and a good farm" (171) on his own and to aspire to a marriage up the social scale but that he has since come to see himself as "a luckless man" (18). In the farm crisis that devastated the South throughout the era, such a history might look less like a tale of personal failing than an example of sectoral decline. A cotton farmer might be understandably reluctant to produce crops that could end up earning him less than it cost to raise them and that might be destroyed by bad weather or pestilence before they ever reached market. He might, also understandably, resent the urban, commercial enterprises that continued to grow throughout the era. "Them that runs the stores in the towns" don't sweat, Anse points out (110).

Faulkner's readers are, of course, predominantly people who live in towns and know stores well. Not surprisingly, the critical reception of *As I Lay Dying* has been marked by a tendency to dismiss such complaints as gratuitous self-justification and to overlook the extent to which they reflect perfectly understandable grievances or desires. Anse's yearning for new teeth, which, as Anse plausibly explains to Jewel, are necessary if he is to "eat God's appointed food," are typically regarded as shallowly cosmetic (191). His children's desires for even the small pleasures of consumer life that more privileged readers take for granted (bananas, recorded music, manufactured toys) often occasion judgments about their capitulation to "the logic of capitalism" (Atkinson 191). Still more striking are those writers who see only culpable signs of "bourgeois, liberal belief" in Cash's objections to the destruction of Gillespie's barn or in the bitter irony that the Bundrens' neighbors express at the likely loss of their crops (Railey 90).

And what is true of Anse's history and of the losses of his neighbors is still more true of the actions Anse takes in the course of Faulkner's narrative. Every reader of *As I Lay Dying* notes that Anse makes use of the trip to Jefferson to get himself a new set of teeth and a new wife. But much less attention is paid to the fact that, were he actually an accomplished villain, Anse might well have set out after those goals without honoring Addie's demand. If he were a Snopes or a character out of Erskine Caldwell, for example, nothing would be less surprising than seeing him ignore his promise. Meanwhile, were he merely hapless, it is unlikely he could have completed his journey by putting together an effective, if costly, bargain with a Snopes or faced down Jewel to complete it. That he hops onto Jewel's wild spotted horse and rides off without trouble to make the deal is a sign that he is not the easily ridiculed figure he often seems.

As I Lay Dying is salted with details of this sort, suggesting a richer and more complex portrait of Anse Bundren and his world than is commonly acknowledged in the critical literature. Those details are rarely considered—in part, because they are not flagged for our attention; in part, because the questions they raise do not appear clearly when framed by the assumptions that Miller refers to as the ideology of the free gift. Because, for example, in burning Gillepsie's barn, Darl tries to end the grotesque mistreatment of his mother's body and because he pays a high price for that act, it is easy to overlook the fact that Cash has a point: Gillespie and his family are made to suffer an enormous (and presumably uninsured) loss solely because they met the customary obligations of hospitality. Against Darl's self-sacrifice, Cash's objection to the loss looks to many readers basely prudent and conventional. Similarly, because Anse is known to have interests in traveling to Jefferson, his fulfillment of his debt to his wife immediately seems doubtful, as does the still more subtle suggestion that he loved Addie. In effect, Darl's arson looks like a "free gift," and the hidden costs borne by others appear unimportant. By contrast, Anse's promise seems illegitimate because it lacks the ostensible selflessness of the gift and thus looks instead like a contract. The high costs he and his children bear to honor it come to seem absurd, because they appear neither wholly disinterested nor rationally tailored to meet any plausible interest. We have, in short, a ready ideological framework for understanding Darl's self-sacrifice—as we do, say, for interpreting Addie's grandeur or Whitfield's hypocrisy. Anse's motivations seem opaque by contrast.

If Faulkner's readers tend to view the events of *As I Lay Dying* in this fashion, it may be because Faulkner gives us, in Addie Bundren's monologue, a fiercely eloquent defense of something near to the spiritual core of the ideology of the free gift. Addie is, of course, not an opaque character. In one of the novel's more subtle structural features, her depiction neatly reverses the representation of Anse: she is at once the character most strongly committed to privacy and the person whose thoughts and feelings are most fully transparent to the reader. Those readers who recognize the harsh self-interest that Addie views as characterizing her world are thus encouraged to view their own intimacy with the character as a kind of alternative, disinterested relationship—again, a gift rather than a contract. More than any other speaker, Addie offers us not only an account of her impressions and observations but also a coherent life narrative and a fully elaborated philosophical vision. Even as she disappears from the narrative present, her voice exercises great influence over how we evaluate what we are told by other narrators.[6] Though she is no longer a schoolteacher, she remains the novel's most effective pedagogue.

As with the depiction of Anse, however, the very power of the psychological portrait that Addie's narrative creates threatens to obscure what we also know about Addie sociologically—that she is not a countrywoman by birth but has come to the Bundren farm from Jefferson and remains determined to return there. That feature of her character may help explain just why she, more than any other character, speaks for the assumptions of "liberal society," as Mauss describes them. Addie is, of course, an intense individualist who aspires to a nearly deific vision of self-authorization. "I would be I," she declares (174), and she is appropriately contemptuous of the customary beliefs and practices that bind other characters. But in addition, running all through her convictions about language, her thoughts about marriage and childbirth—even her ideas about life and death—we see the allure of the ideology of the free gift. Wholly in keeping with the premises of possessive individualism, Addie appears to assume that a fundamental distinction must be drawn between relations of interest and convention, on the one hand, and purely free and original donations that escape the bonds of reciprocity, on the other.

The logic of that thinking can be seen throughout Addie's monologue. In her meditations on language, for instance, she objects to the fact that in conventional speech people "use one another by words" and, at the same time, envisions an alternative "voiceless speech" (175). Because it is a product of "the dark land talking of God's love," the latter language surpasses the intentions and desires of any individual person (174). In her thoughts about sex and marriage, Addie similarly contrasts the conventional duties she "owed to . . . Anse" with the antinomian passion she experiences with Whitfield (174). As in her closely related vision of voiceless speech, that adulterous passion transcends not just social convention but also the differences between individual persons—not only "the clothes we both wore in the world's face" but also the "circumspection necessary because he was he and I was I" (174). With both language and sex, Addie presumes that ordinary life is characterized by conventional systems that enable bargaining between self-interested individuals, each person being characterized by "his and her secret and selfish thought" (170). At the same time, she imagines an alternative that replaces pure selfishness with pure selflessness.

The logic running through Addie's ideas about language and her beliefs about sex is most evident in her attitude toward her children. Anse, we know, expects the children to labor for him; in this way, he represents an unappealing version of the traditional assumptions of patriarchal authority. Addie, however, thinks about her children in the individualist fashion enabled by the assumptions of market society—as either commodities or free gifts. On the one hand, her children can be accounted for on a virtual balance sheet, as contractual obligations negotiated between competing, self-interested agents. "I gave Anse Dewey Dell to negative Jewel. Then I gave him Vardaman to replace the child I had robbed him of. And now he has three children that are his and not mine" (176). On the other hand, they can be imagined as occasions for a perfect intimacy that transcends both the traditional family and the despicable haggling of the market. "My children were of me alone . . . of me and of all that lived; of none and of all" (175).

Not surprisingly, then, in the only dialogue with her most beloved child, Addie articulates something near to a perfect expression of the idea of the pure gift. When she discovers that Jewel has nearly killed himself laboring to earn Quick's horse, she sobs and says, "Jewel . . . I'll give——I'll give——give——" (135). Her sentence is incomplete, strangely nontransitive, and, as a result, highly abstract. In effect, it offers not to give some particular thing but simply giving itself. To the same degree it is impotent. Jewel's face grows "cold and a little sick looking" at the appearance of her offer (135). In these respects, however, Addie's statement can be taken for a perfect expression of the free gift's "paradoxical and self-negating character." As an exchange that aspires somehow *not* to "create obligations or personal connections," the free gift in its ideal state must be intended in a spirit of pure altruism; it cannot even be acknowledged as a gift by either the giver or the receiver, for such recognition would imply the psychic rewards and implicit obligations that would mean the gift was no longer free at all (Laidlaw 618). For Addie's gift to be genuinely free, it must not actually give anything. (Addie herself points to this logic when, while discussing her marriage, she emphasizes that she "did not even ask" Anse "for what he could have given me: not-Anse" [174].) But by this reasoning, even her offer to give herself to Jewel can't help compromising itself. As Jewel's reaction suggests, he takes even her most abstract expression to be making tacit demands on him, and since he is nearly as committed to radical individualism as his mother is, he finds her gift intolerable.

The same logic is apparent in Addie's thoughts about life and death. What we know about those thoughts is that, like her ideas about language and sex and children, they involve the desire to overcome the routine transitivity of conventional social life. "My father said that the reason for living is getting ready to stay dead," Addie states (175). At first glance, the phrasing looks strikingly bleak. But it is worth noting that the sentiment Addie expresses in this sentence resembles an unorthodox expression of the very Christian desire for otherworldly "salvation" to which she refers in the last lines of her monologue (176). In short, what she appears to seek in death is an eternal reward to replace the squalid self-interest, impermanence, and inescapable consequences of living in this world.

Here, Addie articulates the logic of the free gift. In an account of the ideology underlying the idea of the gift and of the social institutions that nurture it, Parry makes a relevant observation. The idea of the free gift flourishes, he notes, in "highly differentiated societies with an advanced division of labor." But the vision of transcendence that the free gift embodies was also nurtured by the rise of "ethicisized salvation religions" (467). Parry argues that the spiritual practices of tribal societies place no particular value on the afterlife and so no special emphasis on the kind of nonreciprocal giving that could be imagined to escape the transitivity of ordinary social exchange. By contrast, the "world religions" that emerged in what Karl Jaspers called the axial age—Buddhism, Hinduism, Judaism, and Christianity—emphasize an "other-worldly orientation" and "the notion of salvation" from the "profane world of suffering" (467, 468). All such religions, Parry points out, also place great stress on the virtue of charity, alms, and unrewarded giving. "The unreciprocated gift becomes" a means of "liberation from bondage" to the sinful world (468).

The most prominent voice of ethicisized salvation religion in *As I Lay Dying* is, of course, Cora Tull, who views the "reward" she expects to receive in the afterlife almost explicitly as compensation (23). In numerous respects Cora is a telling companion figure to Addie. They are each former schoolteachers who, brought to the country from town; have kept their husbands "at work for thirty odd years," and although in differing ways, they each adopt strong spiritual convictions that enable them to make confident moral judgments about the failings of their families and neighbors (33). That Cora presents us with a compromised vision of her beliefs (in which she turns the free gift of salvation into earned compensation) should not obscure the extent to which Addie, as the final words of her monologue suggest, is yet more radically committed to an analogous vision of otherworldly salvation—a vision that, being more than "just words," would aptly surpass her prime example of the conventional bargains of this world (176).[7]

The appeal of that transcendent vision is evident not only in Addie's sentiments but also in the speech and action of Darl, the one child who does most to help her realize her desire "to stay dead." Despite, or perhaps in keeping with, the fact that he expresses little personal feeling for his mother, Darl resembles Addie in many ways, I point out to my students. In particular, the deracination Darl experienced during World War I appears to have made him, like his mother, a marginal figure to the rural community in which he once lived. Cash remarks, "This world is not his world; this life his life" (261), and the ambiguity of his phrasing allows the sentence to refer to the milieu of the Bundren farm, even as it casts Darl as a Christ figure who is ultimately foreign to the whole temporal realm of exploitation and sin. In keeping with that characterization, Darl has few evident emotional or personal connections to the other members of his family. He shows none of the intense grief or need for Addie that leads Dewey Dell, for example, to say, "I wish I had time to let her die" (120). But for that same reason, he alone can hear Addie speak her desire to "lay down her life," and he alone pities the degradation to which she is subjected by the other members of her family (215). He envisions the destruction of her corpse as the occasion for a transcendent emancipation from what Parry calls the "profane world of suffering." When the funeral procession comes to the swollen river, Darl views it as "the place where the motion of the wasted world accelerates just before the final precipice," and he describes the log that nearly frees her as appearing upon "that surging and heaving desolation like Christ" (146, 148).

But, of course, Addie's corpse is not freed from the suffering of this world, either at the river or at Gillespie's barn. Nor does Darl's act of Christian martyrdom actually liberate him from "[t]his world." As it imposes high costs on the Gillespies, it also results in his own, more brutal confinement. There are neither free gifts, it seems, nor free individuals in the world of *As I Lay Dying*. The funeral journey that both fulfills and traduces Addie's last wishes epitomizes this pattern. "[M]y revenge would be that he would never know I was taking revenge," Addie says of the promise she demands from Anse (173). Her formulation is yet another illustration of both the logic of the free gift and of its impossibility. Nothing demonstrates more aptly the cruelty and potential horror of social reciprocity than the cycles of revenge, and nothing is more strongly reviled in each of the ethicisized salvation religions. Addie looks to escape those potentially endless returns by finding a kind of ultimate donation that will somehow escape routine transitivity. Revenge that is not recognized as revenge is the ultimate kind of recompense, she realizes, because theoretically it can never be reciprocated. But the journey to Jefferson, and the degrading treatment to which her corpse is subjected, proves her theory wrong. Anse, who is surely not fool enough to miss the vengeance Addie takes on him, understands how to get his own back.

Seeing Anse Bundren in such a light does not make him any more attractive to most of my students. Indeed, considering *As I Lay Dying* in the manner I have been suggesting only strengthens their impression that Faulkner is a powerful but also a strange and rebarbative writer whose fiction dramatizes beliefs and attitudes deeply foreign to what they most value. But looking more closely at the economic and social implications of Faulkner's story and considering the related ideological conflict that lies at the novel's core help my students get a grasp on a work many of them see as mysterious and unaccountable. In the view of the novel I propose, *As I Lay Dying* turns on the unresolved, unending conflict between Addie and Anse and implicitly on the broader, less evident cultural conflict their battle represents. Even as Addie seeks helplessly to transcend it, it is a conflict, the novel's famous conclusion suggests, that Anse is determined to continue.

To bring home the possible significance of that determination, I ask my students to consider a question strangely unaddressed in most discussions of the novel: Just why does Anse want to replace Addie with a new Mrs. Bundren? He is no longer young or healthy. He has children who will labor in his fields and home and little incentive to find new mouths to feed. What purpose can be served by his taking a new wife?

Noting the Bundrens' perilous economic state, some astute students will plausibly suggest that the new Mrs. Bundren will provide not only a graphophone but also the infusion of capital that Anse needs if he is to maintain possession of his farm and keep control of his family. Others will make a related but more convincing suggestion—that Anse desires a renewal of the emotional and ideological struggle he experienced with Addie and that he needs that goad if he is to survive psychically as well as financially. Kate Tull points to something along these lines early in the book in response to her father's comment that Addie "'kept [Anse] at work for thirty-odd years.'. . . 'And I reckon she'll be behind him for thirty years more,' Kate says. 'Or if it aint her, he'll get another one before cotton-picking'" (33–34).

What Anse seeks in this view is neither, as some critics have suggested, brute labor to exploit nor a soul mate with whom he might find a transcendent union but rather a battle partner who will spur him into fulfilling his customary obligations. Considering that thought leads my students to confront a vision of love and obligation that many of them find distasteful—but one that, as Mauss might predict, they also come to acknowledge as disturbingly familiar.

NOTES

[1] Robert Dale Parker is one of the rare critics who takes seriously Anse's protestations that he loved Addie. See Parker, *Faulkner* 28–31.

[2] For a fuller explanation and for a review of the anthropological and theoretical literature on the subject, see Laidlaw.

[3] See especially Atkinson 176–94; Lester, "As They Lay Dying"; J. Matthews, "*As I Lay Dying*"; Railey 87–96; and Willis, "Learning from the Banana."

[4] Darl remarks that the cultivator and seeder are worth $40 (or approximately $420 in 2007) and perhaps as much as ten percent of a small cotton farmer's net income in Mississippi circa 1920. Mule prices at the time varied depending on region, quality, and breed, but the team of mules the Bundrens lost may have been worth $2,000 or $3,000 (in 2007 dollars) and could have been worth anywhere between a third to a half of a small cotton farmer's net income. The mules with which Anse replaces them, having

been bought at perhaps half that value, are evidently much older and weaker and will presumably be less effective draught animals, therefore intensifying the Bundrens' apparent decline in fortune.

[5] For two especially valuable exceptions to the pattern of dismissive commentary on Anse, see Leyda; Rippetoe.

[6] By comparison, as Dorrit Cohn points out, the novel's next most eloquent narrator, Darl, "tells us what he sees, hears, says, and does in the episodes of the funeral journey, but never what he thinks or feels." The effect is to make it seem "as though the reflective and affective components of the mind had been bracketed" (205, 206).

[7] The extent to which the ideology of the free gift provides the terms on which we intuitively distinguish between Cora and Addie can be seen in Olga Vickery's influential *The Novels of William Faulkner*. In Vickery's account, Cora exemplifies everything Addie resists, and what most characterizes Cora is the fact her gifts are not free: "Her help . . . is offered in the name of duty not love, and it is meant, whether she realizes it or not, to be one more step in establishing her own virtue and her own right to salvation. Kindness such as Cora's is essentially selfish, debasing both the giver and the recipient" (64).

Telling Time: The Use of Montage in the Narration of *As I Lay Dying*

E. L. McCallum

As I Lay Dying is remarkable for its use of multiple narrators and the concomitant fragmentation of perspective, a feature widely construed to be a fundamental mark of modernism. Indeed, modernism's innovations across visual and verbal art, and particularly the visuality of literary modernism, are a critical commonplace. So how might modernist visual culture teach us to read Faulkner's novel? Such a question prompts me to juxtapose *As I Lay Dying* with Dziga Vertov's film *Man with a Movie Camera* in a large-lecture general education course that examines multiple modes of representation. My aim is to give students (many of whom are not liberal arts students, much less English majors) a nuanced appreciation for how representation works. I seek both to build on and to complicate aspects of novels that students are already familiar with—like the omniscient narrator—as well as introduce basic film theory they can use to understand initially difficult texts. By drawing on the lessons of Vertov's avant-garde film to read Faulkner's novel, I direct attention to how, because of modernism's insistence on form, innovative filmmakers and novelists were using principles of composition that can be compared. A seemingly difficult, unconventional film like Vertov's can be understood through narrative principles like point of view, the limits of omniscience, while what seems to be a medium-specific element of form—namely, montage in cinema—can be productively transposed to other media, in this case to aid interpretation of innovative or experimental verbal texts. In this way, students can take what they learn from reading Faulkner to make Vertov's text more meaningful as well.

The fragmentation of narrative perspective in *As I Lay Dying* is an effect found in filmmaking's use of montage, particularly in the Soviet avant-garde work contemporaneous with the novel.[1] Montage is, quite simply, the construction of a film by editing different shots together. Vertov defines montage as "organizing film fragments (shots) into a film-object. It means 'writing' something cinematic with the recorded shots" (88). As articulated by Soviet filmmakers, montage came to mean something more complex than simple editing: it is a patterning that juxtaposes shots on the basis of aesthetic or formal composition rather than exclusively narrative considerations and thus one that does not necessarily craft a spatially or temporally coherent view. Vertov made the antinarrative agenda explicit: "[Montage] does not mean selecting the fragments for 'scenes' (the theatrical bias) or for titles (the literary bias)" (88). Soviet montage provides a compelling alternative paradigm to narrative film organized through continuity editing. By foregrounding it, I urge students to consider how montage might help us see the ways novels engage in nonnarrative meaning making as well.

My lecture before the screening of *Man with a Movie Camera* explains how Vertov's film tells a double story.[2] On the one hand, it depicts a day in the life of a city; on the other hand, in the way it frames and punctuates this chronicle, the film presents an account of its making. Throughout the movie we see the various stages of filmmaking, as if we were watching the creation of this film. The two threads culminate in the metacinematic moment of depicting the screening of the film itself. Although *As I Lay Dying* has a clearer linear plot—driven forward through space as well as time—the novel engages in a similarly doubled strategy of telling a story about representation. By juxtaposing the book with Vertov's film, I hope to tune students in to that second story, how both texts employ a narrative framework that they persistently challenge and even undermine, as well as how both texts include in their range of perspectives a transcendent vantage that is revealed to be impossibly located, purely an artifact of representation itself. Readily seeing this in the shots of the eponymous man filming alone (but obviously requiring a second camera to film him), students can apply that insight and realize that Darl narrates Addie's dying when he is not present to witness it.

Reading the "shot" in fiction requires students to distinguish between narrator and point of view. *As I Lay Dying*'s juxtaposition of different narrators might tempt students to think that the discreteness of each narrator is akin to the discreteness of each shot in a film. Certainly, the composite arrangement of chapters seems to align neatly with montage theory, where the combination of the distinct shots contributes to the meaning. But montage in the novel works at other levels as well. To make the distinction clear, I give students the definition of narrator as the voice telling the story. Drawing on Seymour Chatman's taxonomy,

I then lay out for them the difference between narrated events and either monologue or those events directly witnessed; the degree of intrusion of the narrator's presence, from minimally present (as in diaries or letters or soliloquy) to covert (the narrator mediates our view but does not call attention to himself or herself) to overt (the narrator directly refers to himself or herself); and finally, the trustworthiness of a narrator—whether what we are told accords with what we know. I then contrast the features of narrator with the aspects of point of view, again drawing on Chatman. Seeing from someone's physical perspective exemplifies *perceptual* point of view. Adopting someone's way of thinking—a metaphorical seeing from someone's ideological view or attitude—indicates a *conceptual* point of view. This is not to be confused with metaphorically seeing from someone's advantage or disadvantage, which is an *interest* point of view.

The distinction between the two metaphorical modes of seeing is tricky for some students to grasp, even as I emphasize that if you share someone's interest, you would focus on how things affect their concerns. And of course, interest point of view is key to the novel, since it is often concealed precisely through montage. So to help bring the distinction home, I ask students in their discussion section to consider Anse and Addie and, specifically, why Anse does not "begrudge her it" (117, 163)? We might think that Anse does not "begrudge her it" because he shares Addie's conceptual point of view, her wanting to be buried with her folks. But in fact he does so to conceal his interest point of view: his desire to go to Jefferson to get a new wife.

So with the distinction between narrator-narration as speech and point of view as physical place, ideological position, or practical life orientation to which narrated events stand in relation, we are ready to think of "shot" at a more granular level. To help students perceive the distinction between narrator and point of view, I turn their attention to the first page of the novel.

The opening paragraph, narrated by Darl, plays on the dynamics of spectatorship that the novel engages.

> Jewel and I come up from the field, following the path in single file. Although I am fifteen feet ahead of him, anyone watching us from the cottonhouse can see Jewel's frayed and broken straw hat a full head above my own. (3)

The second sentence of the paragraph posits a spectator and the spectator's vantage—up ahead, at the cottonhouse—while the first posits the vantage of the speaking subject—walking up the path, one behind the other. The present tense used here is the tense of film itself, which is always showing what is as "now"; past or future is marked by reframing that present (the hokey dissolve, for instance, between "now" and "then" only takes us to a now that was then).[3]

A new paragraph marks the narration's shift to a minimally located or even unlocated observer, not one in the cottonhouse but possibly returning to the speaking-walking subject:

> The path runs straight as a plumb-line, worn smooth by feet and baked brick-hard by July, between green rows of laidby cotton, to the cottonhouse in the center of the field, where it turns and circles the cottonhouse at four soft right angles and goes on across the field again, worn so by feet in fading precision. (3)

This unlocated observer is an odd feature for a multiple-narrator novel, and calling attention to it raises questions about the teller's omniscience. It gives me a chance to ask students to compare Faulkner with Vertov, for they can see how the film posits an omniscient viewpoint in some moments, like the overview of the city, sooner than how it shapes a particular perspective at other moments, like showing the film's own editing. They thus can use the lesson of point of view in Faulkner to understand and analyze how film constructs point of view.

I use the "tell" of this unlocated observer to invite students to consider the novel's content in relation to form, again laying out questions for their discussion section. Might it signal Darl's unwillingness to be present in the scene and thus tell us about his disturbed state of mind, or does it merely show his insistence on recording like a machine, a "kino-eye," in Vertov's phrase? In a lecture I note that Darl's unlocatedness, moving from vantage point to vantage point, offers a seductive omniscience or objectivity and suggests a seeing that links people "based on continual exchange of visible fact" (Vertov 87–88). But that exchange of visible fact means that Darl himself can be seen. When students weigh whether Darl's being seen is a way for the novel to turn the camera on him, they start to understand the novel's self-reflexivity about representation as similar to Vertov's. This leads to their discussing when and how Darl is seen and what is remarkable about that climactic moment.

My aim in reading the first page of the book closely is to open up the possibility for students to consider that the "shot" equivalent is not a division between chapters but rather a montage of viewpoints within a chapter. If the switch in the first paragraph is divided by the two sentences, then the second (one-sentence) paragraph more subtly circles different vantages, like the path around the cottonhouse itself. The phrase "straight as a plumb-line" suggests the carpenter Cash's point of view, if he could see across the field from the house on the bluff. The appeal to the tactile—the smoothness and hardness of the path and its situation between green rows—takes us back to the speaker's perspective, while the description of the path's action, how it goes around the cotton house, suggests the more distant, externalized view, one transcending not only space but also time, as the durational sense of the final phrase, the feet's fading precision, intimates.

Because of Vertov's insistence that the kino-eye records objectively, comparison with Darl's opening chapter highlights how the opening scene is surveyed dispassionately, without emotion, even though with sensation. Such seeing is similarly evident in *Man with a Movie Camera*'s opening shots of the city in the morning: textures of shuttered windows; plays of perspective and framing of windows, mirrors, posters; the tactility of a sleeping body draped in sheets; even the smoothness of the road or the thrill of a passing train. All emphasize an aesthetics of sensation without sentimentality or emotion, creating a sense of specific space without necessarily orienting us in it. I draw on the objectivity and emotionlessness in Vertov and ask students to consider whether Faulkner's narrative displays a similar dispassion. It's an opportunity to discuss how emotion—whether the characters' expression of it or our own reactions—is significant in the text.

The radical subjectivism of the novel's telling and the complex play of proximity and distance enable us to question the relation between emotion and reason in how the novel contrasts what the characters see with what we see: foremost, who's sympathetic to Addie's plight? Are all the members of the family, as Diana York Blaine suggests of Dewey Dell, "too preoccupied to notice what's taking place literally under [their] noses" (88)? Or are they so grief-stricken at the loss of their mother that they hardly know how to feel, insisting, as Cash perversely and repeatedly does about his broken leg, "It dont bother none" (196)? There's a peculiar distance from the characters' emotions at work, despite the apparent proximity engendered by the soliloquistic or mentally self-addressed intimacy of the narration. Such distance complicates how readers are supposed to feel about this (on the face of it) repugnant narrative, this black comedy. Blaine observes that we instructors find ourselves "trying to convince students that what seems horrible to them is actually quite humorous" (88). I suggest that some of the formal difficulty of the text—the constantly switching narrators, the unfamiliar cadences of the language, and what critics recognize as its fragmentary, modernist aesthetics—helps students negotiate the dark humor, giving them a distance on the novel. But it is the emotional truths that form the backbone of the novel's sense of reliability in the face of what turn out to be unreliable narrators. Such unreliability emerges for students as they attend more closely to the montage of different kinds of points of view (perceptual, conceptual, interest) as well as different narrators.

The proximity of emotion and reason is just one element that the montage composition reveals to be at work in its gestalt. The point of teasing out these distinctions—whether shifts in perspective within or between sentences, thematic distinctions like reason versus emotion, or contrasting narrators from chapter to chapter—is to enable students to examine in greater detail how the pieces relate and work together. To underscore how the whole is greater than the sum of the parts because of the patterns of relations between those parts, I turn in my next lecture to Sergei Eisenstein's essays on montage in *Film Form*, which offer some of the keenest articulations of montage theory.

Arguing against the idea promoted by Lev Kuhleshov and his followers that montage serves specifically to link pieces together to create unity, Eisenstein espouses the importance of conflict between shots or even within a shot—since, as he puts it, "from the collision of two given factors *arises* a concept" (37).[4] Students are familiar with montage in classical narrative cinema, where montage sequences give a bird's-eye view of the story to advance the narrative, but Eisenstein's exposition of five categories of montage counters this summary model. According to Eisenstein, the highest form is intellectual montage or "conflict-juxtaposition of accompanying intellectual affects" (82). The other four build up from metric montage (akin to a measure of music, pieces of film are juxtaposed on the basis of length); rhythmic montage (which integrates the duration of a shot with its content, such as movement, so that tempo rather than a strict arithmetical meter is the governing feature); tonal montage (which incorporates "*dominant* emotional sound" [76] with rhythmic considerations: elements like lightness, graphical qualities, mood); and perhaps most interesting for reading Faulkner, overtonal montage (which takes into consideration larger tonal arcs of the film, the relation of the whole to the parts).

To apply Eisenstein's insights, I invite students to examine features like the length of chapters and the patterns the length creates, whether regular or irregular (metric montage), who speaks and how often, and how shifts in point of view provide guidelines for mapping rhythmic montage. We also look at what kind of discourse—that is, mode of telling—the chapter uses: monologue or dialogue, for instance, or retrospective, prospective, or present continuous (tonal montage). I then ask them to examine how chapters contribute to larger patterns developing in the novel—the gaps, the silences, the intensities—that cue us whom to trust or believe and whom to empathize with (overtonal). And whereas narrative leads to a culmination that resolves the conflict it portrays, montage, by contrast, leads to a larger, composite image whose resolution might be understood not as an outcome but as a heightened degree of granularity of perception.

Mapping the interplay between narrative and montage helps students understand how a novel is more than its plot and characterization. Faulkner's use of montage simultaneously advances and delays the narrative, creating silences and contradictions that can inform us more about what's going on than telling outright does. Teaching students to read for montage, then, leads to an assignment that asks them to attend to the negative space of the novel—the gaps, the silences, the discrepancies—rather than the positive spaces of character, plot, and so on. Or students might write about the tension between the narrative's linear and causal unfolding and resistances to that drive, the ways the narrative drive is disrupted through delay and deferral (such as: Why does Addie's chapter come when it does? How does its timing affect the montage as opposed to the narrative?). Highlighting the collision between reading forward that narrative impels (syntagmatic) and reading to ponder the rich interlinkage of sensory and intellectual associations that montage facilitates (paradigmatic) is one way to open up students' awareness of the paradigmatic axis. Reading for montage teaches students the pleasures of a more dilatory, more richly interconnected reading.

Read for montage, *As I Lay Dying* can be said to produce a single imagist generalization from the disparate phenomena of each teller—for instance, an ideogram of dependence-autonomy: the bitter self-interest of family members in conflict with the ideals of togetherness in family life and the irony of these ideals' elevation as the highest form of human connection. From Dewey Dell's incipient motherhood or Jewel's bastardy acted out in his efforts to gain financial and transportational independence, both of which question the mythic privilege of marital propagation, to the family's refusal to honor their mother with a timely and decent burial (as neighbors like Samson expect) in deference to Anse's perverse insistence that he keep his promise to Addie and bury her in Jefferson, this conflict takes several forms, both acquiescent and resistant.[5] The montage of these different story strands combines as intellectual montage to chart the dark conflict of autonomy versus familial interdependence.

If this reading of montage seems to reinforce traditional literary approaches to the text, like asking students to discern the theme of the book, I argue that reading for montage offers more—especially in terms of sharpening their critical analysis of patterns at work in the text—just as Soviet montage practice offers more than mere editing. Because the first step requires students to discern what the pieces are and the next step to examine those pieces' relation to one another in formal terms—for instance, scale, repetition, distance, perspective—this approach leads students to a more functional awareness of dynamics in the text. Montage gives them a tool for close reading that connects formal elements with thematic elements—raising questions like, Why is it that Jewel narrates only once, and very early, indeed before Addie dies, yet he looms so large in the story as told by others, particularly Darl? Are the dynamics between Jewel and Darl such that Darl's desire to push Jewel out of the frame intensifies after Addie's death, such that Jewel is squeezed out of the telling of the story as Darl tries to take control of the narrative? What does Darl's edging out his younger brother tell us about his understanding of Addie's death—is Darl refusing it, seeking to punish for it, secretly rejoicing in it, using it as the last straw for his own sanity? If he won't let Jewel tell the story, why does he talk about Jewel so much? What's Jewel's take on the situation? Why can't or won't he leave? As the class attends to both centripetal and centrifugal forces, reading for montage in the novel impels them beyond such narrowly or traditionally thematic approaches.

It is simple enough to sort out how many narrators there are and ask students what patterns they discern about who speaks when and how much or how little (metric and rhythmic montage approach). "What is the nature of their narration?," however, becomes a more fraught question, one that requires students to analyze at the level of tonal montage. As they attend to which narrator presents which soliloquy, which dialogue, which overt narration, they start to question the omniscient narration that the first page of the book seemed to establish. At this point, I bring in Wayne Booth's characterization of *As I Lay Dying*'s narration:

> Our roving visitation into the minds of sixteen characters in Faulkner's *As I Lay Dying*, seeing nothing but what those minds contain, may seem in

> one sense not to depend on an omniscient author. But this method is omniscience with teeth in it: the implied author demands our absolute faith in his powers of divination. (161)

I have students compare this view with Shinya Matsuoka's acknowledgment that "[t]he multiplication of internal narratives by viewing subjects gives the false impression that it is a novel narrated wholly in the third person because it parlays the proliferation of subjectivity into objectivity" (84). Matsuoka's reasoning—that the proliferation of subjectivity becomes objectivity (perhaps akin to how all colors of light combine to make white?) may be found contestable by students. But his observation also gives students a chance to examine how Booth may have reached his claim of "omniscience with teeth" and to debate this idea. (Perchance this perspective is also what Anse strives for, since so much of the novel hinges on what the toothless pater familias does not know or ought not to know.)

The problem of omniscience in *As I Lay Dying* is not merely a problem of critical perception—much as it might open up a useful classroom discussion that moves students toward a more sophisticated view of omniscience—but investing in the "omniscient" view occludes questions of "Who knows?" "Who sees?" and "Who tells?" that the novel troubles very effectively, as students realize from working with the montage of points of view. "In short," Booth concludes, "impersonal narration is really no escape from omniscience—the true author is as 'unnaturally' all-knowing as he [sic] ever was" (161). In some way, then, what reading for montage adds up to is a more nuanced understanding of omniscience that makes students ask what is at stake, interpretively speaking, in asserting a claim about the novel having omniscience or averring that it does not. For instance, does believing omniscience make Darl seem more trustworthy or more manipulative? In addition, this approach calls attention to the paradoxical tension between natural and unnatural representations and turns the question toward the seamless moments as well as the gaps.

Reading for montage gives students a way to move beyond characterization and the like-dislike mode. Cora may be judgmental, but she's also loquacious; her failure to hold anything back contrasts with and thereby elicits silences in Darl's telling. Those silences are not just what Darl does not say; there is also a certain deafness in tone. How does Darl say "It means three dollars" (17)? Is there urgency or reluctance or deadpan in his voice? But Cora has her silences too, which she covers by saying too much. It's Mr Tull's report that Cora relies on to piece together her sense of Darl, so her view of the process is tinged by her not fully articulated feelings toward her husband. Might she be questioning his authority or, instead, using his view as authorization for her own?

The contrast between Vernon's report—"Mr Tull says Darl asked them to wait. He said Darl almost begged them on his knees not to force him to leave her in her condition. But nothing would do but Anse and Jewel must make that three dollars" (22)—and what readers heard from Darl himself in the previous chapter—"'We'll need that three dollars then, sure,' I say" (17)—produces a dramatic tension not merely between characters in conflict but between modes of representation, in the very process of the novel's montage itself. The spatial proximity of Cora's experience to Vernon's, she on the inside of the house and he on the porch (so could she have heard him say "Wait" or not?), combines with the temporal succession of those experiences to seem to produce a continuous narrative progression. But montage reading reveals how the narrative momentum stalls out in these chapters, leaving some of the most important telling to the juxtapositions.

Eisenstein argues that montage is at the core of cinematic practice, "the nerve of cinema" (48), and that it "arises from the collision of independent shots—shots even opposite to one another: the dramatic principle" (49). In the instance above, Cora's view draws out the conflict between Jewel and Darl that will become apparent only later in the novel, yet her sympathy toward Darl, even as it may misread him into the role of dutiful, loving son, paradoxically serves to undermine his credibility. If pietistic Cora likes him, then should we? The conflict in perspectives reveals as well how Darl holds up or staves off the narrative, even as he takes the lion's share of recounting it. Moreover, what's elided in the collision between Cora's view and Darl's view of the sons' departure with their three-dollar load is the question of why there is such insistence on the trip. Cora's judgment that Anse and Jewel must have that money rings hollow to readers distanced by her sanctimony. Juxtaposing Cora's approving account of Darl with his exchange with Dewey Dell helps develop the possibility that Darl's conflict is with his mother, not just with his brother.

The montage here is a form of overtonal montage: "the conflict between the principle tone of the piece (its dominant) and the overtone" (Eisenstein 79), between what's going on in the foreground and what's going on in the background. If the dominant tone of *As I Lay Dying* is one of observer outrage—What are these people doing!—and the participants' various ways of mustering a sense of victimization by circumstance, in the background is the more noble struggle for self-determination that each of the characters engages in, from Vardaman to Anse, a struggle Addie is no stranger to. Addie's effort thus is layered with another overtonal conflict made clear in this montage sequence: that if in the foreground is Darl's conflict with Jewel, then in the background is a conflict with his mother, one that arguably underlies and shapes his tensions with his brother.

Darl's lack of self-location, however, impairs his self-determination; unlocatable, he is ungrounded and lacks boundaries, so he aggressively tries to punish others who transgress, particularly Addie and Dewey Dell, whose plights of extramarital conception, a compound boundary quandary, align them. With Dewey Dell, Darl even charges that she wants her mother to die only so she can go to town and obtain an abortion (39). With Addie, we might not see at first Darl's insistence on taking Jewel with the load as anything but manipulation of his brother, denying him his mother's final moment. Yet Darl's subsequent barn burning is hard to explain except as a last-ditch effort to impede his mother's wish. While Peter Lurie has suggested that "Darl Bundren's burning of Tull's [sic] barn in *As I Lay Dying* seems an act of protest . . . over his family's treatment of his mother" (13), I counter that Darl's incendiary action serves to punish Addie for her transgression in breaking out of the family circle—not by dying but by dating.

Faulkner's use of montage offers a rich vein for analyzing the complexities of *As I Lay Dying*'s art, and attending to the workings of montage shows how the novel is not so much about the destination as about the decomposition—not just of Addie's corpse but of narrative itself. This understanding is a key lesson for students to take away from the juxtaposition of Faulkner and Vertov, the significance of interpreting the novel through montage. After all, even the most conventional reading will indicate that the drive's aim was less the burying of Addie than the restoration of normality or equilibrium, achieved when Anse introduces Mrs. Bundren in the book's final words. But Darl's late speculation—"If you could just ravel out into time. That would be nice. It would be nice if you could just ravel out into time" (208)—is more than a thematic exposition of his own mental unraveling. The raveling out into time is what the montage of the novel effects, using spatial relations, discursive shifts, and movement to mark that raveling.

Jonathan Culler has suggested that *As I Lay Dying* "would not have an omniscient narrator but only a recorder, a presenter of signs, a transmission device" (30). This view brings the novel to the closest point in its orbit to Vertov's notion of kino-eye, which seeks to embrace the possibilities of the machine's seeing for what they reveal to our limited human vision. Vertov suggests that kino-eye "is the documentary cinematic decoding of both the visible world and that which is invisible to the naked eye" (87). At the heart of this recording practice is montage: "Every kino-eye production is subject to montage from the moment the theme is chosen until the film's release in its completed form. In other words, it is edited during the entire process of film production" (88). Vertov posits that every recording is always already an editing, an assembling.

Consider that the transmission device Culler refers to is best thought of as the film editor, the montage. Given the machinic or dispassionate reporting quality of Darl's narration, we might posit that he is the montageur. Like the man in *Man with the Movie Camera*, who films atop the roofs of downtown buildings, in an open-air car running alongside carriages and other cars, or suspended over water rushing over a dam, Darl speaks in montage from everywhere and nowhere. But for Darl, as for the camera operator, someone else must be there to assemble the pieces at another time. So Darl cannot give us the whole picture, much as he aims to. I like to use this limit on Darl's narration to trouble students' sense that they have the whole story given to them, without any interpretive effort on their part. Darl's desire for wholeness, for coherence, might well be seen as aligned with Vertov's expansive grasp for unification through the kino-eye, the visual linkage of everyone in the world (although Darl's world is perhaps more circumscribed than Vertov's). But it is Vertov's assertion of montage in particular as the strategy by which "all points of the universe in any temporal order" (88) might be linked—his reach expanding beyond the world to all of space—that suggests that the camera's power is subordinated to that of the cinema. This is the final lesson I want students to take away: how the media of representation themselves structure meaning and how students can become more alert to that by working across different media.

The recording device never feeds us just what it records—rather, we always engage in some degree of assembling that recording: editing, juxtaposing, montaging. Darl best serves to express the novel's own desire to ravel out into time. It may be that such raveling is a desire to gain access to the unedited version of events. But I suggest, rather, that it aims for a different assembling or ordering to see what might emerge from a remontage, which is what happens every time a reader actively engages with the text. The chance to move purely within the present or to shift paradigmatically away from the linear axis of narrative unfolding, to see not just correlations but larger conceptualizations that emerge from conflicts that are not organized in the plot—this is what montage offers us in teaching *As I Lay Dying*. But in teaching students how to interpret the organization of the pieces, montage requires them to figure out how to put themselves in the picture.

NOTES

[1] Dziga Vertov (b. Denis Kaufman 1896, d. 1954) was a filmmaker working in the Soviet Union in the early twentieth century. His artistic collective, Kino-eye, believed that film's visual language would enable people to transcend the limits of language in communicating across cultures. The Soviet avant-gardists, like Vertov and his compatriot Sergei Eisenstein, sought to make films with a grammar that countered the Hollywood grammar of continuity editing. I have chosen to focus on *Man with a Movie Camera* not only because it is widely available but also because it puts itself in tension with narrative, just as Faulkner's novel does, and aims to reveal truth about the human condition, much as Faulkner's novel does. Despite their overt differences, the two texts describe not simply life as it is but the processes of constructing that reality through representation.

[2] Vertov's film can be offputting or disorienting for noncinephiles, and I lay out the film's arc to help guide students in their viewing, so that they can be more attentive to the patterns the film offers.

[3] Vertov's film actually complicates that sense of the present, as I show in a lecture, using Gerard Genette's dissection of narrational frequency into singulative (telling once what happened once), repeating (telling more than once what happened once), and iterative (telling once what happened more than once). The "day in the life" genre relies on the iterative, but Vertov's concern with truth and specificity elicits the singulative (this woman awoke in this way on this day). But such reading of Vertov's mixed temporalities tempts us to go beyond the scope of this essay's consideration of Faulkner.

[4] Eisenstein's inspiration is the ideogram, which combines two disparate elements to create a third, more abstract and distinct idea. Bruce Kawin's essay on Faulkner and

montage picks up on a convergence between Ezra Pound's source for montage and Eisenstein's in the ideogram to bridge the literary and the filmic. Kawin also suggests that while Faulkner uses both repetition and montage as "two central linguistic and structural devices," Pound and James Joyce veer more toward the side of montage and Samuel Beckett and Gertrude Stein more toward repetition ("Montage" 109).

[5] As Samson puts it, for "a woman that's been dead in a box four days, the best way to respect her is to get her into the ground as quick as you can" (116).

Nonlinear Perspectives in *As I Lay Dying*

Homer B. Pettey

As I Lay Dying can be taught in an interdisciplinary general education survey on the modern period for nonmajors, focusing in particular on the novel's relation to early modern art movements. It also serves well in foundational survey courses on the modernist period that include film, photography, and modern art for undergraduates in majors in the humanities and fine arts. The fragmented quality of the narrative, the multiple perspectives of the narrators, and their distortions of time and space reveal Faulkner's affinity for modern artistic concepts. From the first paragraph, it is evident that Faulkner is concerned with perspective and the act of seeing. In the same way that modern art often requires the viewer to construct meaning, so too does the novel elicit such a strategy from the reader. Faulkner's use of metaphors of framing and composites and his characters' emphasis on visual experience can be related to modernist aesthetics. His interest in modern art is clear from his references to Paul Cézanne and the futurists in his letters from Paris to his mother as well as in his overt use of the phrase "cubistic bug" to describe Addie's coffin (219). Exposing students to early modernist visual culture—impressionism through cubism and futurism to Dada and surrealism as well as artists' fascination with photography and film—before they read the novel provides them with aesthetic concepts and analytical methods to work through the complexities of Faulkner's narrative.[1] *As I Lay Dying* can open up discussion that bridges and integrates approaches to and techniques of modern art, literature, and film. Moreover, such an approach allows students to form their own associations among artistic, literary, and visual experiments and techniques. As they read *As I Lay Dying*, students can draw comparisons between art and literature and evaluate both visual and verbal modernist experiments.

Four concepts in the novel reflect earlier developments in artistic and visual conventions of modernism—multiple perspectives, fragmented perception, plays of time and space, and violations of framing structures. In addition, *As I Lay Dying* seems obsessed with shapes and eyes, with constructing objects and disturbing gazes. First-time readers have difficulty negotiating the different narrative consciousnesses as they attempt to unravel the plot and meaning of the novel. The many viewing selves of *As I Lay Dying* offer diverse perspectives on the events, which, in turn, force the reader, not unlike the viewer of a modernist work of art, to reorient and shift perceptual orientation. Study of multiplicity and nonlinear perspectives from modern art and film can provide students with new vocabulary and taxonomies for these works and also with new experiences of art in its attempt to capture and reproduce an elusive world of perceptions. Modernism is inter-, multi-, and transdisciplinary in its innovations and experiments, particularly the period's paradigms for vision in physics, painting, film, and fiction. Not that there are provable connections among these distinct areas, but they all set about contemporaneously investigating temporal and spatial concepts. Moreover, modernism reorients the spectator in relation to the world, from a purely mechanical, objective vantage point to a subjective creation of the world. *As I Lay Dying* relies on these experiments in visual culture for its paradoxically linear and nonlinear narrative, its relatively simple plotline, and its complex, subjective narrations to convey the story of a family's journey to bury a wife and mother.

Traditional general education surveys and foundational courses for majors emphasize reading rather than visual skills, in part because of assumptions about today's students being a "visual" generation. By that logic, visual issues are assumed to be a part of students' skill set. Of course, this is not the case. Anyone who has tried to teach art or film to undergraduates soon realizes that a host of analytical and interpretive problems can arise, many of them similar to those posed for close reading skills. Comparing the theories and methods of modern art with those of the novel reveals perceptual strategies in both visual and verbal representations. Specifically, a course could begin with artistic movements from impressionism to surrealism, working out details of theory and execution in terms of new perceptions and new representations of reality as well as investigating famous works of the modernist canon, such as Cézanne's *Quarry and Mont Sainte-Victoire* (1898–1900), Edvard Munch's *The Scream* (1893), and Pablo Picasso's *Les Demoiselles d'Avignon* (1907). Useful texts from which to cull background material on the history of modern art include the standard sourcebook, *Theories of Modern Art: A Source Book by Artists and Critics*, edited by Herschel B. Chipp; Robert Hughes's *The Shock of the New: The Hundred-Year History of Modern Art*; Robert Rosenblum's *Cubism and Twentieth-Century Art*; Charles Harrison, Francis Frascina, and Gill Perry's *Primitivism, Cubism, Abstraction: The Early Twentieth Century*; and *History of Modern Art: Painting, Sculpture, Architeture, Photography*, by H. H. Arnason and Marla F. Prather.

Grounding students in modern art history and theory provides them with models for exploring narrative issues. Still essential to this training is the close study of individual works—a training of the eye. Here the emphasis is on defining structure, composition, and technique and then on examining theoretical implications. Students, no matter what their majors, are certainly capable of theoretical analysis, but as in visual and literary analysis, it takes models and repetition to achieve success. With art, having students see the process of analysis of a canvas requires kinds of dissection similar to those used to break down structures in narratives. The instructional strategy, then, is to give students conceptual and analytical training from visual models before exploring the more intricate, complex associations in the novel. More than just identifying visual issues in modern art, students become aware of the nature of and problems associated with perception, perspective, frames of reference, defining and ordering reality, and their own relation to these new, often paradoxical depictions of the world. The process of identifying, conceptualizing, and experiencing visual modernism affords students more precise analysis of the problems facing the Bundren family. Moving from an objective worldview to a subjective reformation of the world is a difficult process for students to grasp, especially when it requires "seeing" or "reading" the world from a character's perspective. Certainly, Darl does not make this task an easy one.

In general, undergraduate surveys follow a chronological order, so that teaching modernist artistic movements occurs before instruction in modernist fiction. Here chronology has instructional benefits, particularly for a novel like *As I Lay Dying,* which relies on and simultaneously questions visual, perceptual, and artistic concepts. Darl, in particular, often uses artistic metaphors to describe others: for Jewel, as "a flat figure cut leanly from tin" (218); Jewel fighting Gillespie in front of the burning barn as "two figures in a Greek frieze, isolated out of all reality by the red glare" (221); and Jewel and his beloved horse as "two figures carved for a tableau savage in the sun" (12). Darl views Anse's face as "carved by a savage caricaturist in a monstrous burlesque" (78) and perceives Jewel as "a figure carved clumsily from tough wood by a drunken caricaturist" (163). In addition, there is the description of Addie's coffin as "cubistic." It is evident that Faulkner employs artistic analogies to convey Darl's consciousness of the world around him. One can draw comparisons between these descriptions and cubism's fragmentary analysis of the world, futurism's fascination with violence and the mechanical, and Dada's and surrealism's reliance on the monstrous, comic, and absurd.

Investigating early modernist problems of perceptions of reality and perceptual reading or interpretation in impressionism and postimpressionism allows students to question traditional assumptions about the nature of sight. Late-nineteenth-century realistic representation in the visual arts moves radically away from academic painting to the more photographic reproduction of the sensory phenomena of light and color in impressionism. Cézanne relied on observations of nature as he conceived of the reaction by the eye. He painted in perceptual units of nature—cylinder, sphere, and cone—because they give "concrete shape to sensations and perceptions" (20). Cézanne's planar reduction of nature represented the constructs of the world as they hit the eye. In a corresponding fashion, Cash's thirteen-point discussion of the bevel, the shape best suited to represent the human body, might well be seen in conjunction with postimpressionist assessments of the forms, shapes, and constructs that artists must use to represent the natural world. Cash, relying on visual evidence, aptly makes clear the function of the bevel in nature:

> 10. You can see by an old grave that the earth sinks down on the bevel.
> 11. While in a natural hole it sinks by the center, the stress being up-and-down.
> 12. So I made it on the bevel. (83)

Cubism, though, went further, as evidenced by *Les Demoiselles d'Avignon*, to reveal that the Renaissance's single perspective was neither the true representation of reality nor the way the eye functions but instead a visual deception. Figural distortions and fragmentation of the objects into planes in cubism actually are more closely aligned with the dynamic movements of the eye than with the static, traditional notion of linear perspective. Like cubism, *As I Lay Dying* is concerned with redefining the concepts of representation and seeing.

Nonlinear elements in cubism, then, concern transformation in spatial and temporal relations, so that a new awareness of reality is made available to the viewer. To produce on a two-dimensional surface—the canvas for Picasso or the page for Faulkner—the three-dimensionality of the world, modernism must address the problems of boundaries and thereby redefine reality. Spatially, *Les Demoiselles d'Avignon* contorts forms, combines almost inexplicably foreground and background, allows for a fruit bowl to morph into a hand or the other way around—it all depends on the various positions taken by the viewer and the multiplicity of eye movements. Hence the painting gives us not a single perspective but multiple perspectives. In a similar manner, *As I Lay Dying* is divided into chapters not by traditional demarcation but instead by characters' names, without any numbered sequence, with fifty-nine monologues spoken by fifteen different narrators.

On first reading the novel, most readers are struck by the excessive amount of blank space that begins and separates chapters. Clearly, Faulkner wants his novel to take on an appearance of a work of art, not merely comment on it. As is well known, Faulkner wanted the publisher of *The Sound and the Fury* to print Benjy's section in different colored inks, so that the time differences would be more readily apparent (Brooks, *First Encounters* 45). Such an effect would transform the page into a kind of canvas. In this sense, *As I Lay Dying* belongs to the modernist tradition of visual poetics, such as the visual typeface experiments of Guillaume Apollinaire or Vicente Huidobro's poetics of the "square horizon" that suggests "a framing process that may be reflected in the shape of the poem" (Breunig 196). Showing students the multitextured and papiers collés of cubism, such as Picasso's *Guitar, Sheet Music, and Wine Glass* (1912), which has part of a headline from *Le Journal* cut out and pasted to the canvas, can give them a sense of modernism's attempts to break free from restrictions of traditional art, whether the two-dimensional frame boundary of the canvas or the linear narrative conventions of the novel.

Image making in the early twentieth century was nonlinear in its experimental attempts at multiplicity, and it drew on a variety of sources, among them instantaneous photography and chronophotography, film editing, and experiments in painting. Having students view Picasso's *Les Demoiselles d'Avignon* for the first time will immediately require training them how to see, in much the same way that *As I Lay Dying* trains students how to read. Both Picasso and Faulkner present the viewer-reader with a series of modernist problems to solve, initially grounded in linear structures but quickly recognized as violating linear principles. In *Les Demoiselles d'Avignon*, students can "read" from left to right an evolution or devolving of images, from nearly classical, almost realistic feminine poses to abstracted distortions of the female form. The progression, though, does not follow a clearly logical, linear method.

Like the impressionists, cubists were attracted to the new possibilities offered to the artist by the camera. Unlike the impressionists, who found a quasi-scientific view of the world in daguerreotypes, cubists transformed objective photographic results into new modes of breaking up or analyzing the world. Étienne-Jules Marey produced various types of chronophotography in the late 1880s, such as the extended exposure of a strip of film, which revealed human being's movement as a continuous sequence to reveal the structural or mechanical aspects of human motion. By means of a timed shutter, chronophotography superimposed images onto a single plate, producing a series of motion images. Also in the late 1880s, Eadweard Muybridge's series photography, or instantaneous photography, broke up human movement into numerous separate shots taken at very short intervals, which were then re-presented as a development series from the beginning of an action to its end, such as a woman walking down steps, a man running, or the famous Leland Stanford experiment that proved that a horse raised all four legs off the ground during a gallop. Both Marey and Muybridge captured human and animal locomotion as fragments, as a series of successive moments of motion. For Marey, the result of these superimposed images was a kind of collage of multiple movements, giving a sense of continuous motion. For Muybridge, the result of distinct photographs spaced at minute time intervals was a sequence of shots that the viewer could put into a succession of movement.

Space and time are thus broken down and revealed to be perceptually fragmentary. Perception of continuous motion is an illusion whereby the viewer formulates a progression where gaps, pieces, and spaces actually exist. *Les Demoiselles d'Avignon* relies on both the Marey technique of collage and the Muybridge discrete fragment. So, too, does *As I Lay Dying*, in the structure of its multiple narratives about the same event. The reader, similar to the viewer of Marey, Muybridge, or Picasso, recognizes the discontinuity and fragmentation of the novel's structure but also perceives a linearity, a continuity where none actually exists. Faulkner's novel, then, is a verbal representation of space and time in the very sense of modern art's experiments with motion.

In *Les Demoiselles d'Avignon*, are we observing one woman in various positions over time, as in the instantaneous photography of Muybridge or the motion studies of Marey? Are we observing several women who share an affinity, such as being prostitutes, but reveal multiple aspects of that shared experience, from the traditional emotional gestures to primitive and animalistic responses? The same types of questions may be posed about *As I Lay Dying*. Are we confronted with a sustained consciousness with the dominance of Darl's narratives? Do we observe a devolving of that central consciousness over time? Are there affinities among the related narrators of the Bundren family? Are we experiencing radical shifts from classical narrative to abstracted forms? Are we experiencing shifts in emotional responses to Addie's death from the classical, if comic, stoicism of Anse to the violent, animalistic reactions of Jewel? Of course, the comparison between Picasso and Faulkner is not one to one; rather, studying the premises of cubism opens up visual paradigms that can be useful for exploring the complexities of modernist narrative strategies and multiplicity of expression. Picasso and Faulkner were interested not in reproducing Marey's and Muybridge's studies in motion but in experimenting with space, time, and movement in their own ways.

These chronophotographic and instantaneous photographic images were the sources for much of futurism's dynamism experiments, such as Giacomo Balla's *Dynamism of a Dog on a Leash* (1912) and Umberto Boccioni's *The City Rises* (1910). There are numerous examples in *As I Lay Dying* of experimenting with dynamic or kinetic motion and also arresting movement not dissimilar to these modernist experiments. Examples include Darl's observations of time and space:

> He watches Jewel as he passes, the horse moving with a light, high-kneed driving gait, three hundred yards back. We go on, with a motion so soporific, so dreamlike as to be uninferant of progress, as though time and not space were decreasing between us and it. (107–08)

> It is as though the space between us were time: an irrevocable quality. It is as though time, no longer running straight before us in a diminishing line, now runs parallel between us like a looping string, the distance being the doubling accretion of the thread and not the interval between. (146)

Clearly evident in Darl's depictions of time and space are their paradoxical correspondences and distinctions. In both examples, visual analogies are needed to express the complex concepts of temporal distortion and displacement in the first passage and spatial-temporal conjunction or correlative in the second passage. The first passage nearly evokes a chronophotograph by Marey, while the second passage almost describes the effect of putting together the intervals of a Muybridge series.

Recent discoveries at the Musée Picasso in Paris have shown not only that Picasso had a vast photographic collection, particularly of African tribesmen, nineteenth-century portraits, and reproductions of great masterworks of European painters, but also that Picasso himself dabbled in photography, including superimposing images, as evidenced by his own self-portrait over numerous works in his studio (Baldassari 289). *Les Demoiselles d'Avignon*, as well as many futurist works, can be seen as painterly reproductions of photographic superimposition. Certainly, the photomontages of the early 1920s by the German Dadaists Hannah Höch, George Grosz, and John Heartfield function as composite representations. Whether as a new realism for cubists or a new visual poetry for futurists and Dadaists, fragments, differentiations, and dispersals of images are reassembled into a composite perception of the multiplicity of space and time. *As I Lay Dying*, in its fragments of narratives and repetition of narrative voices, shares an affinity with these modernist visual collages. Most evident from the novel is Darl's description of Cash's showing Addie the coffin he builds for her, which is based upon multiplicity and combination of images to represent his mother:

> He looks up at the gaunt face framed by the window in the twilight. It is a composite picture of all time since he was a child. He drops the saw and lifts the board for her to see, watching the window in which the face has not moved. He drags a second plank into position and slants the two of them into their final juxtaposition, gesturing toward the ones yet on the ground, shaping with his empty hand in pantomime the finished box. For a while still she looks down at him from the composite picture, neither with censure nor approbation. Then the face disappears. (48)

This short paragraph relies on the conceit of a composite. It is Darl's narrative of Cash performing the death ritual for his mother, Addie. Cash, through visual, not verbal, gestures, assembles the board fragments into the coffin, which now is a composite or collage that represents Addie in the future, Addie in death. Addie, though, is a composite of all the images from Cash's past, and in the window she appears not as a human being but as a representation of a human being—a face that is itself a collection of representations. Addie's face is a "composite picture" suggestive of a framed image, which is framed by the window, which itself is framed by Darl's narrative, which itself is framed by the novel.

Of course, this passage suggests spatial-temporal problems in terms of past and present but also in terms of the assembling yet breaking of the boundaries of the frames. *Les Demoiselles d'Avignon*, for example, makes use of space by recontextualizing its functions, its emptiness, its gaps, and its divisions. In *As I Lay Dying*, Faulkner draws correspondences between the visual and the verbal by paradoxically including empty spaces in the text, divisions, and interstices. Moreover, the novel is fascinated with the limitations of boundaries, particularly types of framing devices; among the metaphorical frames employed are coffin, window, door, wheel rim, coin, spyglass, womb, and grave. Creating frames, like relying on single-point perspective, is a way to contain and make the world static. Modernism, however, desires to break frames, to reorient frames, and to challenge the very nature of frames, boundaries, and limitations. In the first chapter, *As I Lay Dying* relies on the breaking of a frame to suggest its own structure: Darl follows Jewel as they approach the dilapidated cottonhouse with "a single broad window in two opposite walls," through which Jewel "steps in a single stride" (4). Jewel's action of walking through the perceptual structure of the frame alludes to the novel's structural breaks. Using the visual contexts of modernist frames, then, provides students with an understanding of Faulkner's attempts to make visual and narrative divisions in the novel.

Modernism's fascination with cinema is also evident. Showing students examples of modernist filmmaking will enhance their understanding of painting and poetics. Futurists, Dadaists, and surrealists experimented with cinematic techniques, especially the close-up, editing, superimposing, and framing experiments. While initially relying on the work of Marey and Muybridge, futurists went further in their braggadocio and radically impossible-to-produce theories, such as claiming that they would exceed the limitations of chronophontography with photodynamism, which obtains "intermovemental" stages "that trace in a face, for instance, not only the expressing of passing states of mind . . . but also the immediate shifting of volumes that results in the immediate transformation of expression" (Bragaglia 40–41). This ambitious technique is what Faulkner carries off successfully in the Addie as a "composite picture" passage, as evident from the shifts from past to present to future and back with the same image of Addie.

Fernand Léger's *Ballet mécanique* (1923–24) is an extension of his cubo-futurist theories of cinema, which can enlarge an object or a fragment of an object and thus grant it, as Léger claimed, "a personality it never had before and in this way it can become a vehicle of entirely new lyric and plastic power" (279). In addition to its mania for human and machine rhythms, not unlike the early photographic experiments, *Ballet mécanique* concentrates on distorted views through prisms to reveal visual tempos and on close-ups of eyes and mouths, both open and closed, to draw connections between visual and verbal interdependence. The fixation on the eye and ways of seeing is analyzed in the psychosexual surrealist tour de force by Luis Buñuel and Salvador Dali, *Un Chien andalou* (1928). The eye-splitting of the woman is as grotesque as Vardaman's prodding "at the eye-bump" of the fish "with his toe, gouging at it" (31).

As I Lay Dying also concentrates on characters' shifting between the verbal and visual contexts. Faulkner's characters suffer from perceptual problems, which result from their fixation on the visual. No other novel by Faulkner describes eyes so often or in such detail. Most narratives in the novel focus on eyes, stares, glances, observations, and looks from others and the gaze of the narrator. Bundren family members and others comment on how Darl's eyes disturb them. They believe that Darl has a kind of clairvoyant vision, an ability to penetrate into their innermost desires and secrets. After being with Lafe in the secret shade, Dewey Dell suspects that Darl

> knew without the words like he told me that ma is going to die without words, and I knew he knew because if he had said he knew with the words I would not have believed that he had been there and saw us. (27)

Both Addie and Darl can fix others with their eyes. Modern art often makes us aware of the disturbing effect of gaze from the subject of the painting on the viewer, as observed in Édouard Manet's *Olympia* (1863) and *Le Déjeuner sur l'herbe* (1863), before which the viewer becomes voyeur. *Les Demoiselles d'Avignon* confronts the viewer with stares that are blank, bland, and blindly indifferent, all of them disturbing because the viewer must interpret their meaning. The viewer shifts from perceiving subject to perceived object before these paintings. A similar sensation is experienced by the characters in *As I Lay Dying* who confront those knowing, interrogating, and powerful gazes of Addie and Darl. Contemporary readers of the novel understood the viewer's uneasy position from their experiences at the movies, especially the remarkably startling use of the close-up in, for example, the final moments of Edwin S. Porter's *The Great Train Robbery* (1903), when a gun fires at the audience; the tension produced by the menacing faces of the criminals overtaking the screen in D. W. Griffith's *The Musketeers of Pig Alley* (1912); the hideous face and dead eyes of Count Orlok in F. W. Murnau's *Nosferatu* (1922); and the grotesque and alarming visages of Lon Chaney in *The Phantom of the Opera* (1925) and *The Unknown* (1927) and of Conrad Veidt in *The Man Who Laughs* (1928).

Another correlation to early film can be made with the novel's sections and intertitles, particularly as they introduce characters. A common practice in film was to introduce plot elements along with characters and to return to characters' names to repeat thematic, imagistic, and narrative issues. *The Wishing Ring: An Idyll of Old England* (1914), by Maurice Tourneur, introduces actors and their roles in the opening sequence and also provides four different yet intertwined threads of the narrative. This complexity of plots is represented initially as four different points of view, a technique that corresponds to Faulkner's narrative approach. More commonly, audiences understood plot by having to juxtapose two characters' differing views of the world. *The Sheik* (1921), directed by George Melford for Paramount Pictures, introduces Zilah (Ruth Miller) with an intertitle card claiming her lowly status as a prize for the marriage lottery, which is followed immediately by an intertitle about Ahmed Ben Hassan (Rudolph Valentino), who has inherited the burden of princely leadership. Such silent film examples draw connections between the verbal and visual as a matter of course. *As I Lay Dying*'s chapters, particularly the very brief ones, appear almost as though they were intertitles. Faulkner's narrative divisions break up the plot in a similar manner. *As I Lay Dying*'s narrative structure can be viewed in terms of the nonlinear quality that editing gave to early films, as Tom Gunning explains:

> Once story action extends over cuts, temporal relations become more complex. . . . The temporal relation occurs when an action is continual over a cut and the shots are in close spatial relation. The action of one shot (filmed from one viewpoint) is repeated either wholly or in part in the shot that follows (filmed from another viewpoint). The time of the film, instead of presenting a continuous linear flow, is staggered, stutters, repeats itself. (96)

In *As I Lay Dying*, the multiple narratives act both as intertitle shifts for character and plot and as visual repetitions of scenes—but told or shown from another vantage point.

It would be misleading to present modern art to undergraduates in a context that does not pay attention to modern visual culture, especially photography and early cinema. By the same token, it would be difficult to teach *As I Lay Dying* outside the contexts of the visual culture of its era. Studies of early modern art and popular visual arts that deserve looking into include *The Image in Dispute: Art and Cinema in the Age of Photography*, edited by Dudley Andrew; *Peinture, cinéma, peinture*, edited by Germain Viatte; *The Visual Turn: Classical Film Theory and Art History*, edited by Angela Dalle Vacche; and *Moving Pictures: American Art and Early Film, 1880–1910*, edited by Nancy Mowll Matthews and Charles Musser.

As I Lay Dying allows students to explore modernist visual culture from a new perspective, a perspective that makes associations between visual and verbal constructs. As multiplicity and repetition are central to the visual distortions of cubism, futurism, Dada, and surrealism, so too are they crucial to Faulkner's telling of the Bundren tragicomedy. My suggestion for teaching visual culture before engaging students in the complexities of *As I Lay Dying* is premised on the following concepts being addressed in modern art, photography, and film:

Dominance of vision and the visual as defining modernism
Reevaluation of perception
Perspective or point of view as dynamic, kinetic
Fragmentary aspects of visual constructs
Spatial-temporal transformations
Framing constraints and breaking boundaries
Subjectivity replacing objectivity
The viewer participates in the construction of a visual text
The ontological play of "eye" and "I" in art

With these concepts developed through viewing and discussing modern art, photography, and film, students will become grounded in relatively complex theoretical issues without the necessity of first reading selections from Walter Benjamin, Jean-Paul Sartre, Maurice Merleau-Ponty, Roland Barthes, or Michel Foucault on vision, visual culture, and the interdependence of spectacle and spectatorship. Of course, any of these theorists could be included in a survey of the modern period, but the point of this instructional model is to allow students the opportunity to arrive at these concepts through the process of viewing art and reading the novel. Learning how to see analytically and evaluatively and how to read closely and critically are skills that are becoming more and more necessary in our era of global media.

NOTE

[1] The term *modernism* here covers several disciplines and refers to the period from the 1860s, with the first impressionist exhibitions, to the late 1920s, with the publication of *As I Lay Dying*. During this period the confluence of aesthetic and technological innovations in art, photography, film, and literature influenced and transformed concepts of perspective and perception.

As I Lay Dying: A Modernist Epic

Heide Ziegler

William Faulkner's novel *As I Lay Dying* is suffused with political, religious, and social preoccupations and prejudices of the American South, but they are nowhere fully stated or deployed. Instead, they inform the narrative, creating a subtext of mythical proportions. The intention of the following discussion is therefore pedagogical—to help the reader grasp some of the narrative strategies that turn Faulkner's novel into a modernist epic. I begin by noting that a crucial context for teaching the fiction of William Faulkner is the web of classical and biblical allusions present in nearly everything he wrote. The title *As I Lay Dying* refers to Homer's *Odyssey*: "as I lay dying" are words spoken by the dead Agamemnon to Odysseus in Hades, the ancient Greek underworld. The gods have decreed that Odysseus, on his journey back to his family and society after the Trojan War, must descend into Hades to learn his fate from the seer Tiresias. There Odysseus's former military leader recounts his own homecoming and murder by his wife, thereby unconsciously contrasting his fate with what will turn out to be Odysseus's happy reunion with Penelope. Or does Agamemnon divine Odysseus's fate—at least the part that concerns him most? How much can a dead or dying soul know if he or she is not a seer? And how does he or she communicate with a person whose level of existence is different from his or her own?

Agamemnon's plight illuminates that of Addie Bundren, matriarch and center of the Bundren family of Yoknapatawpha County, Mississippi. Yoknapatawpha is the old Indian name—meaning "water runs slow through flat land," according to Faulkner (*Faulkner* 74)—for the flooded river the Bundrens have to cross on their way to Jefferson, where Addie wants to be buried. The river resembles Lethe, the mythic river the dead have to cross on their way to Hades. Speaking like Agamemnon from the netherworld to the reader, who, since he or she is alive, takes the place of Odysseus, Addie relates that only two of her five children—her firstborn, Cash, and Jewel, product of her clandestine affair with Minister Whitfield—truly belong to her; she has "given" the other three to Anse, her husband.[1] Yet all five children accompany Anse, the head of the clan, to Jefferson, and they follow his orders, offering their most prized possessions to help him fulfill his promise to bury Addie with her relatives. Each goes to Jefferson, however, pursuing a particular motive, which is revealed in the monologues identified by his or her name; in addition to their explanations, there is Addie's speech, a voice from the dead, from beyond the realm of mundane motive and desire, that knows and explains her life.

The main tension in Addie's life has been between (conventional) words and (secret) deeds, a tension she explicitly addresses:

> And so when Cora Tull would tell me I was not a true mother, I would think how words go straight up in a thin line, quick and harmless, and how

> terribly doing goes along the earth, clinging to it, so that after a while the two lines are too far apart for the same person to straddle from one to the other. (173)

Addie's marriage to Anse gradually became static and conventional, a relationship in which the word *love* became meaningless, so that only the secret liaison with Minister Whitfield and its sinfulness (which she insists on) could replenish her life. Faulkner sympathizes with Addie;[2] still, the outrageousness of the plot results directly from her attitude. The tension between words and deeds, which Addie could not resolve during her lifetime, not even when she lay dying (she takes the secret of her affair with Minister Whitfield to the grave), is manifested in her speech and repeats itself in the tension between her sons Darl and Jewel—albeit in another mode.

Of the novel's fifty-nine interior monologues, or sections, the largest number (nineteen) is allotted to Darl, who, more than anyone else, embodies language and recollection among the living. Only one interior monologue is uttered by Jewel, who appears to be almost incoherent with fury at having to speak at all. Jewel represents almost pure action. Thus Addie, who always believed that only the deed has significance, correctly prophesied that her son Jewel would be her savior, thereby deliberately dumbfounding her conventional neighbor, the pious and hypocritical Cora Tull, for whom Addie's words amounted to sacrilege.

> He is my cross and he will be my salvation. He will save me from the water and from the fire. Even though I have laid down my life, he will save me. (168)

What Addie foresaw and described, not only in biblical but also in Homeric terms (Troy went up in flames, just like Sodom and Gomorrah; Odysseus and his comrades had to fight the perils of the sea in their effort to get home, just as Noah had to fight the flood), was a vision of what happens after her death. When the Bundren family sets out to take Addie's body home to Jefferson, a hard rain and the consequent flooding of the river compound their journey dangerously; instead of the usual two days' travel by wagon, nine days pass after Addie's death before they reach the Jefferson cemetery. Moreover, the trip takes place in the hottest season of the year, causing the corpse to disintegrate. During that journey of increasingly epic and—under the pressure of the Bundrens' present-day circumstances—more and more grotesquely distorted proportions,[3] Jewel almost single-handedly saves the coffin from being carried away by the flood as well as from being burned in Gillespie's barn, which his brother Darl has set on fire. Jewel prevails, as Addie foresaw, while Darl, who attempts to undermine her design, fails. The family conspires to have Darl committed to an insane asylum to evade Gillespie's demand that he be paid for his barn. The difference between Darl and Jewel thus resolves Addie's dilemma as one who lies dying, silent and immobile, yet is the source of present violent action.

The whole burial journey has been described as dramatizing the traumatic eruption of privacy and secrecy into public view (Wadlington, As I Lay Dying 29). But while it cannot be doubted that Addie's secret liaison—which she reveals only to the reader and only after her death, just as the dead Agamemnon talks only to Odysseus, a living human being who is able to visit with the dead—is the pivotal event of the novel, and while it cannot be doubted that Addie's privacy and secrecy influence all the members of her family and radiate to those who come into contact with them, it is the nature of that secret that must be explored and ultimately questioned. For it does not erupt into public view; in fact, it remains a secret within the confines of the plot. But it becomes tantalizing precisely because it is revealed only to the reader—and in such a way that the novel asks us to read secrecy while preventing us from changing the relation of secret knowledge to speech and action.

Addie believes that her affair with Minister Whitfield secures her an entrance into the kingdom of everlasting sin or lasting significance. She believes this in part because the existence of Jewel, the unlawful but beloved child of the affair, does not permit her to forget it. She also believes that, in waiting for Whitfield in the woods, she had been waiting for a representative of God, who she felt created sin in the first place. Finally, and perhaps most important, she thinks that her secret liaison with a minister (a mortal sin, in her view) justified her keeping it hidden from other human beings throughout her life, entitling her to redeem the deed over the word. It is Addie's sin that grants her privileged status—the privileged status of a mother whose illegitimate son will eventually become her savior, despite the fact that her ordinary life continues to be that of a poor white farmer's wife.[4]

Yet just like Agamemnon in the *Odyssey*, where he is described as having held a privileged position among the Greeks, Addie is hemmed in by fate. Nature, which each of them has violated, reasserts itself with a vengeance by granting a longer lifespan to those they do not consider their superiors. Agamemnon is doomed to walk among the shades, in a realm where he is no longer able to compensate for the sacrifice of his daughter Iphigeneia, while his listener, Odysseus, is free to shape a new phase of his life. Addie's interior monologue in *As I Lay Dying* is framed by sections attributed to the hypocritical Cora, on the one hand, and the no less hypocritical Whitfield, on the other; while she is confined to her coffin and her final truth, they, like the reader, can still interpret the world. Agamemnon and Addie may both foresee that their children will complete their revenge on their spouses, but what they do not take into account are the disintegrating forces of nature that are going to undermine their notions of power and glory once their own dominating personalities are gone. Orestes, Agamemnon's son, will be haunted by the furies after he has killed his mother to avenge his father. In planning her revenge, Addie has overlooked the fact that all she will leave to her children is a longing for the maternal love she denied them during her lifetime and that they will now never be able to acquire. The despair that results from her attitude is most intensely voiced by her unhappily pregnant daughter, Dewey Dell:

> I heard that my mother is dead. I wish I had time to let her die. I wish I had time to wish I had. It is because in the wild and outraged earth too soon too soon too soon. It's not that I wouldn't and will not it's that it is too soon too soon too soon. (120)

As long as Addie was alive, she was able to control her children and keep other influences at bay. Even her last words—"You, Cash!" (a summons spoken in a voice "harsh, strong, and unimpaired" [48])—once more assert the influence of her personality on her firstborn and, through him, on the whole family. Addie has made Anse promise to take her back to Jefferson after she dies, telling him that she wants to be reunited with her father. Anse, she knows, will not understand that she is thus getting her revenge on him, which is that he will never know she has taken revenge by refusing to be buried next to him. But in turning her children into instruments of that revenge, she actually delivers them into Anse's hands; it is Anse they will have to depend on at the end of their journey to restore them to whatever minimal sense of community and familial belonging is still in store for them.

Anse told Addie that he loves her, but for Addie, marital love is only a convention. Moreover, she did not want to be loved by Anse—not after she discovered how lazy, selfish, and dependent he is on the support of others. For Addie, Anse has been dead as a man since Cash's birth; Darl, the son she gave birth to after Jewel, has thus become her "death child," the child who made her turn in on herself. Anse can no longer represent "doing" for Addie since she has come to despise him. Although Anse is a farmer and supposedly works the land, he tells people that if he ever sweats, he will die. In similar fashion, Minister Whitfield, though God's ordained instrument, has perverted the divine word for Addie as the betrayer of her husband. Only passion, which is clothed in sin and thus directly related to God, who forbade sin and thus caused it, could still acquire a terrible life for her.[5] "I would think of the sin as garments which we would remove in order to shape and coerce the terrible blood to the forlorn echo of the dead word high in the air" (175). After Jewel is born, that passion, the "wild blood boiling along the earth, of me and of all that lived; of none and of all" (175), passes away, and Addie consciously begins to construct her death-in-life. Following the advice of her father, who exhorted her that living means getting ready to stay dead, she now meticulously prepares her own dying; in naming the novel *As I Lay Dying*, Faulkner seems to confer on Addie the paradoxical authority to control her own death as a character. Thus Addie makes up her mind that she must still give two more children to Anse—Dewey Dell and Vardaman—in order to balance the account between her and her husband—or, as she puts it, to "negative" Jewel and to "replace" Cash, the two sons who belong to her (176). After applying this "secret home economics" (Wadlington, As I Lay Dying 31), she feels free to prepare her revenge on Anse. She never allows love to succeed to the place of passion, nor does she substitute the milk of human kindness for the boiling blood of passion.

While Addie superficially obeys conventions, she secretly despises motherhood, and as soon as she dies and her corpse begins to disintegrate, nature begins to avenge itself. Suddenly, the Bundrens are faced with situations that spin out of their control, defying the best efforts of all of Addie's offspring. During the prolonged burial journey, the natural elements seem to persecute the Bundren family until, finally, after Addie's burial is eventually completed, all her children have become losers, left to cope with life as best they can. Cash, despite his fortitude and moral integrity, is left with one of his legs permanently maimed and the burden of the fate of his brother Darl on his conscience; Darl, despite his intelligence, eloquence, and apparent clairvoyance, is sent away to an insane asylum; Jewel, despite his single-minded and furious devotion to his mother, has lost his horse, his mother replacement and main reason for living; Dewey Dell, despite her cunning and deviousness, has to bear the child she has conceived almost by accident; and Vardaman, despite his sensitivity and childish goodwill, will not be able to establish an identity. His father forces him to cut up the big fish he has caught, which was to have been *his* mother replacement, and the toy train he craves so that he can dream of getting away has been replaced by a sack of cheap bananas he has to share with the rest of the family.

By the novel's conclusion, the question becomes whether there is an escape strategy for the reader from the cycle of action, retribution, and reaction in which the Bundrens are caught up: can Addie's dying provide any form of insight that serves as a response to this naturalistic scenario? In teaching *As I Lay Dying*, such a question acquires greater importance as the novel's thematic and stylistic concerns inform the manner in which the novel imbricates its own reading. Addie's passionate belief in the irreconcilability of words and deeds, which has caused the mutual hatred of her sons Darl and Jewel, is taken over by the novel as such, surfacing as a structural separation of narrators, on the one hand, and, on the other, characters who are agents within the narrative.[6] All fifteen speakers who share the fifty-nine sections of *As I Lay Dying* are characters in the novel as well as narrators, independent actors as well as beings who are linguistically and stylistically dependent on the author.[7] As characters, they differ as if arranged on a scale: there are those who come close to representing nothing but the word, like Darl or Cora Tull (who cannot sell her cakes because, as Addie puts it, she "could never even cook" [174]), and those who are almost pure doing, like Dewey Dell and Jewel. As narrators, however, all these speakers are infused with the author's consciousness—a fact that accounts for their much-debated rhetorical skills—but this authorial consciousness is made to serve and express their individuality as characters acting within the plot.[8]

The stylistic differences that can be observed between a speaker speaking as a character and one speaking as a narrator might, of course, simply be accounted for by considering that a character, as long as he or she participates in the development of the plot, generally speaks in the present tense, while a narrator always speaks from hindsight—which accounts for his or her greater perceptiveness. Still, some critics have wondered why Faulkner chose to make his Yoknapatawpha poor whites so eloquent; they have, for instance, tried to excuse the sometimes ornate speech by calling it the "poetry of madness" (Darl) or the "poetry of the child" (Vardaman) (Brooks, *Yoknapatawpha County* 94). What is more remarkable, however, and heightened precisely by Faulkner's elaborate rhetoric, is the resistance of the "doing" characters to their dependence on the author's consciousness. They seem to withdraw into themselves—to the point where they "negative" (176) their own identity.[9] Thus Dewey Dell may be unwilling to accept her pregnancy, but, more important, she seems to reject her whole narrative existence, the role as character that the author has assigned to her.

> *I had a nightmare once I thought I was awake but I couldn't see and couldn't feel I couldn't feel the bed under me and I couldn't think what I was I couldn't think of my name I couldn't even think I am a girl I couldn't even think I. . . .* (121)

The narrator who is closest to the author, thereby enabling him to enter into a true dialogue with the reader, is the son whom Addie has rejected: Darl. At times Darl indulges in Faulkner's most elevated style, leading some critics to conclude that he represents the artist or the author himself (Putzel 212; Wadlington, As I Lay Dying 58). But that would imply that Darl verges on being an omniscient narrator, which he is not. His insight into the development of the plot is clearly limited. Like Addie, he implicitly knows that his true addressee can be no one but the reader, because he is Addie's "death child," the son born without an identity he can forfeit. Therefore, he cannot truly consort with the living, the community that his brother Cash can easily relate to and that his father knows how to exploit. To the neighbors, Darl appears strange, if not altogether mad. He comes close to being a noncharacter and close to being an ideal, although not an omniscient, narrator. Thus Darl, the poet and seer of the Bundren family—who even when he is miles away suddenly knows that Addie has died, knows that Dewey Dell is pregnant, and knows that Anse is not the father of Jewel—does not understand that his family is conspiring against him, contriving to send him to the insane asylum in Jackson after he has set fire to Gillespie's barn.[10] Darl sees more than the others because he possesses a heightened sensitivity and an obsession with hidden sin. His mother clothed her deeds in sin to give them significance in a community steeped in conventionality; but she achieved this significance only by hiding the deed and thus flaunting its sinfulness. Darl therefore learns to equate sinfulness with lying. He is convinced that if he uncovers the sin, he will arrive at the truth—which will, in turn, help him acquire an identity. This belief isolates him from the rest of his family and from a community that accepts conventionality as a lifestyle. As a consequence, Darl is unable either to foresee his role as scapegoat or to understand the behavior of his family as a form of self-defense.

The limited, though sometimes shared, perspective of the speakers of *As I Lay Dying* initially appears to be an authorial device for withholding important information from the reader, thus creating a feeling of suspense. While we can look into the minds of the Bundrens and occasionally gain insights, we strive to participate in their clandestine world and look for answers to their unspoken questions. But when we listen to the voices of the non-Bundrens—Cora and Vernon Tull, Peabody, Samson, Armstid, Moseley, and MacGowan—we begin to understand why especially those Bundrens who turn to the reader to be understood are different. The speakers who represent the Yoknapatawpha community do not withhold any information, nor are they opaque or threatening (with the Snopesian exception of MacGowan, who gets involved with Dewey Dell). On the contrary, they are outspoken and often helpful: they offer their teams of mules to draw the Bundrens' wagon and their houses and barns as shelters during the family's ill-fated journey. Moreover, Dr. Peabody, Samson, and Moseley offer not just help but good advice as well. And they all generally display common sense. For example, Samson suggests that since all bridges over the Yoknapatawpha River are gone the Bundrens bury Addie in New Hope and not try to cross the river to get to Jefferson; Armstid tries to make the Bundrens fetch a doctor to fix Cash's broken leg; Moseley, the first druggist Dewey Dell encounters when she seeks an abortion, tells her to take the money her lover, Lafe, gave her and "get married with it" (203); and Armstid and Gillespie both advise the Bundrens to send word ahead that they want to bury Addie in the Jefferson cemetery.

Cash, the oldest and most responsible of Addie's children, eventually comes closest to accepting these communal values. He desperately calls on them when he attempts to justify to himself that Darl, the brother he loves best, should be sent to the asylum in Jackson:

> But I dont reckon nothing excuses setting fire to a man's barn and endangering his stock and destroying his property. That's how I reckon a man is crazy. That's how he cant see eye to eye with other folks. And I reckon they aint nothing else to do with him but what the most folks say is right. (233–34)

Yet as long as they are under Addie's spell and hampered by their own secret devices and desires, the Bundren children are beyond common sense and are incapable of acting on good advice. During their mother's initially mental but increasingly physical dying process, their identities too begin to dissolve. Darl's one true action, his setting fire to Gillespie's barn, suddenly reveals to him Addie's well-kept secret: that words and deeds, mind and body, cannot be harmonized. Up to this point, Darl has seemed to live almost exclusively in a mental realm; he takes action in a desperate attempt not to lose his hold on his slipping identity. Burning the barn that houses the corpse of his mother is supposed to anneal the separation between body and mind by effectively destroying Addie and her uncanny influence and thus save him. Darl's deepest anxiety is that he does not truly exist, because he was Addie's "death child," the child whose advent symbolized the end of her relationship with Anse. "I cannot love my mother because I have no mother" (95), he says, and although he says it after Addie has died, it is a portentous statement.

The experience of a mentally or physically threatened identity in each of Addie's children is counteracted by a deep desire for bonding in the family as a whole. This desire is concentrated in the family patriarch, Anse, who keeps repeating that they can fend on their own and "be beholden to no man" (19). Although not only Anse but the whole family depends on the support of the community to achieve their increasingly unnatural goal of burying Addie in the Jefferson cemetery, they shrink from anything that would endanger their frail family identity. This is most evident in the occlusion of family secrets, and the Bundrens' secrecy requires a closer look at the Darl sections of the novel. By relentlessly attempting to reveal any secret he discovers, Darl risks, and finally achieves, being ostracized by the rest of the family—thereby upsetting the precarious structural balance not only of his family but also of the novel itself, since its creator shares the Bundrens' secrecy. Faulkner hides his preoccupations and prejudices regarding the American South to become a modernist writer.

Darl is the first narrator the reader encounters, and it has been pointed out by many that Darl, who is walking fifteen feet ahead of Jewel, should not be able to see how Jewel steps in a single stride through the window of a barn sitting in the middle of their path and then out through the opposite window and onto the path again—with the result that he is now walking ahead of Darl (Mellard 229–30). Darl's description is seen as early evidence of his clairvoyance. Of course, his description can in part be accounted for by the fact that, as a narrator, Darl concludes from hindsight what must have happened, since it is only in this fashion that his brother could catch up with him and overtake him. Much more important than answering the question of how Darl was able to see what his brother did, however, is the fact that his clairvoyance is restricted to what concerns Jewel and those closest to Jewel: Addie and Dewey Dell. Darl hates Jewel because he is his mother's "jewel." He also seems to understand that Addie only began to hate Anse when she was pregnant with him, Darl, and that she made Anse promise to bury her in Jefferson after he was born. Darl is singled out and rejected from the very beginning; he is a narrator who must sublimate being denied his development as a character within the Bundren family.

Thus Darl's clairvoyance—his striking ability to discover the family's most hidden secrets—targets nothing but secrets related to Jewel, and Jewel is, for him, the embodiment of Addie's sin. Whereas Addie embraces sin as life-giving, Darl knows and reveals Addie's sin for what it is: the denial of love to himself and the children Addie has given to Anse after Jewel. When Darl watches Addie crying at Jewel's bedside after she discovers how Jewel, with months of secret hard labor at night, has bought the horse that will replace his mother, and when Darl finds out that Jewel secretly feeds his horse with hay that belongs to Anse and that Jewel denies he is taking, he learns how to hate Jewel—and the scope of his clairvoyance is limited by this hatred. Although he intuitively knows, for instance, that Anse is not the father of Jewel, he does not realize that Minister Whitfield is Jewel's father, and although he intuitively knows that his sister is pregnant, he does not realize that Lafe is the father of Dewey Dell's child. Darl hates Jewel because Jewel is loved by his mother, and he lusts after Dewey Dell because he discovers that his sister loves Jewel too. Darl is obsessed with hidden sin because he is obsessed with Jewel, and he thus taunts him whenever he can:

> "Jewel," I say, "whose son are you?"
>
> . . . .
>
> "Your mother was a horse, but who was your father, Jewel?"
> "You goddamn lying son of a bitch."
> "Dont call me that," I say.
> "You goddamn lying son of a bitch."
> "Dont you call me that, Jewel." In the tall moonlight his eyes look like spots of white paper pasted on a high small football.
>
> . . . .
>
> *Jewel, I say, Who was your father, Jewel?*
> *Goddamn you. Goddamn you.* (212–13)

Here Darl speaks to Jewel both as a character (when their dialogue is rendered within quotation marks) and as a narrator (when their unspoken dialogue appears in italics). When Darl speaks as a character, Jewel rejects the taunt, calling Darl a liar; however, when Darl asks him the same question in his role as narrator, Jewel seems to admit that Darl's insinuation may be justified, blaming him at the same time for not letting it remain a secret. As a character, Darl taunts Jewel into unwittingly calling their mother a "bitch" (212), thus asserting his own intellectual dominance by making Jewel state forthrightly what he, Darl, is only implying; as narrator he is content to imagine Jewel's rage as being commensurate with his own.

Darl's empathy with Dewey Dell's predicament takes a more ambivalent form, yet it also is rooted in his hatred of Jewel. Darl is the only one in the family who has fathomed his sister's passionate attachment to her brother Jewel. Dewey Dell will take care of the rest of the family—fanning her mother for days when she lies dying; repeatedly wiping Cash's mouth with the hem of her dress when he vomits after he has broken his leg; mothering Vardaman, who trusts her completely; cooking dinner for the family and the neighbors—but it is Jewel whom she adores. It is to him, for instance, that she desperately calls out when several members of the family seem to be in mortal danger as their wagon disappears in the flood. Addie gave Anse Dewey Dell in order to "negative" Jewel; Jewel and Dewey Dell complement each other; and just as Darl suffers from the knowledge that his mother does not love him, he desires Dewey Dell because she secretly loves the brother he must hate. Jewel and Dewey Dell (bearing remarkably consonant names) become the novel's corresponding male and female principles. For Darl, they are both desirable yet unattainable: Jewel, solitary and proud; Dewey Dell, the archetypal female whom he cannot approach, because she is his sister.

Like Quentin Compson in *The Sound and the Fury*, Darl is preoccupied with incestuous desire, a desire that is all the more devastating for being secondary and taboo:

> Dewey Dell carries the basket on one arm. . . . She sets the basket into the wagon and climbs in, her leg coming long from beneath her tightening dress: that lever which moves the world; one of that caliper which measures the length and breadth of life. (103)

> Squatting, Dewey Dell's wet dress shapes for the dead eyes of three blind men [Cash, Jewel, Vernon Tull] those mammalian ludicrosities which are the horizons and the valleys of the earth. (164)

Darl understands but will not embrace sin like his mother, and his infrequent, if violent, actions—like setting fire to Gillespie's barn, where his mother's coffin has been put up on two sawhorses "like a cubistic bug" (219)—serve only to sever him from his family and his Yoknapatawpha neighbors. Like Faulkner, he has the mind of a modernist artist—an artist, however, who lacks the conviction of his art, because it alienates him from his community. Thus Darl can only watch helplessly as Jewel saves Addie's body from the fire, just as he had saved it from the flood; and Darl must also suffer the loss of the trust of his youngest brother, Vardaman, who confides the reason for the barn burning to Dewey Dell, who in turn tells Gillespie about Darl's deed and thus gets Darl committed to the insane asylum. Dewey Dell understands that Darl not only knows but condemns her double-edged secret and realizes that she will be in his power if she does not manage to get rid of him. Her rising hatred of Darl takes the rest of the family, especially Cash, by surprise when it finally vents itself:

> But the curiousest thing was Dewey Dell. It surprised me. I see all the while how folks could say he was queer, but that was the very reason couldn't nobody hold it personal. . . . And then I always kind of had a idea that him and Dewey Dell kind of knowed things betwixt them. . . . But when we got it filled and covered and drove out the gate and turned into the lane where them fellows was waiting, when they come out and come on him and he jerked back, it was Dewey Dell that was on him before even Jewel could get at him. (237)

As Cash here tells the reader in passing, Addie has finally been buried in the Jefferson cemetery. Her will has been done—yet her dignity has been lost in the process. Darl, the only one of her sons who could have completed her revenge by turning it into art, has become the family's scapegoat, and while he may have unified the other members of the family in their desire to get rid of him, he cannot assume the traditional burden of scapegoat and restore peace through his suffering, because they will not let him acquire an identity by naming their secrets and thus becoming a purveyor of truth: "I dont know what I am. I dont know if I am or not. Jewel knows he is, because he does not know that he does not know whether he is or not" (80). Without Darl, each of his siblings is driven back into his or her privacy and isolation until the secrets will, as they eventually must, either reveal themselves or become insignificant. When Darl grasps that his being sacrificed will make matters worse for his siblings, not better, he begins to laugh and cannot stop laughing. The outrageousness of his family's design and the meaninglessness of his fate become, for him, emblematic of the absurdity of the world.

At this point, even the reader must part from Darl, since, for Faulkner, the existential experience of the absurd must engulf Darl both as a character and as a narrator. In the last Darl section of the novel (253), Darl the narrator and Darl the character communicate in schizophrenic fashion exclusively with each other and no longer with the reader. Only now does the reader detect that Darl has long since become his or her guide on the epic journey through the Bundrens' *Inferno* or *Purgatorio*—much as Vergil, the Roman Homer, was the designated guide for Dante through the netherworld and the *Purgatorio* of the *Divina commedia*. Only with the help of Darl has the reader come to understand that the Bundrens' ill-fated journey parallels an inner movement of frustrated desire and impossible revenge that achieves mythic proportions. Darl's vivid perception and his powers of description, analysis, and interpretation managed to make the underlying psychic portent of the epic events transparent. He also had command of most of Faulkner's well-known rhetorical and stylistic devices, because the author granted him the role of privileged narrator. But insofar as all narration is the quintessential form of customary knowledge (Lyotard 19), Darl's strong narrative position fails him as soon as he loses all ties to his family and to the community of Yoknapatawpha County:

> Darl has gone to Jackson. They put him on the train, laughing, down the long car laughing, the heads turning like the heads of owls when he passed. "What are you laughing at?" I said.
>
> "Yes yes yes yes yes." (253)

Darl the narrator is forced to attempt to create himself as Darl the character—an impossible enterprise. In this last Darl section, Darl not only represents the first person in "I said" but also speaks of himself in the third person: "Darl has gone to Jackson." Darl the character answers nothing but yes to the various questions put to him by Darl the narrator in a final but vain attempt to assert himself when his author has already deserted him.

> "Is it the pistols you're laughing at?" . . . "Is it because you hate the sound of laughing?"
>
> . . . .
>
> "Is that why you are laughing, Darl?" (253–54)

Darl's repeated yeses (nineteen in total) not only remind the reader of the final sentence of Molly Bloom's interior monologue at the end of *Ulysses*, thus indirectly indicating another Homeric and modernist parallel,[11] but also show how Darl, by invariably saying yes exactly nineteen times, is, in retrospect, desperately attempting to reclaim for himself the nineteen sections he has been permitted to narrate. He must attempt to reclaim them because he did speak them, he was there; at the same time, his yes, senseless in its absurd iteration, blots out any meaning that his life and character might still have for his family and his environment, in keeping with the sad statement of his favorite brother, Cash: "Down there it'll be quiet. . . . It'll be better for you, Darl" (238). While Darl the narrator is still speaking, Darl the character already begins to foam at the mouth and cling to the bars of his cage. Darl, who has been the narrative guide for the reader throughout the novel, is being expelled from his family, the community, and eventually from the novel, for knowing too much. As Addie Bundren's most faithful son, he knows too much about sin and revenge without, however, being able to perpetrate either.

By contrast, being incapable of understanding Addie Bundren at all—that is, being like her husband, Anse—ensures sanity. Anse is selfish, lazy, and stubborn, but he has always seen himself as part of the community, and he has never failed to receive his neighbors' support, although, like Armstid, the neighbors seek in vain to grasp what motivates them:

> Because be durn if there aint something about a durn fellow like Anse that seems to make a man have to help him, even when he knows he'll be wanting to kick himself next minute. (192)

While Addie in her strength could retreat into secrecy and privacy throughout her life, her husband needs to rely on others to survive. Yet he can create a group consciousness where even shared laughter becomes possible. Anse provides the novel with the much-needed comic relief that is the other side of the coin of the absurd. By making others, most notably his family, work for him, he manages, even if outrageously, to retain his role as patriarch and not lose his dignity, despite his ridiculousness when seen from the perspective of the reader.

While all of Addie's children become maimed in one way or another when they attempt to carry out their mother's revenge, it appears that Anse, the target of that revenge, instead of suffering from it, ultimately gains by it. He takes from his children everything they possess and prize to get to Jefferson, yet he wants to get there not to bury his dead wife (he even forgets to take along a shovel) but to get himself a new set of teeth and a new wife to take care of him. Therefore, some critics, in defiance of the novel's title, have hailed Anse as the main or at least the most successful character (Swiggart 110–11; Putzel 202–03). Set within the mythic scope provided by Addie as character and Darl as narrator, however, this shifty and shiftless character should rather be seen as an antihero:

> I told Addie it want any luck living on a road when it come by here, and she said, for the world like a woman, "Get up and move, then." But I told her it want no luck in it, because the Lord put roads for travelling: why He laid them down flat on the earth. When He aims for something to be always a-moving, He makes it long ways, like a road or a horse or a wagon, but when He aims for something to stay put, He makes it up-and-down ways, like a tree or a man. . . . Because if He'd a aimed for man to be always a-moving and going somewheres else, wouldn't He a put him long-ways on his belly, like a snake? It stands to reason He would. (35–36)

Anse is rooted in Yoknapatawpha and the South; he does not wish to move elsewhere. He is therefore not happy when a road is built that runs close by his farm, because the road seems to invite him to travel and he does not want to meet that challenge. Man is not made for travel, he reasons. Man is made to "stay put" like a tree (36); a tree does not leave its appointed place. According to Anse's logic, everything that is destined to move is stretched out horizontally, like a road or a horse or a wagon or a snake. God's will can be deduced from the shape of a thing. Anse does not take into account that roads and wagons are human-made and that, at most, God is responsible for the shape of the horse and that of the snake. Nor does he take into consideration that all animals (including himself) need to move to survive. But his argument conveys his point: he is too lazy to exert himself, and in defiance of the American dream, he employs whatever logic he can to justify his antiwork ethic. Tragedy, according to Aristotle, is tied to action; if so, then Anse Bundren undermines the very notion of tragedy—and by the same token seems to inhabit the realm of comedy.[12]

Addie leads her life on a large, if secretive, scale; like a tragic heroine, she is willing to act and to transgress all boundaries defined by God and human law,[13] whereas Anse reduces action to a minimum, thus making it tractable and safe to laugh at. Still, Anse is not a true comic antihero, just as Addie is not a true tragic heroine. On the one hand, Addie's attitude does not allow for a tragic flaw for which she accepts responsibility in the end. She believes in her right to sin, and she expects her children to collaborate in her secret revenge on Anse for not coming up to her standards—a revenge Anse escapes only because he does not understand it. On the other hand, Anse lacks the fortitude of the comic hero or antihero. In *As I Lay Dying*, the tragic might thus be termed pathetic and the comic farcical,[14] but even these terms lose their significance in view of the spectacle of the author's having to abandon the one narrator who kept him in touch with the reader and having to take sides with a society that, according to his own deepest belief, was "killed by the Civil War" (Faulkner, *Essays* 291).[15]

For the present-day reader, just as for Darl, the overpowering force of untameable nature in *As I Lay Dying*—inner passions and outer violence, symbolized by flood and fire—welds tragic-pathetic and comic-farcical elements together with such intensity as to make the world of the novel appear absurd. Indeed, as the novel develops, the reader witnesses an accelerated blending of preliminarily tragic or comic elements, leading to a confusion of the realms.[16] *As I Lay Dying* eventually turns into a nightmare from which the reader wants to be delivered, even at the cost of having to accept the banal for the comic or inconclusiveness instead of the cathartic effect of tragedy. At the same time, the reader experiences the end of the novel and Anse's triumph over his family—his successful acquisition of a new set of teeth and a second wife—as a kind of emotional betrayal, a loss of narrative significance.

> And there we set watching them, with Dewey Dell's and Vardaman's mouth half open and half-et bananas in their hands and her coming around from behind pa, looking at us like she dared ere a man. . . .
>
> "It's Cash and Jewel and Vardaman and Dewey Dell," pa says, kind of hangdog and proud too, with his teeth and all, even if he wouldn't look at us. "Meet Mrs Bundren," he says. (260–61)

In terms of plot, Anse's behavior after Addie has been buried and Darl disposed of clearly leads the Bundren family back to normality and back into the confines of Yoknapatawpha County. Yet even if the Bundren family and their author are reintegrated into Faulkner's fictional southern community, the reader is not. Darl was the narrator who set the reader off and led him or her into the novel; Cash, who among all the Bundren siblings comes closest to accepting community standards, is the final narrator, and he lets Anse, the patriarch, have the last word. However, for the reader, the meaning of the story has come to depend on Darl, the most memorable narrator of the Bundren family, and since Darl has become mad as a character and unreliable as a narrator in the end, the reader too has become alienated from the Bundrens' world. True, other consciousnesses besides Darl's have intermittently come into focus, modifying his perspective and providing alternate interpretative possibilities,[17] but by the novel's end Darl, like Addie, the most memorable character of the novel, refuses to be forgotten by the reader. For the reader, Addie and Darl have become part of the modernist tradition as it has developed from its classical and biblical roots. Only the reader is in a position to evaluate the implications of the novel's title, for only the reader can call up the Homeric tradition Faulkner has drawn on in the title; and only the reader can interpret the story in such modernist terms as they have been evoked throughout the novel. Although the reader must read Addie's confinement in a coffin and Darl's confinement in an insane asylum as instances of familial death-in-life; and although, as characters, Addie and Darl remain committed to the American South, even in extremis; and although the author's loyalty is to his home county and his own family traditions—yet, as a modernist artist, Faulkner has implicitly created ways for the reader to resist him, taking a clue from that narrator whose narration belongs not to the American South but to modernist literature. In this fashion, Faulkner wills the reader to re-create "was" as "might have been" or even "should have been." *As I Lay Dying* is a novel the reader will not be able to forget.

NOTES

[1] Faulkner often seems to presuppose a role of the reader beyond that of implied reader, an independent role that becomes more and more pronounced. In Faulkner's late novel *Requiem for a Nun* (1951), the reader appears as the imagined "stranger" from almost a hundred years away.

[2] "If there is a villain in that story it's the convention in which people have to live" (*Faulkner* 112).

[3] "The plot is . . . that of the oral epical tradition of quest or journey" (Mellard 221).

[4] In *As I Lay Dying*, Faulkner takes Hester Prynne's situation in Nathaniel Hawthorne's *The Scarlet Letter* to the extreme by giving Addie a son who resembles her, instead of giving her a daughter who is her very opposite, like Pearl in *The Scarlet Letter*. The parallels and differences between the two stories demonstrate the grotesque deformation every story about the transgression of norms—for instance, a story about New England's Puritan hypocrisy—must undergo when transformed into a myth of the South. See also Matthews, "Intertextuality."

[5] "Addie believes in her own way that only sin can give a sense to existence" (Weisgerber 194).

[6] "Faulkner's subjects are products of linguistic narrations in at least as many ways as they are producers of it" (Kelly 118).

[7] For Faulkner, any character he created took on a life of his or her own. He treated them as individuals who might very well write their own autobiography. This is nicely described by Meta Carpenter Wilde: "'Now, Bill, in this scene you say—' I began. 'I didn't say it,' he corrected me. 'The character said it.' 'The character?' 'Yes.' Although I nodded as if I understood, I did not really comprehend that Bill was telling me that his characters had a life-force of their own. What they did, what they said, came from them. Once he had created them, given them shape and color, they were then the authors of their own speeches and triumphs and follies" (Wilde and Borsten 84–85).

[8] "It is a writer's privilege to put into the mouths of his characters better speech than they would have been capable of, but only for the purpose of permitting and helping the character to justify himself or what he believes himself to be" (Faulkner, *Essays* 186).

[9] John T. Matthews here recalls the influence of Henri Bergson on Faulkner's language: "Language cannot render all that is present in perception or experience" (*Play* 37).

[10] "Because of Darl's power to intuit others' thoughts and our own access to his mind, the reader may feel like replying, 'I thought you would have known, Darl, and told me. I never thought you wouldn't have'" (Wadlington, As I Lay Dying 28).

[11] "The great mythic journey is the journey home, from the Trojan wars to Ithaca or, in Joyce's version, through the night sreets of Dublin to Molly Bloom. For modernist

authors, the journey from one place to another is a form of dislocation, even though the goal might be home" (Parini 143).

[12] "*As I Lay Dying* is not a mock-epic in the traditional sense of possessing a style too grandiose for action. . . . But the over-all contrast between public and private reality produces a comparable effect" (Swiggart 110).

[13] "Tragedy is mimesis not of persons but of action and life; and happiness and unhappiness consist in action, and the goal is a certain kind of action, not a qualitative state" (Aristotle 51; Ar. 1450a15).

[14] "*As I Lay Dying* . . . was an extremely original book. . . . One real originality was its juxtaposition, startling for 1929, of the tragic or pathetic and the farcical" (Guerard 72).

[15] In 1946 plans were made for a Modern Library double volume of *The Sound and the Fury* and *As I Lay Dying*. At this point, Faulkner rejected an unpublished introduction for *The Sound and the Fury* that he had written in 1933. The introduction can be found in *Essays, Speeches, and Public Letters* (289–300).

[16] "Faulkner learned a great deal from the movies before he was forced to earn a living from them" (Putzel 205).

[17] Darl "openly becomes one side of a dialectic that opposes him to the larger community" (Kinney 176).

"Seeing into the Heart": Teaching the Vardaman Narratives of *As I Lay Dying*

Michael Zeitlin

I typically spend eight fifty-minute classes on *As I Lay Dying*, and I have always found it productive to focus attention, usually in the second and third classes, on Vardaman, who never fails to fascinate most students. (For purposes of this discussion, the students I have in mind are those in the second year of college.) Why Vardaman fascinates is worth contemplation and discussion in the classroom, but my initial goal is to enable the students to grasp the powerful narrative logic of Vardaman's two most baffling monologues—his first, beginning "Then I begin to run" (53), and his third, consisting of the single line "My mother is a fish" (84). Reading these monologues is an especially good way to explore Faulkner's mysterious modes of identification and omniscience in their elemental forms. As we follow his representations of the little boy in the first third of the novel, we move from a series of brief but vivid descriptions of his face and figure to the sudden, spectacular revelation of his inner being and consciousness. For Cora, only the Lord "can see into the heart" (7) (although she often claims something of his power in this respect). In Vardaman, Faulkner enables us to "see into the heart" of the traumatized child.

Vardaman is literally invisible through the first seven monologues. He is out of sight and virtually out of mind. Only Cora thinks of him: "that little one almost old enough now to be selfish and stone-hearted like the rest of them" (23). Then, in the eighth monologue, Tull's first, Vardaman comes into view and instantly becomes an object of sustained fascination:

> That boy comes up the hill. He is carrying a fish nigh long as he is. He slings it to the ground and grunts "Hah" and spits over his shoulder like a man. Durn nigh long as he is.
>
> "What's that?" I say. "A hog? Where'd you get it?"
>
> "Down to the bridge," he says. He turns it over, the under side caked over with dust where it is wet, the eye coated over, humped under the dirt.
>
> "Are you aiming to leave it laying there?" Anse says.
>
> "I aim to show it to ma," Vardaman says. He looks toward the door. (30–31)

This passage introduces the major themes to be developed in the course of Vardaman's journey: his relentless exposure to the reality of flesh in decay; the guilty association of the fish with a beast to be butchered and devoured; the ugly gaze of the "eye coated over" in death; the dying mother who cannot witness the boy's pride; the distant yet proscriptive father; and the child's essential isolation in the unfolding scene of virtually unimaginable loss.

The text is insistent that before the fish can become a mythological entity (whether symbol of Christ, sacrificial totem beast, or mental icon of the dead mother), it is a brutish, smelly, smeary *thing* with which the little boy literally grapples:

> "You clean it," Anse says. He dont look around. Vardaman comes back and picks up the fish. It slides out of his hands, smearing wet dirt onto him, and flops down, dirtying itself again, gapmouthed, goggle-eyed, hiding into the dust like it was ashamed of being dead, like it was in a hurry to get back hid again. Vardaman cusses it. He cusses it like a grown man, standing a-straddle of it. Anse dont look around. Vardaman picks it up again. He goes on around the house, toting it in both arms like a armful of wood, it overlapping him on both ends, head and tail. Durn nigh big as he is. (31)

The dead fish assumes psychologically immense proportions, and a major part of Faulkner's genius is to place the small child at the center of the engagement with this enormousness. The contest of the little boy with this reality of harrowing magnitude is registered in Vardaman's discourse as a series of poignant attempts at negation:

> "I can feel where the fish was in the dust. It is cut up into pieces of not-fish now, not-blood on my hands and overalls. Then it wasn't so. It hadn't happened then. And now she is getting so far ahead I cannot catch her." (53)

> *My mother is not in the box. My mother does not smell like that.* (196)

To develop the meaning of negation here, as a psychological agency that one can discern in the discourse of the human subject, I introduce a passage from Sigmund Freud's essay "Negation":

> When a patient says, "You ask who this person in the dream can be. It's *not* my mother." We emend this to: "So it *is* his mother." In our interpretation, we take the liberty of disregarding the negation and of picking out the subject-matter alone of the association. It is as though the patient had said: "It's true that my mother came into my mind as I thought of this person, but I don't feel inclined to let the association count." . . . Thus the content of a repressed image or idea can make its way into consciousness, on condition that it is *negated*. Negation is a way of taking cognizance of what is repressed; indeed it is already a lifting of the repression, though not, of course, an acceptance of what is repressed. (235–36)

It is worth discussing why Freud's primary example of negation concerns, as its point of reference, the figure of the mother. Is this merely coincidental? Why feelings for the mother might need to be negated can be a good way to begin a discussion of the Oedipus complex and so make Freud's conception of the matter anything but reductive or abstract: How is the mother involved in the fundamental human questions of life, love, and death? In Vardaman's case, the word *not* and other verbal negations are to be explored as signs of intense psychic struggle, of Vardaman's attempt to absorb, assimilate, or ward off the force of a shattering recognition (which at this point in the discussion we are merely approaching).

To give some additional perspective to the logic of the psychological processes at work in Vardaman's soul—on the day he catches the biggest fish of his life and his mother passes away—I often turn to a rich pairing of psychoanalytic narrative sources, Jacques Lacan's discussion of Freud's famous dream of "Irma's injection." In a general way, Lacan and Freud give us a vocabulary to describe the novel's oneiric qualities (which, profoundly present and operative throughout the narrative, become explicit, for example, in Dewey Dell's dream—"I saw Vardaman rise and go to the window and strike the knife into the fish, the blood gushing, hissing like steam but I could not see. . . . I rose and took the knife from the streaming fish still hissing and I killed Darl" [121]). More specifically, they enable us to focus on what is at stake in the present instance: the atrocious recognition (bound up with all sorts of complicated unconscious fantasies) of the pathological fate of all biological substance. Here is the critical part of Freud's dream:

> A large hall—numerous guests, whom we were receiving.—Among them was Irma. I at once took her on one side, as though to answer her letter and to reproach her for not having accepted my "solution" yet. I said to her: "If you still get pains, it's really only your fault." She replied: "If you

> only knew what pains I've got now in my throat and stomach and abdomen—it's choking me."—I was alarmed and looked at her. She looked pale and puffy. I thought to myself that after all I must be missing some organic trouble. I took her to the window and looked down her throat, and she showed signs of recalcitrance, like women with artificial dentures. I thought to myself that there was really no need for her to do that.—She then opened her mouth properly and on the right I found a big white patch; at another place I saw extensive whitish grey scabs upon some remarkable curly structures which were evidently modelled on the turbinal bones of the nose. (*Interpretation* 107)

Lacan's reading of this dream is brilliant and of the utmost pertinence:

> Having got the patient to open her mouth . . . what he sees in there, these turbinate bones covered with a whitish membrane, is a horrendous sight. This mouth has all the equivalences in terms of significations, all the condensations you want. Everything blends in and becomes associated in this image, from the mouth to the female sexual organ, by way of the nose. . . . There's a horrendous discovery here, that of the flesh one never sees, the foundation of things, the other side of the head, of the face, the secretory glands *par excellence*, the flesh from which everything exudes, at the very heart of the mystery, the flesh in as much as it is suffering, is formless, in as much as its form in itself is something which provokes anxiety. Spectre of anxiety, identification of anxiety, the final revelation of *you are this—You are this, which is so far from you, this which is the ultimate formlessness*. (154–55)

Hence (in accordance with the unconscious gaze into the interior flesh of the woman's body) disavowal, negation: I am not this; my mother is not this; I am not, she is not, mortal. The revelation here, in Lacan's words, is of "something which properly speaking is unnameable . . . this something faced with which all words cease and all categories fail, the object of anxiety *par excellence*" (164). The state of disintegration, the irreversible process, cannot be undone. The damage is beyond reparation, and the "impossible" meaning of this truth is the traumatic kernel of the text. It is utterly fascinating how Faulkner situates this deep knowledge within the living soul of the little child. "My mother is a fish" is thus to be read as a mental image of the utmost psychical and affective condensation.

In suggesting that the one-line monologue might be read as if it were a dream (in a sense, it *is* a dream), I like to quote from the sixth chapter of Freud's *The Interpretation of Dreams*, the section entitled "The Work of Condensation":

> Dreams are brief, meagre and laconic in comparison with the range and wealth of the dream-thoughts. . . . As a rule one underestimates the amount of compression that has taken place . . . whereas if the work of

> interpretation is carried further it may reveal still more thoughts concealed behind the dream.
>
> . . . it is in fact never possible to be sure that a dream has been completely interpreted . . . the possibility always remains that the dream may have yet another meaning. Strictly speaking, then, it is impossible to determine the amount of condensation. (279)

To define Faulkner's text as essentially oneiric is to encourage the students to develop a feeling for its manifest and latent dimensions: there is the surface of the flowing river, and there are the objects that loom in the depths. We sense their presence, and their sudden emergence can seem a fulfillment of premonitions and presentiments: "The log appears suddenly between two hills, as if it had rocketed suddenly from the bottom of the river. Upon the end of it a long gout of foam hangs like the beard of an old man or a goat" (148). How should we read the imagery here? What is being said in what is being said? I feel it is important to let the students have their full say here, to let them free-associate for a while and not give them too much in the way of prescription. In the presence of the dream text, one reads it, but one also allows oneself to be read by it. When a student, in the presence of what is often felt as the passage's lecherous and disturbing qualities, attempts to interpret the symbolism in sexual terms, I respond with these questions: Who is describing the scene, and how does it reflect his deepest preoccupations? Does reading the symbols in a Freudian manner amount to a reduction or an expansion of the passage's meaning? Here I follow Freud's suggestion that, when discussing sexual and bodily matters (as one must to engage this novel in a serious way), one should adopt a dry and direct tone.

After this brief foray into the psychoanalytic theory of condensation, I let Faulkner himself speak to the question posed by the one-line monologue. I cite this passage from *Faulkner in the University*, in which we are reminded of Vardaman's isolated situation in the larger family drama:

> Q. Mr. Faulkner, why did Vardaman say "My mother is a fish"?
>
> A. That was the child, nobody had paid any attention to him. He saw things that baffled and puzzled him, and nobody—none of the adults would stop long enough to show him any tenderness, any affection, and he was groping and that occurred to him that because of the—now, that's another book I should have read, I don't remember exactly what happened, except when he brought the fish home, something that happened from the outside got the fish confused with the fact that he knew his mother's body was in a room and that she was no longer his mother. She couldn't talk or—anyway, suddenly her position in the mosaic of the household was vacant. . . . He was a child trying to cope with this adult's world which to him was, and to any sane person, completely mad. That these people would want to drag that body over the country and go to all

> that trouble, and he was baffled and puzzled. He didn't know what to do about it. (110–11)

Faulkner's comments elicit from the students all sorts of thoughtful remarks about childhood feelings of isolation, loneliness, and fear. But I suggest that the author can tell us only so much—that the textuality knows and tells more than the author ever can, even when we take him or her to be an authoritative public spokesperson on its behalf. The work of interpretation must go beyond what the author says in any given instance, and this is why a close reading of the text, along with a full commitment to the collective work of interpretation, is always a necessary part of any serious engagement.

For example, as a way of pressing beyond what the author might say of his or her text, there is a dimension of its deep knowledge that might also be worth exploring, in a speculative way, in the classroom: that the damage that has been done to the body of Addie Bundren (and I believe Faulkner suggests this strongly) is an effect of the family's unconscious hostility toward her. (That is, there are good, historically specific reasons for putting the matter in these modernist Freudian terms.) When one considers the manner in which Addie's corpse, like the body of Madeleine Usher in Edgar Allan Poe's famous story, becomes the object of an astonishingly grotesque, seemingly relentless exertion of violence (her body is dragged, dropped, bored into, "crucified," burned, allowed to rot openly, and so on), it is hard not to postulate the presence (but at what level?) of some unmistakably purposive and destructive agency. In an important sense, *As I Lay Dying* (borrowing the words of Don DeLillo from another context) is "the story of a body that the living did not want to yield" (*Mao II* 192). The living are not yet ready to give up their claim on Addie Bundren, as an object of love and mourning but also of resentment and even hatred. Given the libidinal connection of the living to the dead, what happens to Addie Bundren is always what is done to her. In *As I Lay Dying*, that is, we are in a resolutely animistic universe in which all seemingly natural processes are inseparably bound up with the "omnipotence of thoughts" (Freud, *Totem* 83), and in these terms, Addie has not so much died as been killed. This is how Vardaman immediately understands the matter, fixing (at least for a moment) Doctor Peabody as the cause of the effect:

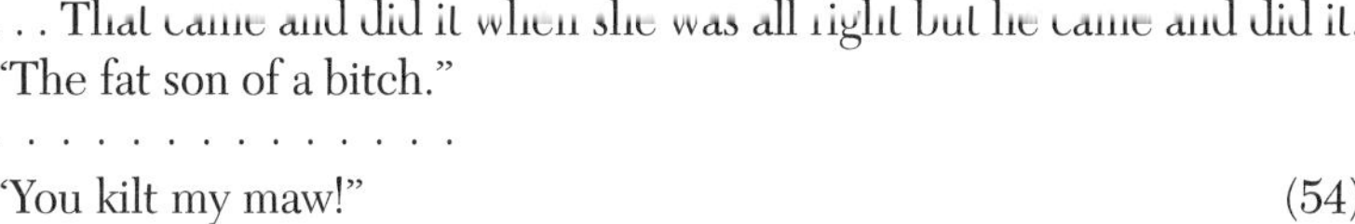

> . . . That came and did it when she was all right but he came and did it.
> "The fat son of a bitch."
> . . . .
> "You kilt my maw!" (54)

The mother is dead, but in the strange logic of the novel, which we can trace to the boy's sense of the matter, she remains alive, awake with living force, as do her suffering and her resistance. Here Faulkner represents the boy's sense of her living presence yet tantalizing elusiveness:

> . . . because in the water she could go faster than a man and Darl had to grabble for her so I knew he could catch her because he is the best grabbler . . .
>
> . . . because in the water she fought to stay under the water but Darl is strong and he was coming in slow and so I knew he had her because he came slow and I ran down into the water to help and I couldn't stop hollering because Darl was strong and steady holding her under the water even if she did fight he would not let her go he was seeing me and he would hold her and it was all right now it was all right now it was all right
>
> *Then he comes up out of the water. He comes a long way up slow before his hands do but he's got to have her got to so I can bear it. Then his hands come up and all of him above the water. I cant stop. I have not got time to try. I will try to when I can but his hands came empty out of the water emptying the water emptying away*
>
> "Where is ma, Darl?" I said. "You never got her. You knew she is a fish but you let her get away. You never got her. Darl. Darl. Darl." I began to run along the bank, watching the mules dive up slow again and then down again. (150–51)

This poignant passage is worth lingering over. Putting things into words is what we do, I tell the students. Who can accept the challenge to articulate what Vardaman is feeling here, about his mother, about his brother? How is his mind working? And what about the word *grabbler* in a novel so rich with colloquial poetry? Why is it so expressive?

One might say the entire novel is an attempt to "grabble" with Addie Bundren as she eludes us. Yet just as she seems to vanish, she returns in waves of unsettling power. Darl observes:

> The breeze was setting up from the barn, so we put her under the apple tree, where the moonlight can dapple the apple tree upon the long slumbering flanks within which now and then she talks in little trickling bursts of secret and murmurous bubbling. I took Vardaman to listen. (212)

The equation of wood and flesh lies at a fundamental level of the novel's logic, and it is in these terms that the complex of ideas involving the oneiric continuance of the mother's suffering might be approached. Somehow, everybody participates (unconsciously) in the crucifixion of Addie Bundren. This is suggested when we read the letter as well as the spirit of the text's utterances (by Anse, Tull, Peabody, Darl, Vardaman):

> ". . . and she will rest quieter for knowing it and that it was her own blood sawed out the boards and drove the nails." (19)

> He goes on around the house, toting it in both arms like a armful of wood, it overlapping him on both ends, head and tail. (31)

> Beneath the quilt she is no more than a bundle of rotten sticks. (44)

> . . . *he pries with a slipping two-by-four, with a piece of rotting log for fulcrum, at the axle. Jewel, I say, she is dead, Jewel. Addie Bundren is dead* (52)

> . . . and I said "Are you going to nail her up in it, Cash? Cash? Cash?" I got shut up in the crib the new door it was too heavy for me it went shut I couldn't breathe because the rat was breathing up all the air. I said "Are you going to nail it shut, Cash? Nail it? *Nail* it?"
>
> Pa walks around. His shadow walks around, over Cash going up and down above the saw, at the bleeding plank. (65)

"Are you going to nail it"? I often mention Poe again—"The Cask of Amontillado," for example, or "The Fall of the House of Usher" and Poe's attempt to imagine what it is like to be shut up alive inside the tomb or coffin. Let us all close our eyes, I invite the class, and really imagine it. Premature burial. Vardaman's claustrophobic identification with his mother is radically unsustainable beyond a few moments. This is the limit experience Faulkner is trying to represent. I also talk about what it must be like to explain the matter of Christ's crucifixion to a young child for the first time: Christ was put on the cross. But how? His hands and feet were nailed into the wood. How else can one say it? How can the thought of iron nails through bone and soft tissue not be terrible to a young child? (I.N.R.I., as Leopold Bloom puts it in *Ulysses*: "iron nails ran in" [Joyce 81].) Why is this act repeated (unwittingly) when Vardaman bores through the wood, and the flesh, with the augur?

At this point, it is productive to contemplate Addie explicitly as a sacrificial figure in the novel. Why is she being punished, crucified? What is her sin or crime? Are the sins and crimes hers alone, or has she taken them on for the sake of the community? The first question is elementary: What are some of the possible sources of animosity toward Addie Bundren in the novel? (A related discussion of Anse is always lively; the discussion of Addie always turns out to be more solemn and difficult.) I ask whether the hatred Addie herself has learned to feel in response to a long series of violations might be thought of as returning to her as "a sort of obverse reflection of the . . . people [she] lives among" (to borrow Quentin Compson's phrase from *The Sound and the Fury* [86])—and so on in a *mise en abyme* of echoing reflections. A focused discussion of this passage in Addie's monologue thus becomes necessary:

> . . . instead of going home I would go down the hill to the spring where I could be quiet and hate them. . . .
>
> . . . I would hate my father for having ever planted me. I would look forward to the times when they [not only her students but also, I suggest, her children] faulted, so I could whip them. (169–70)

Why does Addie whip the children? How might such key terms as *sadism*, *masochism*, and *displacement* help us understand? What, after all, does each of these terms actually mean? How and to what extent might human psychology and human emotions be illuminated by such terms? When Addie claims, "Then I gave [Anse] Vardaman to replace the child I had robbed him of. And now he has three children that are his and not mine" (176), does she enable us to grasp the extent to which Vardaman (like Darl, like Dewey Dell) experiences himself as something of an empty center, as a walking symbol of the mother's negation in himself of the precious and beloved "jewel" who displaced him before he was born?

The text suggests that Addie's gaze possesses a terrible annihilating power: her death wish is all too clear. (It is a power seemingly passed on to her daughter: "and then I found that girl watching me. If her eyes had a been pistols, I wouldn't be talking now. I be dog if they didn't blaze at me," says Samson [115].) As Addie stares at her youngest son, her look (we must imagine ourselves in Vardaman's place, on the receiving end of it) is uncanny and terrifying. I even call it sadistic, offering such a strong reading to generate discussion, which often becomes quite animated at this point. Clearly, this is no tender and loving goodbye to the baby of the family. Here is Peabody's description:

> She looks at us. Only her eyes seem to move. It's like they touch us, not with sight or sense, but like the stream from a hose touches you, the stream at the instant of impact as dissociated from the nozzle as though it had never been there. She does not look at Anse at all. She looks at me, then at the boy. Beneath the quilt she is no more than a bundle of rotten sticks.
>
> "Well, Miss Addie," I say. The girl does not stop the fan. "How are you, sister?" I say. Her head lies gaunt on the pillow, looking at the boy. "You picked out a fine time to get me out here and bring up a storm." Then I send Anse and the boy out. She watches the boy as he leaves the room. She has not moved save her eyes. (44)

In Darl's clairvoyant rendering of the scene, the dying mother's gaze is focused unmistakably on Vardaman's face:

> She lies back and turns her head without so much as glancing at pa. She looks at Vardaman; her eyes, the life in them, rushing suddenly upon them; the two flames glare up for a steady instant. Then they go out as though someone had leaned down and blown upon them. (48)

This passage epitomizes the novel's insistence on placing the boy's small body and little mind (which, on first reading, remains relatively opaque) against realities of the greatest possible magnitude. Focusing on Faulkner's technique here, I suggest that the consistent perspective given to the littleness of the boy is akin to the manner in which a painter or photographer accentuates perspective by placing a small human figure in the foreground of the awesome panorama. Vardaman is represented dialectically in this sense, the focus alternating between the "backdrop of cosmic scale" (Millgate 110) and the child's diminutive isolation:

> The durn little tyke is sitting on the top step, looking smaller than ever in the sulphur-colored light. (45 [Peabody])

> "That poor boy," Cora says. "The poor little tyke." (34 [Tull])

> They had done put him to bed in the trough in a empty stall. (117 [Samson])

> So when Cora waked me it had set in to rain. Even while I was going to the door with the lamp and it shining on the glass so he could see I am coming, it kept on knocking. Not loud, but steady, like he might have gone to sleep thumping, but I never noticed how low down on the door the knocking was till I opened it and never seen nothing. I held the lamp up, with the rain sparkling across it and Cora back in the hall saying "Who is it, Vernon?" but I couldn't see nobody a-tall at first until I looked down and around the door, lowering the lamp.
>
> He looked like a drownded puppy, in them overalls, without no hat, splashed up to his knees where he had walked them four miles in the mud. "Well, I'll be durned," I says. (69 [Tull])

After peering out into the rain, Tull locates the source of the thumping. He lowers his lamp, and Vardaman's face is suddenly illuminated. "He looked at me, his eyes round and black in the middle like when you throw a light in a owl's face" (70). Wide-eyed with secret and terrible wisdom, Vardaman is a composition of round shapes—head, face, pupils, all encircled by the light of Tull's lamp. When Vardaman says, "You mind that ere fish," we might well imagine Tull's equally baffled and rounded expression as he mirrors the boy's face. (Tull is astonished and paralyzed; it is Cora who comes to the door and pulls the child in out of the rain.)

Here I use the overhead projector to show a reproduction of Edvard Munch's *The Scream*, a painting Faulkner probably knew, to suggest the kind of traumatic intensity being represented in the imagery of drastically dilated facial features:

> Pa stands beside the bed. From behind his leg Vardaman peers, with his round head and his eyes round and his mouth beginning to open. (47)

> From behind pa's leg Vardaman peers, his mouth full open and all color draining from his face into his mouth, as though he has by some means fleshed his own teeth in himself, sucking. He begins to move slowly backward from the bed, his eyes round, his pale face fading into the dusk like a piece of paper pasted on a failing wall, and so out of the door. (49)

Unlike Anse, who ignores Vardaman throughout the ordeal, and against Addie, who appears deliberately if not maliciously to horrify and madden her youngest son with her death-glazed eyes, Peabody, Tull, and Darl are showing how we should be sensitive to the pathos of Vardaman's isolation:

> It was about a mile from the house we saw him, sitting on the edge of the slough. It hadn't had a fish in it never that I knowed. He looked around at us, his eyes round and calm, his face dirty, the pole across his knees. (92 [Tull])

> He too has lost flesh; like ours, his face has an expression strained, dreamy, and gaunt. (226 [Darl])

We are now ready to engage Faulkner's representation of Vardaman's interiority in the boy's first monologue. In an outburst of rage and anguish following Addie's death, Vardaman runs down to the barn where he vomits his crying and attacks Peabody's team. In the "warm, smelling, silent" barn, Vardaman is suddenly felt from the inside (56). His vocalized utterances frame the spectacular stream-of-consciousness passage at the heart of the monologue:

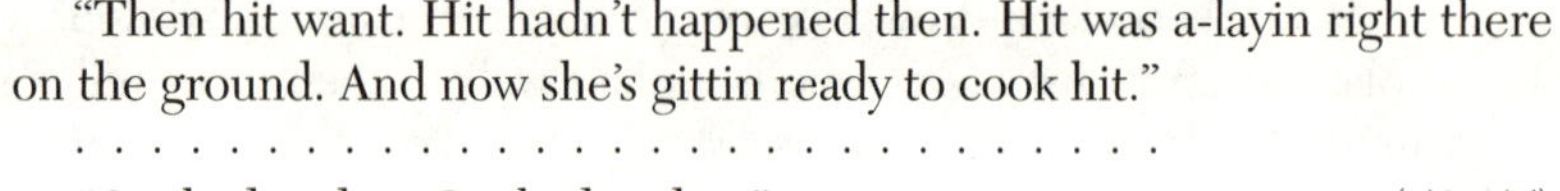

> "Then hit want. Hit hadn't happened then. Hit was a-layin right there on the ground. And now she's gittin ready to cook hit."
>
> . . . .
>
> "Cooked and et. Cooked and et." (56–57)

A radical linguistic contrast is produced: on the one hand, there are Vardaman's words and thoughts; on the other, within him there "lurks a wisdom too profound or too inert for even thought" (49), a preverbal mode of knowing represented as a kind of negative capability or radical impressionability:

> It is dark. I can hear wood, silence: I know them. But not living sounds, not even him. It is as though the dark were resolving him out of his integrity, into an unrelated scattering of components—snuffings and stampings; smells of cooling flesh and ammoniac hair; an illusion of a co-ordinated whole of splotched hide and strong bones within which, detached and secret and familiar, an *is* different from my *is*. I see him dissolve—legs, a rolling eye, a gaudy splotching like cold flames—and float upon the dark in fading solution; all one yet neither; all either yet none. I can see hearing coil toward him, caressing, shaping his hard shape—fetlock, hip, shoulder and head; smell and sound. I am not afraid. (56–57)

The passage must be read aloud, slowly, which makes Vardaman's voice anything but abstract. How should the monologue sound? I feel it is important to ask various students to read from Vardaman's passage aloud, and especially to read across the transition from his own colloquial voice to the interior diction of this special passage. Having sounded the narrative textures here, we can then move quite profitably in some explicitly philosophical directions (providing an occasion to introduce such terms as *ontology*, *epistemology*, and *phenomenology*) as the class attempts to provide a definition of the self who speaks, thinks, feels. On the one hand, there is the self we all believe in—what Faulkner in *Absalom, Absalom!* calls "the I, myself, that deep existence which we lead" (109) and "the citadel of the central I-Am's private own" (112). On the other, this centrality is often a temporary or provisional "clotting" readily susceptible to dissolution, to being overwritten by a more powerful being (as when, for example, Darl contemplates the rushing river much later in the novel):

> It looks peaceful, like machinery does after you have watched it and listened to it for a long time. As though the clotting which is you had dissolved into the myriad original motion, and seeing and hearing in themselves blind and deaf; fury in itself quiet with stagnation. (163–64)

Locating the subject becomes a matter of grasping the nature of the exchange being represented in such scenes.

After giving a brief account of Benjy's narrative in *The Sound and the Fury*, I ask the students to summarize in their own words the kind of representational problem Faulkner encountered in Vardaman and to compile an inventory of Faulkner's narrative solutions. The students recognize in Vardaman a kindred spirit whose impressions of the world sink deeply into the soul. Thus they are ready to read the words of his interior monologue as expressions of profound feeling and perception and to defend him against the charge of illiteracy or ignorance. A slow, line-by-line reading is necessary here for bringing out the richness of Faulkner's representation. I then divide the class into small discussion groups and ask them to contemplate representative critical responses to Vardaman's first monologue:

> [Vardaman's language] is not appropriate to the mind of a child. Good rhetoric or not, as a verbal medium the passage gives little plausibility to its referent, and the existence of another person—that of the author-narrator—is postulated even though . . . the narrative arrangement of *As I Lay Dying* includes no narrator. (Franklin 59)

> [T]he author attributes his own ornate rhetoric to the thoughts of ignorant children. (Ross, "Shapes" 723)

> [V]erisimilitude at times is stretched to the breaking point by unexpected variations in tone and linguistic competence. (Pitavy 40)

> [Faulkner] . . . clearly [puts] terms in Darl's descriptions to which a simple country boy could hardly have access. (Allen 191)

> [Vardaman implies an] astonishing violence to plausibility (in the reflections and language of reflection, of the characters). (Aiken 653)

> [Darl uses] a highly sophisticated diction certainly incongruent with his condition as a farmer. (Pitavy 40)

I have found that the students readily perceive the ideologies of class and region that seem to be inherent in such claims and that they almost always find an eloquent way to respond to them, in defense of both Vardaman and Faulkner. Together, in (often polemical) dialogue with the critics, we come to define and appreciate the revolutionary nature of Faulkner's narrative experiment: how, within the bounds of a formal first-person narrative voice, Faulkner invents a way to represent the richly textured and vivid complexity of an experience and state of being that Vardaman could not himself put into words. In Vardaman's first monologue, we encounter the depths of consciousness, the life of the senses, the moment-to-moment affective utterances of a traumatized soul, the sound of the voice, and the way in which the verbal personality is drowned out by the silent visual power of the image (in this case that of the horse, defamiliarized). It's all enough to make your "heart hurt" (216).

"Salvation Is Just Words Too": Addie Bundren and the Language of Motherhood

Annette Wannamaker

> And when I knew that I had Cash, I knew that living was terrible and that this was the answer to it. That was when I learned that words are no good; that words dont ever fit even what they are trying to say at. When he was born I knew that motherhood was invented by someone who had to have a word for it because the ones that had the children didn't care whether there was a word for it or not. (171–72 [Addie Bundren])

> Addie cannot escape the Symbolic. What she can and does do, however, is to enunciate the lack that fuels signification and grounds the Symbolic on which patriarchy itself depends. (Porter, "Symbolic Fathers" 96)

While quite a few contemporary critics see Addie Bundren as a potentially subversive character, many students reading *As I Lay Dying* for the first time see her simply as a bad mother. She is one of Faulkner's most maligned characters, chastised for being a cold and unfeeling mother whose children have suffered as a result of her neglect and sin. This reaction may be based in part on the contradictory cultural tropes about motherhood that Faulkner invokes but then leaves unresolved. In the character of Addie, Faulkner depicts ambivalent images of the mother: the monstrous mother, personified by flood, who threatens to engulf her family; the consuming, castrated, castrating m(O)ther, from whom the child must distance himself as part of the passage into subjectivity; the muted mother, silenced and spoken for in patriarchal culture; or the mother who is forced to take the blame for all childhood trauma, familial dysfunction, and psychic wounds that linger into adulthood. It is no wonder, then, that many college students, few of whom are themselves mothers, often react negatively to Addie.

In *Faulkner's Women: The Myth and the Muse*, David Williams characterizes the Bundren family as victims of an unnatural, loveless mother. The theme of *As I Lay Dying*, he claims, is "the lack of mother-love and its consequent impact upon a family" (97). Students reading the novel for the first time often echo this interpretation of the text, often want to blame Addie for the lack of communication and love in the Bundren household. And, indeed, they find ample evidence to support this interpretation: Addie beats her students, favors Jewel, has an affair with a preacher, stubbornly refuses to confess her sins, and asks to be buried in Jefferson—the request that sets the macabre events of the novel into motion. With the exception of the single chapter she narrates, Addie is mostly described as a grotesque, rotting body: "You get this thing buried," says the marshal (204); "*My mother does not smell like that,*" says Vardaman (196). Metaphorically,

Addie's body exceeds the space of her coffin: she is the smell that attracts buzzards, she is the entrails of a fish, the rain that swells the land, the flood that kills the mules; she is an excessive maternal body, morphed into the earth and the weather, threatening to engulf and consume all her children. One could easily therefore argue that Faulkner's portrayal of Addie is misogynistic and represents a fear and loathing of the feminine. And this would certainly be the case if Addie had not been given a space in the novel from which to speak.

Addie, especially in her monologue, is more complex and also, perhaps, more sympathetic than she might initially seem. Her stream-of-consciousness monologue moves beyond the concept of the monstrous mother to anticipate contemporary feminist theories that both respond to and critique negative, narrow perceptions of women and mothers. Furthermore, Faulkner gives Addie a space from which to speak while also adeptly acknowledging that it is an uneasy space of indeterminacy where Addie is used by language in her every attempt to use it. Or as Carolyn Porter states in her essay "Symbolic Fathers and Dead Mothers: A Feminist Approach to Faulkner," Faulkner's depiction of Addie and other mothers demonstrates "how women can be positioned as both other and as speaking subjects" (81). Even though Faulkner, a male author, is speaking for Addie, her chapter is a sympathetic and sophisticated (though at times ambivalent) portrayal of the silenced mother struggling both within and against her exclusion from language. Even if it is not possible for Addie, the character, to win this struggle, the novel makes visible the interplay among language, gendered identity, and access to power in patriarchy. Although most Faulkner characters find themselves distanced from the symbolic, Addie is distinct in that her struggles with language are marked as specifically feminine and, more specifically, maternal: they are directly tied to her body and sexuality, to her relationships with men, to her identity as a mother, and to her ambivalence about Christianity and the roles prescribed for her therein. Therefore, while Addie has been harshly criticized for being an adulterer and an uncaring mother by some critics and by many students, Faulkner's rendering of her reveals an empathetic understanding of women's troubled relation with language and the way it mirrors their troubled existence in patriarchal social structures. The novel does this in a way that anticipates some of the foundational texts and ideas of feminist psychoanalytic theory and that can help students work through and understand those texts.

Many students approach critical theory as they might approach a textbook, as if a theoretical essay is a transparent, instructional text from which they can glean a collection of facts. But theoretical texts are not textbooks. Indeed, some have more in common with works of literature in terms of tone, style, and aesthetic qualities. There are theoretical texts that use the same tropes and rhythms as literary texts, and, conversely, there are works of literature that playfully and experimentally use language to deconstruct meaning, that seek to understand the human condition in ways that feel very much like theory. Perhaps if we used the same reading strategies for theory that we use to understand a work of literature, and vice versa, new, more fluid, more intertextual and creative readings of both might develop. Faulkner's texts, because of their self-conscious use of language and their focus on the role of language in shaping the self, are ideal sites for such intertextual work.

Although professors of literature often teach critical theory in such a way that theoretical concepts are presented as utilitarian tools for deciphering literary texts' meanings, the best literary texts often anticipate critical theory, often function in ways similar to theory by examining and challenging the roles of discourse, powerfully and sophisticatedly. Texts like *As I Lay Dying* can be read in tandem with theoretical texts and can even be used as tools to decipher the meanings of theoretical texts. With this shift in reading strategy, students can gain a richer understanding of both literary and theoretical texts and learn new ways of reading that can challenge assumptions about the functions, genres, and connections among different sorts of texts. Ultimately and ideally, the best works of literature can help us interrogate and reexamine theoretical concepts we have come to accept as truisms. Conversely, engagement with critical theory can help students move beyond the surface reading of a text, which is often focused on plot development and character identification.

Like much of Faulkner's writing, *As I Lay Dying* carefully examines connections among language, identity, and power. The novel can be used in an upper-level undergraduate or graduate-level critical theory course or feminist theory course in ways that can deepen students' understanding of both literary and theoretical texts and expand on and complicate ideas concerning discourse and gender. *As I Lay Dying*, because of its complexity and ambiguity, can be taught in dialogue with a variety of critical texts. As an example, I focus specifically on teaching the novel in dialogue with selected works by Luce Irigaray, Julia Kristeva, and Hélène Cixous. Essays by these French feminist theorists are often difficult for students to grasp, partly because they are critiques of various psychoanalytic theories with which students must have some familiarity and partly because these writers use language in experimental and disconcerting ways to make visible women's difficult relation with language. If we read Faulkner's characterization of Addie as Porter does, as a way to "enunciate the lack that fuels signification and grounds the Symbolic on which patriarchy itself depends" ("Symbolic Fathers" 96), then Faulkner's depiction of Addie serves the same purpose as the work of these feminist theorists and uses similar rhetorical strategies to do so.

Language preexists us all, and we—male and female—must use words created long before we existed for defining and expressing ourselves. Some feminist theorists argue that women are doubly distanced from language because it has been constructed predominantly by patriarchal cultures. Girls and women must define themselves and their relations with the world using discourse largely created by men (the patriarchal symbolic order), from which they have historically been denied full access. Furthermore, according to some theorists, the mother is the most silenced and most "spoken for" of women. Kristeva refers to "the difficulty a mother has acknowledging (or being acknowledged by) the symbolic realm" (13). Because many women have felt excluded from discourse, some theorists, like Irigaray and Cixous, have worked to define and differentiate a feminine writing (*écriture feminine*) based largely on women's sexuality or women's bodies that would differ from male writing not only in subject matter but also in form, structure, rhythm, and cadence. Irigaray and Cixous tried to create a space for women to write outside—or at least on the margins of—the symbolic, though many, including Kristeva, argue that they were unsuccessful. Creating a space outside traditional forms of representation from which to speak (even if not possible) is a political act meant to empower women and give them an authentic voice or perhaps to imagine how such an authentic voice might sound.

On women's exclusion from the patriarchal symbolic order, Cixous writes:

> Every woman has known the torture of beginning to speak aloud, heart beating as if to break, occasionally falling into loss of language, ground and language slipping out from under her, because for woman speaking—even just opening her mouth—in public is something rash, a transgression. A double anguish, for even if she transgresses, her word almost always falls on the deaf masculine ear, which can only hear language that speaks in the masculine. (98)

Therefore, dismantling the patriarchal symbolic order by making visible the gaps and spaces where language fails to represent the feminine, by marking those aspects of discourse that are masculine, and by working to create a space for an alternative feminine mode of discourse becomes part of a larger feminist project. Reading and discussing these theories in dialogue with Faulkner's work is not to say, of course, that Faulkner was a feminist. Nanci Kincaid writes about Faulkner's depiction of Addie and other female characters: "I think Faulkner admires women mightily—but his fear of them is equal to if not larger than his admiration." No matter what his intentions might have been, Faulkner's writing—the way he interrogates the complex relations among discourse, power, and identity and the way he often writes in the interstices of language—has been read as being akin to *écriture feminine* by several theorists.

Although texts written by male authors are not often included in feminist theory or women's literature courses, *As I Lay Dying* is an ideal text to use to introduce students to the concept of *écriture feminine*, perhaps especially because its male authorship raises important and interesting questions about the relation between gender and language. Cixous writes:

> [R]are are the men able to venture onto the brink where writing, freed from law, unencumbered by moderation, exceeds phallic authority, and where the subjectivity inscribing its effects become feminine. (95)

Faulkner is such a rare writer, able to write the other, able to move in spaces between words where the oppositions that structure discourse and determine gender are made visible, though never in simple or transparent ways. Addie's monologue, the center around which the narrative of *As I Lay Dying* is structured, serves on one level as an example of the sort of writing the body that Cixous calls for and practices. But it also serves as an example of the elusiveness of any distinct definition of the relation between discourse and gender, the way that discourse shapes gender, and the way that discourse is gendered.

Addie's monologue raises myriad questions (none of which can or should be easily answered) that consider the relations between discourse and gender: How, within discourse, is motherhood defined? How is woman defined? How is a woman's sexuality defined? How is the feminine self, one's gendered subjectivity, defined in relation to others? Can a mother have an identity separate from her children? When a woman is pregnant, gives birth, or nurses, what part of her is outside her body and what part is inside? What is self and what is other? Is language gendered? Do men and women view language differently? Do they use language differently? Does language use them differently?

These and other questions, which feminist theorists like Irigaray, Kristeva, and Cixous have worked to understand, are raised eloquently in Addie's monologue in ways that can make some theoretical concepts more accessible to students. And, conversely, feminist theories about the relation between language and gendered subjectivity can help students better understand Addie and the linguistic gaps made visible through her struggles with(in) dominant discourse.

In a classroom discussion about *As I Lay Dying*, students can cite instances in Addie's monologue where language fails to define her as a woman, wife, lover, and mother. For example, after having two children, Addie says:

> The shape of my body where I used to be a virgin is in the shape of a   and I couldn't think *Anse*, couldn't remember *Anse*. It was not that I could think of myself as no longer unvirgin, because I was three now. (173)

Useful questions to ask students about this passage are, What does Addie mean by "unvirgin," and what words do we have in our vocabulary that mean "unvirgin"? Why is the shape of her body where she "used to be a virgin" unrepresentable? Is that part of herself gone, and has it been replaced by something else? What failures of language are made visible by the blank space that Faulkner inserts in the text, and why is the blank space used in place of a woman's reproductive organs? In *Speculum of the Other Woman,* Irigaray writes that women are made to use masculine language framed by patriarchal understandings of sexuality and power to describe female bodies and sexuality in ways that force a woman into "a discourse that denies the specificity of her pleasure by inscribing it as the hollow, the intaglio, the negative, even as the censured other of its phallic assertions" (140–41). Irigaray explains that Freud's theory of penis envy denies female sexuality and distances women from their own bodies:

> Woman's castration is defined as her having nothing you can see, as her *having* nothing. In her having nothing penile, in seeing that she has No Thing. Nothing *like* man. That is to say, *no sex/organ* that can be seen in a *form* capable of founding its reality, reproducing its truth. *Nothing to be seen is equivalent to having no thing. No being and no truth.* (47)

In this patriarchal economy, a girl longs for and searches for a phallus to fill a void. She is misdirected in her search, mistaking something for no thing. In this system, "no economy would be possible whereby sexual reality can be represented by/for woman. She remains forsaken and abandoned in her lack, default, absence, envy, etc. and is led to submit" (48).

Addie exists in such an economy and tries to resist it but does not have the weapons available to her to help her do so. As she struggles with attempting to represent her role as wife and mother and her sexuality, she initially thinks of her "unvirgin" state as "Anse," inserting the name of her husband who took her virginity in place of her missing virginity. The only terms available to her are *thing* (phallus) and *no thing* (lack, empty space). It is not a choice between different terms but instead a choice between representation and invisibility, between being and not being. She tries to refuse this imposed definition of herself: "and I couldn't think *Anse*." She is unwilling to see her sexuality as an empty space defined only in opposition to the phallus meant to fill that space. Indeed, she goes one step further and empties Anse's name, making it a lack as well. She meditates it into nothingness:

> I would think about his name until after a while I could see the word as a shape, a vessel, and I would watch him liquify and flow into it like cold molasses flowing out of the darkness into the vessel, until the jar stood full and motionless: a significant shape profoundly without life like an empty door frame; and then I would find that I had forgotten the name of the jar. (173)

This rejection, however, does not empower her, because in rural Mississippi, in her marriage, and in the patriarchal culture in which she must live, her options are few.

Addie tries to choose another course of action and another word from the limited vocabulary available to her: the word *sin*. "I believed that I had found it," she says of her briefly satisfying affair with the Reverend Whitfield (174). She chooses the word *sin* to describe her affair with him perhaps because *sin* is the only word available to her to describe her sexual desire or perhaps because it implies activity instead of passivity or perhaps because it represents an act of defiance against patriarchal marriage laws and religion.

> I would think of sin as I would think of the clothes we both wore in the world's face, of the circumspection necessary because he was he and I was I; the sin the more utter and terrible since he was the instrument ordained by God who created the sin, to sanctify that sin He had created. (174)

Of course, her affair with Whitfield does not free her, because her flight from Anse leads her from one symbol of patriarchal power to another, from husband to religious leader, and both relationships, both ways of being (wife and adulteress), have already been defined for her.

The ways Addie is trapped within a patriarchal discourse directly connected to Christianity are further highlighted by the structure of the novel. Her single monologue is framed by the words of her father (her mother is not mentioned) when she says at the beginning that "my father used to say that the reason for living was to get ready to stay dead a long time" (169). This statement is alluded to several times in the chapter and structures Addie's sense of identity because it represents the word of the father (both her actual father and God) in and against which she must define her actions and existence. Her monologue also is framed, in a larger sense, by the "word of the Father," because it is sandwiched between the monologues of Cora and the Reverend Whitfield. Cora Tull, a "good" woman who self-righteously and un-self-consciously speaks for the patriarchy, admonishes Addie, saying, "Who are you, to say what is sin and what is not sin?" (167), reminding Addie that the discourse they use has already been defined for them and that their role as women is to submit to it. While Cora parrots religious dogma, the Reverend Whitfield skillfully uses words to absolve himself of the affair he has with Addie and to thank God for "His infinite wisdom that restrained the tale from her dying lips as she lay surrounded by those who loved and trusted her" (179). While Addie painfully struggles with discourse and while Cora uncritically ventriloquizes the word of the Father, Whitfield seems able to exist within the symbolic and use language with ease to rationalize his actions. He thanks God that Addie has died without confessing their affair to her family; it is her inability to speak that allows him to retain his position of power and respectability. Words do not fail him as he enters the Bundrens' house and, over Addie's dead and silent body, speaks the word of the Father with certainty: "God's grace upon this house" (179). The self-righteousness of Cora and the hypocrisy of the Reverend Whitfield are easy for students to recognize and discuss. It is helpful, also, to ask students about differences of language use. Why do Cora and Whitfield seem to be at ease with language, while Addie does not?

The ironic certainty with which the Reverend Whitfield and Cora are able to use language is in direct opposition to Addie's uncertainties about language. The patriarchal symbolic order, or the word of the Father, conflated with the Christian platitudes mouthed by Cora and Whitfield, is the only language available to Addie, even though she tries to find a space outside this language. Ultimately, she must choose words like *sin* or to struggle with nonwords, the gaps between words, or the spaces on the margins of what is representable. When Addie tries to speak, each word she utters carries with it meaning she does not intend. And most significant, Addie is painfully aware of this gap. She knows that language speaks for her and that even in the act of trying to move beyond language, she, ironically, must use language. To convey the meaninglessness of words, she must use words. For example, to express the separation between signifier and signified, she says:

> I would think how words go straight up in a thin line, quick and harmless. And how terribly doing goes along the earth, clinging to it, so that after a while the two lines are too far apart for the same person to straddle from one to the other. (173)

To Addie, words always fall short of the deed, the thing, the meaning they represent. They signify an existence that is not hers but that she is forced to inhabit, that cannot represent her way of seeing and understanding the world, that can only mimic patriarchal constructions of what she is supposed to be but can never actually be. The distance between word and deed is dramatically illustrated through the events of the novel. The deeds that follow her words—her wish to be buried in Jefferson—are a perversion of that spoken desire. Her husband and children trek across the county with her coffin because they are obeying her word. "I done my best," Anse says. "I tried to do as she would wish it" (106). Anse's doing, however, does not match Addie's intent. When she asked to be buried in Jefferson, she did not intend her stinking, battered corpse to be dragged through water, burned by fire, and displayed throughout the county as the centerpiece in a macabre parade. The events of the novel ironically illustrate Addie's inability to use language. Instead, language uses her—because the deeds her words produce do not match their intent. However, the events that transpire after her death probably would not surprise her. She says, "And I would think . . . of how the high dead words in time seemed to lose even the significance of their dead sound" (175).

Kincaid connects Addie's distance from language to her distance from a religion that condemns the female body. She writes:

> What can we say about a religion that teaches that the body is, of itself, sinful? Can we escape our bodies? Is it our fault that the encasement of the soul is something vile and filthy, something we are to be ashamed of and to apologize for and to hide as best we can?

She argues that Addie is a character who is acutely aware that "[a] woman's body does not belong to her, but to her family, her church, her God." Within the Christian discourse that Addie has learned, her sexual desire can be described only as sin, something filthy, evil, and unnatural. Kristeva writes, "The brimming flesh of sin belongs, of course, to both sexes; but its root and basic representation is nothing other than feminine temptation" (126). The different attitudes toward sin expressed by the Reverend Whitfield and Addie help illustrate for students the ways that words are gendered and also the ways that gender influences how we interpret those words.

The idea that words like *motherhood*, *virgin*, and *sin* are loaded with signification is not one that students have difficulty grasping, because there are many examples of language about "good" and "bad" mothers, and "good girls" and "bad girls," available in popular culture, public discourse, and other literature. One exercise that works well is to solicit words, which I write on the board, that define "good girls" and "bad girls." It illustrates the ways we are confined by language and cultural expectations. What options exist for girls and young women in the spaces between *tease* and *slut* or between *virgin* and *whore*? Are there ways to break these binaries? In what ways do girls and women attempt to reimagine these terms? Are they always successful? How might these terms be defined differently in a society that is not patriarchal? Is such an economy possible, or is it merely a utopian ideal? Cixous proposes a "bisexual" approach to writing that does not privilege binaries and hierarchies, which can be written by both men and women "who are complex, mobile, open. Accepting the other sex as a component makes them richer, more various, stronger, and—to the extent that they are mobile—very fragile" (102–03).

Some theorists argue that Faulkner is such a writer. In *The Feminine and Faulkner: Reading (beyond) Sexual Difference* Minrose C. Gwin suggests that Faulkner's writing is a paradox:

> The paradox is that Faulkner himself, although very much *of* his culture, becomes in his greatest works the creator of female subjects who, in powerful and creative ways, disrupt and sometimes even destroy patriarchal structures. (4)

Others argue that this interpretation is too idealistic, that while Faulkner's women may call attention to their marginalized positions, they are helpless to change their lot. Porter writes that, speaking from the space of mother within a patriarchal family, Addie is trapped despite all her and Faulkner's attempts to free her.

> If Addie is a speaking subject, the space of lack from which her voice emerges is not the much wished-for space of *l'écriture feminine*, of a *jouissance* lying somehow beyond the phallic signifier, but rather the space of lack itself. ("Symbolic Fathers" 99)

The usefulness, then, of putting *As I Lay Dying* into dialogue with French feminist theories is not to transparently apply theory to a literary text but instead to open up a discussion about the complex relation among language, power, motherhood, religion, bodies, sexuality, and gendered identities for which there are no straightforward answers. Faulkner's novel works both to explicate and to complicate these theoretical concepts. Addie's monologue, after all, is not just about the failure of language, because her fumblings with words create the most moving chapter in the text. Perhaps the greatest paradox of Addie is that her awkward attempts to express the inexpressible are precisely what give her chapter such power and eloquence.

NOTE

The quotation in the title of this essay are the last words of Addie Bundren's monologue, on page 176.

"It Aint Balanced Right": Repositioning the Body in and of *As I Lay Dying*

Lisa K. Perdigao

It seems that all critical discussions of William Faulkner's *As I Lay Dying* begin with the caveat that the text is complex, problematic. I remember the first time I encountered it as an undergraduate and was informed that it would be a difficult read. Now as I try to prepare my students for this task, I do not promise that once they work through the many layers of the text it will become clear, its meaning made tangible. Instead, I emphasize that the text, like Addie's body represented in it, resists easy containment in critical discourse—including our own. In courses where I emphasize the shift between modernism and postmodernism, *As I Lay Dying* performs as a metatext, representing what is at work with the changing theories by illustrating the defining characteristics of the twentieth century and its linguistic turn. These characteristics—for example, the recognition of a loss of centers and the accompanying sense of crisis or opportunity—can be traced in the responses to Addie's death as well as to her dead body. The novel demonstrates the crisis induced by a loss of centers and also the possibility of narrative transaction at the site of loss.

Addie's body and its role in the narrative suggest this simultaneous crisis and opportunity as the characters re-member her body—a body that, in its materiality, literally rots at the center of the novel. By examining how it is continually repositioned, reconsidered, and reevaluated—in Vardaman's high symbolist mode, in Cash's structural principles (a type of pseudoscience), and in her own language, so resonant with deconstructive and poststructuralist discourse—I demonstrate how the novel echoes new concepts of body, self, and language that emerge during the modern period. Analyzing how the novel reflects modernist and postmodernist theories yields opportunities for understanding literature and literary theory in the twentieth century. An apt metaphor emerges: as Addie's body resists burial, the novel resists containment in monolithic critical categories.

In this essay I explore how instructors can use the body *in* the text as a metaphor for the body *of* the text; neither is "balanced right" (108) because each straddles the critical divide between the modern and the postmodern, between loss and the recovery of meaning. My approach is to offer a guide on how to use the text in a general survey course such as American Novels as well as in a thematic course like the one I teach called Death, Burial, and Entombment in Twentieth-Century American Fiction. In both courses I focus on the representations of Addie's body, which is the center of the narrative, and on the ways the heteroglossic narrative continually repositions Addie in discourse—in effect, reconfiguring the body. I embrace the complexities of the novel, how it signifies both crisis and possibility, both a crisis of representation and a narrative transaction. The issues I raise in relation to critical constructions of literary histories and periodization, as well as concerning contemporary theory, offer a comprehensive approach to the novel.

As I describe the two strategies I use—one focusing on the broad perspective of a literary tradition and the other focusing on the representation of death and burial—I suggest ways of teaching the novel in introductory literary courses, advanced electives, and graduate courses in literary theory. By using critical theory in a range of courses, instructors can better position the novel in the tradition and in their own discourse. In American Novels I examine issues of periodization—the transition from modern to postmodern fiction—and lead students through Willa Cather's *The Professor's House*, F. Scott Fitzgerald's *The Great Gatsby*, *As I Lay Dying*, Kurt Vonnegut's *Slaughterhouse-Five*, John Gardner's *Grendel*, Toni Morrison's *Beloved*, Alice Walker's *The Color Purple*, and Don DeLillo's *White Noise*. In Death, Burial, and Entombment I concentrate on the representation of death and the problems and possibilities of remembering the dead while constructing meaning at the intersection of loss and recovery. Students read *As I Lay Dying* as an originary text for these tropes; from there, they consider the novel in relation to Gloria Naylor's *Linden Hills*, Morrison's *Beloved*, Jeffrey Eugenides's *The Virgin Suicides*, and Alice Sebold's *The Lovely Bones*.

While the two courses have different foci and objectives, *As I Lay Dying* is central to each and serves as a bridge to and between the other texts we explore. Since both are undergraduate classes and only some of the students are English majors, I take particular care to establish a solid framework for this complicated novel. I concentrate on presenting a picture of the twentieth century and its cultural, historical, literary, and theoretical traditions. This allows the students to see the connections—and gaps—between Faulkner's novel and other modernist and postmodernist texts. Both courses are conducted as seminars, with discussion and oral presentations, so I can see firsthand how well the students are able to negotiate these complicated terms. I find that giving short lectures to introduce the texts, themes, and critical readings is essential, because the lectures allow the students to enter the larger critical and historical conversation with a secure foundation. The seminar format works well; the students can work through the terms to find a critical language that, like that of the novel, at first seems elusive, ephemeral, and unyielding.

As I Lay Dying works particularly well as a means of exploring a perceived crisis in representation traceable through creative writing as well as the literary theory that emerges in the twentieth century. While my course on death, burial, and entombment is more concerned with the representation of dead bodies in literature, in my American novel course we focus on the crisis of representation depicted in canonical texts. By examining the scenes of violence—scenes of abuse, dying, and death—we are able to trace how the historical and cultural contexts of the twentieth century are represented in fiction. To help students see how the novels fit within these frames, I have them read essays about the novels alongside essays that more broadly define modernist and postmodernist literatures. One text is Michael Levenson's introduction to *The Cambridge Companion to Modernism*. His description of the twentieth century as "an epoch of crisis, real and manufactured, physical and metaphysical, material and symbolic" (4) is applicable to what we find in Cather, Fitzgerald, and Faulkner. Levenson argues that the "inescapable forces of turbulent social modernization" gave "subjects to writers and painters" and "forms suggested by industrial machinery, or by the chuffing of cars, or even, most horribly, the bodies broken in the war" during this period (4); here students are provided with a language for connecting the contexts surrounding the novels.

As I Lay Dying is an important text in our examination of the writers' representations of the struggle between tradition and modernization. It introduces a central crisis during the period, identified by Tim Armstrong's question: "Why is the body so important to Modernism?" (2). Armstrong suggests that "modernity saw the body as the locus of anxiety, even crisis; as requiring an intervention through which it might be made the grounds of a new form of production" (4). Faulkner's novel grounds these abstract notions by asking what do we literally do with the body? Presenting this logistical question, the novel asks what do we do with the loss of the mother? These questions provide a link to Cather and Fitzgerald. After students analyze Professor St. Peter's sense of crisis about modernity and his near asphyxiation, they explore Nick Carraway's reaction to the deaths of Myrtle Wilson and Gatsby and his desire to return to the Midwest. Faulkner's novel offers a connection between *The Great Gatsby* and postmodern works like *Slaughterhouse-Five* by demonstrating how the entire landscape of America (and American fiction) changes with these new crises of representation and interpretation.

As I Lay Dying is like Addie's body in its resistance to containment. It seems to exist in a liminal space between modernist and postmodernist literature, straddling the divide, yielding seemingly infinite possibilities for critical readings. But rather than feel a sense of crisis when introducing the novel, I (perhaps like Faulkner) consider it a site of opportunities. In my course on American novels we have already discussed the modernism of *The Professor's House* and *The Great Gatsby* when we turn to *As I Lay Dying*; we have considered how both Professor St. Peter and Nick Carraway long for a return to an earlier period. Faulkner's novel provides a wonderful opportunity to show the class how the two periods overlap, so much so that some critics do not discern a difference that warrants the characterization of postmodern. The divide between Faulkner's modernism and postmodernism is described clearly in *The Cambridge Companion to William Faulkner*, edited by Philip M. Weinstein, specifically in the essays by Richard C. Moreland and Patrick O'Donnell. I assign Moreland's "Faulkner and Modernism" and O'Donnell's "Faulkner and Postmodernism" for students to read on completion of the novel. We use these two texts as the foundation for a discussion of how *As I Lay Dying* bridges the modern-postmodern divide, and I show how the critical constructions of literary modernisms and postmodernisms become pluralized, blurred, and contestable in the novel. Describing *As I Lay Dying* as "Faulkner's most successfully autonomous modernist text" (23), Moreland argues that the novel is "marked by powerful currents but also by persistent disturbances, differences, transferences, renegotiations, reconfigurations, and change" (25). At the same time, Moreland's definition of Faulkner's modernism is determined in part by the postmodernist aspects of Faulkner's work:

> This postmodern-sounding dimension of Faulkner's work grows out of the failures, impasses, and emotional dryness of modernism when it is put to a social test, as Faulkner's work usually insists that it is. . . . Whereas the modernist focus of Faulkner's work is on centers that cannot hold, a more postmodernist dimension of that same work listens fitfully for other stories as signs of life in a culture differently conceived. (25–26)

For Moreland the distinction between modernist and postmodernist is located in the ways in which writers (and critics) conceive the function of representation. For modernist writers the shift from centers signifies a loss; for postmodernist writers the multiplicity of stories is an opportunity for reconsidering the relation between the individual and a larger culture, a larger history.

Faulkner's novels are involved in this transformation of centers, as characters focus on the limitations and possibilities of representation. For example, in *As I Lay Dying* the multiple narrators offer possibilities for representing the dead. By questioning the function of language, its ability to represent, Faulkner's text speaks to its modern moment and becomes a foundation for what emerges as postmodernism in literature and theory. Exploring Faulkner's postmodernism, O'Donnell, like Moreland, discusses how Faulkner's texts

> resist, disrupt, or exceed both Modernism (with a capital "M") and Faulkner's own modernism—his intended response to the perceived literary, cultural, and historical contexts of his writing. ("Faulkner" 31)

Also like Moreland, O'Donnell turns to *As I Lay Dying* as a representative text:

> Whatever Addie Bundren may have been in life, however she may have been viewed by the members of her family, each of whom "reads" her differently, there is no discounting the presence of her decaying body in the coffin: just the opposite of being ineffable, "a word to fill a lack," her body is all too scandalously real to the offended passerby who smells it in *As I Lay Dying*. (48)

In O'Donnell's terms, the "readings" of Addie by family members and townspeople—fifteen, in total—offer possibilities for the transaction of narrative and serve as an example of the heteroglossic text. The novel rejects the traditional narrative voice (a voice students have found in Cather's and Fitzgerald's texts) and instead introduces new opportunities as well as radical uncertainties, particularly when Addie's prosopopoetic narration (through a voice speaking beyond death) criticizes the functions of words.[1] Here Faulkner highlights the problems with language, ideas popularized by deconstructionist critics predominantly, showing language's inability to function as a stable system. Expanding on this point, he counters the ephemeral, metaphorical representation of the dead by constantly reasserting the materiality of the corpse. Addie's body cannot be transformed into something other—the language does not work and is no longer available to the characters and, perhaps by extension, the modernist writer.

In class discussion and essay prompts, I ask students to focus on the complexities highlighted in the text and in the critical discourses surrounding the text. In my American novels course each student completes one- to two-page responses to the individual novels, an oral presentation (like a four- to five-page conference paper), and a final paper. Each student must write a short response to Faulkner, which he or she can then draw on for the oral presentation. Additionally, students can use *As I Lay Dying* as one of three novels considered in a final eight- to ten-page paper, which must use some of the critical essays. The prompts for the short response (and what may come to serve as the basis of the oral presentation) are questions that consider the placement of the novel between modernism and postmodernism and in the American literary tradition more broadly, as well as the readings of the work in the text of Addie's body. One prompt I use is the following:

> In "Faulkner and Modernism" and "Faulkner and Postmodernism," Richard C. Moreland and Patrick O'Donnell, respectively, create a conversation about Faulkner's role as a modern or postmodern writer. How does *As I Lay Dying* fit into (or challenge) those categories?

Another prompt draws on David Minter's statement about Faulkner's fiction in *A Cultural History of the American Novel*:

> Like much modern fiction, his is often pessimistic and violent, even brutal and despairing. He is a poet of deprivation and loss. Affluence and plenty mark his work only in style and imagination. Yet we find other things there: . . . the persistence of the exuberance of the twenties, which was experimental as well as escapist; and the difficult hope against hope that sprang to life during the Great Depression, of creating anew an imperfect community, knit together by imperfectly possessed and painfully held memories and by imperfectly shared and practiced values. (229)

My question for the students pertains to how we place *As I Lay Dying* in conversation with Minter's terms and the other novels we have discussed by considering how it is like or unlike other works of modern fiction.

The last prompt translates well into my course on death, burial, and entombment as it focuses on the different revisions of Addie's identity and body. I ask the students to consider whether the multiple voices construct a definitive or incomplete portrait of Addie in answer to the questions raised by her presence: Who is Addie Bundren? And is she different to different characters? What type of language is used to define her?

In the final essay one of the four prompts I present offers a frame for using *As I Lay Dying* as the center. It draws on Levenson's description of the "general preoccupations" of modernism:

> the recurrent act of fragmenting unities (unities of character or plot or pictorial space or lyric form), the use of mythic paradigms, the refusal of norms of beauty, the willingness to make radical linguistic experiment, all often inspired by the resolve (in Eliot's phrase) to startle and disturb the public. (3)

Added to the preoccupations is modernism's use of "forms of creative violence" that represent the "violence of the art." I ask students if violence is a general preoccupation of twentieth-century American writers, and then I ask them to identify what form the violence takes in modern and postmodern American fiction. Faulkner's text reveals undeniable violence at the center of the text, a locus of anxiety, of crisis. In the short responses, presentations, and final papers, I have found that students' readings of the text reflect the complexities that have emerged in our discussions, offering self-conscious analyses of Faulkner's language as well as the students' own attempts to make meaning.

In my American novels course, *As I Lay Dying* invites multiple readings as students try to decipher and articulate Addie's seemingly uncontainable presence. In my course on death, burial, and entombment, the text yields a distinction between modernism and postmodernism in its approaches to representing the dead; rather than trace contexts (critical discussions of modernism and postmodernism, for example), I begin with the novel's representations and consider the larger theoretical issues, both epistemological and ontological, that those representations suggest. In studying the dead body, we are like forensic scientists, finding clues and constructing the larger story.

The tension between the materiality of the body and the discourse surrounding it reflects the ideas about language in the space between modernism and postmodernism. If the linguistic turn results in a perceived crisis about language's ability to represent, Faulkner's novel exposes the limits of language—the space surrounding a dead woman. According to O'Donnell, her body is "all too scandalously real" ("Faulkner" 48); the limits of materiality—the rotting corpse—reassert the metonymic function of representation. Ronald Schleifer describes "'the facticity of death, a facticity wholly resistant to reason, to metaphor, to revelatory representation'" (1–2) and argues that metonymy stands "more generally . . . for the materiality of language" and functions as a "material language" for death (6, 7). His language and the definitions of metaphor and metonymy highlight the divide in the text regarding the characters' representations of Addie's body.

In Death, Burial, and Entombment I am able to introduce more theoretically complicated ideas; the novel becomes a marker of modernist (and postmodernist) experimentation with the cultural construction of death and burial, representing the ways funerary rituals intersect with the foundations of narrative form as convention, ritual. The perversity of the burial rites is like a breaking of form and convention, a central strand of both literary modernisms and postmodernisms. Postmodernist theories about language abound in the class—first introduced by the critical readings and then adeptly used by the students themselves. In fact, I am amazed by what my students are able to achieve. By focusing on this specific (and morbid) topic, they glean more about literary theory than I am able to show them in a survey of those ideas. And perhaps what is most amazing is that I find the discussions of the novels to be expansive and even profound rather than limited by such a singular focus.

While terms like *metaphor* and *metonymy* are introduced in most introductory literature courses, the applications of these critical terms and others (like *trope* and *metatextuality*) become a type of poststructuralist exercise. As we explore the ways in which the members of the Bundren family attempt to articulate their loss—and describe their relationships with Addie—we find that they employ a range of styles and figures. We ground our discussion through metaphors and metonyms, two basic principles constantly negotiated and renegotiated throughout the novel. According to O'Donnell, the introduction (or reemphasis) of the material (which can be connected to metonymy) marks the postmodern text and Faulkner's corpus. Faulkner tests the boundaries of language, showing that the dead cannot be neatly buried through the gesture of metaphor (perhaps negating the overarching metaphorical ending of *The Great Gatsby*, which buries the dead in a green landscape). As the characters experiment with metaphors and metonyms to represent the Addie who lies dying (not dead), she is continually repositioned in language, and these repositionings echo shifts in ideas about language that emerge in the late twentieth century.

In Death, Burial, and Entombment we analyze strategies of representation—the uses of figurative language—of the dead body. Vardaman's metaphoric configurations and Cash's metonymic constructions serve as strong examples for considering how the writers (and narrators) re-present the dead. This approach works well as we discuss the other novels in the course. After analyzing *As I Lay Dying*, we examine how Beloved exists both metonymically (as an exhumed body) and metaphorically (as the symbol of those lost in the Middle Passage), how the boys remember the dead Lisbon girls in Eugenides's *The Virgin Suicides*, and how, in *The Lovely Bones*, Susie Salmon recounts her relationship with her own dead body from a place "[i]nbetween" (34), like Addie's narration.

Beloved is another complicated text for students to decipher. I have found that teaching *As I Lay Dying* as a prelude to *Beloved* makes Morrison's text more provocative and intriguing, as students examine how Beloved, like Addie Bundren, will not be buried. While Addie questions language's efficacy, Beloved facilitates its unraveling. If a burial plot (like Nick's concealment of bodies in *The Great Gatsby*) is, in some ways, a device that modernists employ to conceal their anxieties about the modern world, its technologies and threats to the body as a stable system, the exhumation plot is the substance not only of many postmodernist novels but also of contemporary forensic television. *As I Lay Dying* shows both competing drives—a body that must, yet cannot, be buried.

In American Novels I draw on critical discussions of modernism and postmodernism; in Death, Burial, and Entombment I offer students selected readings that highlight some of the complexities of representing the body in language. I have students read from Elisabeth Bronfen's *Over Her Dead Body* as well as O'Donnell's "The Spectral Road: Metaphors of Transference in Faulkner's *As I Lay Dying*" so they can consider how figurative language represents the dead body—by way of metaphor and metonymy—and examine what cultural assumptions and constructions are represented through tropes and figures. For example, Bronfen's consideration of the relation between woman and death is useful for helping students reflect on how Addie's role in the narrative represents larger issues involving the formation of gendered identities. We can then make a transition into psychoanalytic theory, exploring how the loss of the mother leads to Darl's insanity, as it constitutes a loss of center and of centering itself. O'Donnell's essay provides the students with a language for discussing how these notions about the problems in representing the body, representing death itself, are contained in Faulkner's writing.

Using the language of body theory and theories about language, we examine Faulkner's representations, his employment of metaphors and metonyms, lacunae, and pictures. O'Donnell writes that "[t]he ironic and complex metaphorical notions of the novel define its subject as a reflection upon the meaning of both funereal and metaphorical journeys," and he suggests that Faulkner, "by means of the metaphors he creates, questions the tenuous connection between fictional language and the apparent 'world' to which it refers" ("Spectral Road" 62). Reading *As I Lay Dying* as a "metaphor for death, in which all meaning and motion, all the diverse, metaphor-filled, Addie-filled perceptions of fifteen voices focus around an ultimate, significant act—Addie's burial," O'Donnell argues that the novel "allows the satisfaction of closure" and the possibility of a new Mrs. Bundren, a new journey (64). Yet O'Donnell identifies the problems with this resolution as well, stating that, despite the overarching metaphorical drive of the novel, "the novel's metaphorical ambivalences" suggest that Faulkner is "undertaking to try the power and limits of metaphorical language" (64). Barry R. McCann writes that the coffin becomes a "metaphor, a shape that is built and filled," yet it also functions metonymically, "binding together the Bundrens, the narrative, and the nature of language" (272). We use these terms in class to explore how Faulkner's text vacillates between metaphor and metonymy as well as between modernism and postmodernism, between burial and exhumation.

While one difficult task of teaching the novel is approaching its narrative voices, the analysis of their representations of Addie's body becomes a means to better understand Faulkner's ideas about language. Some students have read *The Sound and the Fury*, and for them I suggest that *As I Lay Dying* is more straightforward. While they grasp the multivocality of the narration, they seem to have trouble with the language. Early in the readings I turn the discussion to issues of prose and poetry; by studying Vardaman's language, the students and I are able to examine how Faulkner is working between genres. By comparing the rhetorical strategies of the different characters, students are better equipped to consider how Faulkner is questioning the function of language as well as its form. In American Novels this helps clarify the novel's placement in relation to other twentieth-century American texts; I extend this line of discussion to the critical debates surrounding Faulkner's representations of poor, rural families, which works well with our examination of *The Great Gatsby* and Nick's narration.

In both of my courses I focus on how the range of narrative voices represents ideas about language in the twentieth century—from high modernist to poststructuralist. The terms are complicated, but we begin to unpack them with close readings and examples; as a result, students begin to better understand what is at stake in *As I Lay Dying* and in the larger tradition. I demonstrate how this works by focusing on Vardaman, Cash, and Addie herself, three distinct examples of types of representations (and their limitations). As the youngest child, Vardaman suggests the symbolist imagination in his constructions of metaphors to describe his mother. He continually renegotiates Addie's position in highly metaphorical terms: "*She's in the box. . . . My mother is not in the box*" (196); "It was not her. . . . It was not my mother"; "she is just like the rabbit. . . . she is not a rabbit" (66). Judith Lockyer argues that

> [i]t is through Vardaman and Darl . . . that Faulkner most carefully delineates the process of making perceptions understandable and thus real through language. . . . Central to that relation is the need and ability to make metaphor. Metaphor respects the gap between word and thing while it strives to close it. (168)

Just as Faulkner uses Vardaman's and Cash's language to make perceptions understandable, students use the characters' metaphors as a way of understanding Addie's position in the novel.

In a stark contrast to Vardaman's language, Cash's language reads like that of a structuralist; his emphasis on the construction of the coffin affirms the structural principles by which the coffin will contain Addie's body. His language is metonymic as well; the sounds of the adze open the novel, and his narration is focused on the coffin throughout the journey. I have found that students are initially more capable of grasping how Vardaman's language is metaphoric and poetic than they are of understanding how metonymy guides Cash's language. But once they begin to work with the terms and discover the moments when Addie is defined by the box rather than by her relation to other characters, they understand better how metonymy and tropes work. This exercise becomes more intriguing when we turn to the passages where Cash's terms become complicated—for example, his set of structural principles for the coffin and for the body come undone:

> 5. In a bed where people lie down all the time, the joints and seams are made sideways, because the stress is sideways.
> 6. Except.
> 7. A body is not square like a crosstie. (82–83)

In one of his chapters, Cash describes the construction of the coffin and the metonymic basis for the characters' identifications of Addie. Throughout the narrative, Addie gradually becomes the box, as Cash, then other characters, begin to call her "it." Cash links the body and box: "In a couple of days now it'll be smelling"; "It aint balanced right" (108). Cash's construction of the coffin literally positions Addie within the narrative.

The difficulty the characters experience trying to bury Addie is akin to their inability to represent her—as mother, wife, fish, horse, and box—since the body resists such constructs; as these representations come undone, Faulkner turns to Addie and, through a prosopopoetic voice, offers a poststructralist approach to language. Reflecting the linguistic turn (from within her box), Addie is able to question the arbitrariness, the artificiality, of language. She states that "words are no good" and "dont ever fit even what they are trying to say at" (171). For her, words are "like spiders dangling by their mouths from a beam, swinging and twisting and never touching" (172); words are "just the gaps in people's lacks" (174). Students have explored poststructuralism in theory; when they see it in practice here in Addie's chapter, they see the gaps within language, where signification comes undone. We examine what Addie says about language, and turn to the representations of the coffin and the blank space where she "used to be a virgin" (173) to analyze how Faulkner is representing the act of representation itself. Robert Dale Parker writes:

> Addie's medley of unnameables (shape, blank space, couldn't think, couldn't remember) is therefore not simply the blank space that some critics have called it. It is neither a fault in language nor a castratingly feminized absence or lack. Addie's blank space, her writeable anatomy, is full with gendered discourse. It is language. . . . ("Sex and Gender" 76)

I introduce students to this quotation so they can consider how Addie's chapter is a metatext for the entire novel. It demonstrates the possibilities for articulating how and where language fails; when it does, Addie turns to other forms—blank space as writing, as language.

In both courses the students and I ultimately tackle the novel's problematic ending. For each class I create a handout with the final passages from all the novels we have discussed during the semester, listed in the order that we read them. In Death, Burial, and Entombment this approach is particularly symbolic, as the passages suggest, in Frank Kermode's phrase, "the sense of an ending" provided by the individual texts and the final gaze afforded at the semester's end. I use this occasion to discuss what "the sense of an ending" suggests for narratives about loss and a loss of meaning.

Despite our acknowledgment of the difficulty of the novel, students want the ending to represent closure, and it is this desire that creates the complexities (and frustration) we have discussed throughout our reading. *As I Lay Dying* cannot be neatly categorized as modernist or postmodernist in American Novels, nor can it represent either a modernist burial or a postmodernist exhumation in Death, Burial, and Entombment. The plot fittingly travels in circles, despite the forward progress to Jefferson and burial. Throughout, the family stalls in its attempts. Even Anse acknowledges their failure, stating, "We ought to have done like Armstid and Gillepsie said and sent word to town and had it dug and ready" (228). When Cash's leg worsens, Darl says, "Let's take Cash to the doctor first. . . . She'll wait. She's already waited nine days" (234). But although the Bundrens stall the plot and admit their failures, by the novel's end they become insistent about burying the dead, about resolving the plot. They say, "We got the digging to do, too" (235) and concede that "[i]t was better to get her underground" (235). In both courses we focus on these moments when the language does not yield a definitive progression of plot but rather exhibits a vacillation between the terms and concepts. Despite the characters' admission of their need and desire to bury Addie (and thus resolve the plot), by the end of the book, burial is an impossibility. O'Donnell offers students a way of understanding the complex ending, its limitations and possibilities. He writes:

> In a concrete sense, as the scene toward which the entire novel gestures is not portrayed—Addie's burial—so Faulkner avoids the "death" of his own novel in favor of its ungrounded, unended "life" of incomplete journeys and fractured relations. ("Spectral Road" 77)

While Professor St. Peter and Nick Carraway ultimately face the crisis of modernity and resolve it with grand metaphorical gestures, Faulkner's characters highlight this crisis at the novel's end. When my American Novels students turn to *Slaughterhouse-Five* next, they connect Faulkner's representations of this crisis to Billy Pilgrim's problem of having come "unstuck in time" (23). In Death, Burial, and Entombment, when students read about Beloved's being remembered, disremembered, and dismembered, they return, in class discussions and in their writing, to Faulkner's Addie—her notions of language and the characters' representations of her. Ultimately, Addie's body represents a center that cannot hold and offers the possibility of "other stories as signs of life in a culture differently conceived."

The assignments in Death, Burial, and Entombment resemble those in American Novels in that they ask students to consider how Faulkner's representations reflect ideas about language as well as notions about closure and recovery of meaning in the twentieth century. Students are assigned two essays, one of four to five pages and the other of eight to ten pages. Many of the prompts focus on the ending of the novel, how the ending's trajectory (including those vacillations along the way) reflects what is at work in literary and critical traditions. For the first paper I supply the students with three prompts; two of them offer solid frames for a critical reading of *As I Lay Dying*. The first draws on Elisabeth Bronfen's terms in *Over Her Dead Body*—specifically, the relation between woman and death. I ask students to consider what the phrase "over her dead body" means in the context of the works we have discussed. In another prompt I cite Bronfen's suggestion that "[f]emininity and death cause a disorder to stability, mark moments of ambivalence, disruption or duplicity and their eradication produces a recuperation of order, a return to stability" (xii). I ask students to discuss what is repressed and what is articulated in representations of death in literature. *As I Lay Dying* can be positioned as a frame for reading the other texts. Following the terms of the first question, students may focus on how Addie is represented as a dead bride, what the significance of her role of woman and mother is within the text, and how these roles influence the representations of her. In regard to the second question, students may draw on *As I Lay Dying* as a bridge to the postmodernist texts and the refusal of burial—this is the "disorder to stability," signifying ambivalence and disruption.

As the novel moves to Jefferson and to burial but ultimately evades such a plot, it highlights the complexities of the drives and desires Bronfen discusses. In one of the two prompts for the second essay, I ask students to draw on the sense of the novels' endings—their completion or elusion of the burial or exhumation plots. I ask them to construct an argument about what entombment and exhumation signify by discussing why these two issues are so central to the literature that is focused on death and how these notions are literally and figuratively employed. Finally, reflecting the larger goal for the course, I ask students to consider how they can represent a study of contemporary American literature in relation to these issues. By posing these questions, I am able to reflect the trajectory of our discussions, from a consideration of how the novel represents death to its placement in relation to other works, and, finally, to the construction of a twentieth-century American literary tradition. In essays, students can draw on Faulkner's text as a frame for the modernist burial and then consider the postmodernist texts *Linden Hills*, *Beloved*, *The Virgin Suicides*, and *The Lovely Bones*.

From its placement in courses on American novels and death, burial, and entombment, *As I Lay Dying* functions as a solid (yet destabilized) foundation for constructing traditions in literature and theory. Because it vacillates between modernist and postmodernist strategies (as well as tropes and figures), it introduces questions of meaning surrounding literature through its representations of scenes of interpretation. Faulkner's novel illustrates the "persistent disturbances, differences, transferences, renegotiations, reconfigurations, and change" (Moreland, "Faulkner" 25) that define modernist and postmodernist writing, and it reflects students' own problems in interpretation. As students examine this text, they become able to reposition themselves in relation to the body in and of *As I Lay Dying*, ultimately discovering that Faulkner's text is a center that cannot hold and a site that invites interpretations "differently conceived."

NOTES

A portion of this article first appeared in my *From Modernist Entombment to Postmodernist Exhumation* (Ashgate, 2010) and is republished with permission.

[1] In "Willa Cather's *The Professor's House*: Sleeping with the Dead," Lisa Marie Lucenti defines the prosopopoetic as "the illusion of voice, rather than its presence" (253). I use the term here, as Addie's narrative distinctly performs this trope.

"It Means Three Dollars": Following the Money in *As I Lay Dying*

Deborah Clarke

There are, of course, numerous ways of approaching *As I Lay Dying*. But given many students' initial difficulty—for example, Who are these people? What is going on?—it can be useful to begin not with the psychological drama of the novel but with some of the economic realities the characters face. What's the big deal about selling another load of wood for three dollars? Why does Cora keep obsessing about her cakes and eggs? Why are we told that Kate's necklace cost twenty-five cents? What is the reader to make of Vardaman's questioning the meaning of the cost of flour and sugar and coffee?

There are a remarkable number of economic references in the novel, and they can provide a way of understanding some of the trials and tribulations of not just the Bundrens but most of the rural residents of Yoknapatawpha County as well. By focusing on the financial details, instructors can help students gain some awareness of the Depression-era South and the extent to which poverty shaped family and identity. Such an approach not only highlights Faulkner's searing presentation of the lot of rural southerners, it also allows students to see that many of the difficulties faced by the Bundrens may not be so far removed from their own lives and the lives of people around them. To some extent, everyone is shaped by his or her economic situations. Faulkner often spoke of the ability of the human spirit to prevail; in the Bundren family we see not only the flaws but also the resiliency that he so admired. Following the money helps students appreciate the full extent of Faulkner's artistic genius.

Instructors must begin with the region so central to Faulkner's work—the South, an area many nonsouthern students still don't know much about except that it practiced slavery and lost the Civil War. That war, of course, devastated the southern economy. In addition to the turmoil surrounding the end of slavery, the enormous loss of life—particularly of men in the prime of their working capacity—and the destruction of cities, villages, and farms wreaked economic havoc on the region for generations to come. Even before the advent of the Great Depression, the South was, and had been, in serious economic trouble. As Joel Williamson puts it, "When the Great Depression came to the South in the 1930s, it was not news; it was simply more of the same and deeper" (330). In 1938, President Franklin D. Roosevelt commissioned a report on the economic conditions of the South, declaring, "It is my conviction that the South presents right now the Nation's No. 1 economic problem" (qtd. in Carlton and Coclanis 42). The report concluded:

> [S]ince the War between the States the South has been the poorest section of the Nation. The richest State in the South ranks lower in per capita income than the poorest State outside the region. In 1937 the average

> income in the South was $314; in the rest of the country it was $604, or nearly twice as much. (54)

Even within the South, Mississippi's situation was dire. In 1929, a year before the publication of *As I Lay Dying*, Mississippi ranked second to last in the country in per capita income ($287), exceeded only by South Carolina at $261 (Carlton and Coclanis 119). By 1933, Mississippi's income had dropped to $117 (Daniel 11).

Faulkner was well aware of the situation, as Ted Atkinson has persuasively detailed in *Faulkner and the Great Depression*. He lived in the second poorest state in the country and could hardly escape the visibility and depth of the poverty that surrounded him—and that he himself was constantly battling. According to Williamson:

> He seldom mentioned the depression explicitly in his stories, and yet those stories were undergirded by a keen awareness of the long history of poverty in the South, one that really began with the Civil War and, in effect, put the South as a region in the position usual among the underdeveloped regions of the world. (227)

It is against this backdrop that Faulkner's family dramas play out: Jason Compson's obsession with recouping his family's fortunes and position; Thomas Sutpen's battle to restore his plantation and his dynasty; Flem Snopes's inexorable rise to wealth and power; Isaac McCaslin's desperate attempt to repudiate his family's legacy of slavery and incest; the Bundrens' struggle to bury their wife and mother and enjoy a few of the modest material rewards available in Jefferson. Financial hardship in *As I Lay Dying* determines much of the plot, psychological complexity, and tension of the novel, as John T. Matthews has observed:

> The Bundren family accounts actually flush the original economic sediment of the nuclear family to the surface at the moment of highest consumer desire (which is also the moment of greatest personal loss), for it is clear that the Bundren family has the meter running on all the relations that the myth of agrarian familiarity upholds against the assaults of modern commercialism. Money silently constitutes and openly mediates the family in the agricultural South. ("*As I Lay*" 76)

Money, or lack thereof, is critical to *As I Lay Dying*. Students need to understand what it means to live without sufficient cash and also without easy access to credit. In these days of almost universal credit and debit cards—even for college students—they may need to be prodded to think a bit about what it means to live in a cash-based economy when cash is scarce.[1] What happens when cash runs out? What did debt mean in a pre–American Express society? In the agricultural South, real money was an extremely rare commodity. The historian Lu Ann Jones cites a Depression-era interview with a rural woman who states, "In all those years this woman has never been hungry. But there's many, many years I didn't know what a piece of money was" (6–7). Most small farmers lived on credit and barter; when Anse needs to buy new mules, he has to find something to mortgage, which sends him still deeper into debt.[2] It might be useful to let students know about Ab Snopes's horse trading in *The Hamlet*; Snopes allows himself to get involved with Pat Stamper, the most dangerous horse trader around, simply to try to redeem the "actual Yoknapatawpha County cash dollars" Stamper managed to start "rattling around loose." As Ratliff, the traveling sewing-machine salesman and raconteur, points out, "When a man swaps horse for horse, that's one thing and let the devil protect him if the devil can. But when cash money starts changing hands, that's something else" (38). To lose cash money is to lose face and honor as well.

The concern over "cash dollars" may also reflect the larger financial situation in the country. With the gold standard becoming increasingly shaky—it was abandoned in the United States in 1933—the meaning of money becomes increasingly fluid. When one can no longer exchange dollars for gold, what does a dollar mean? It requires a leap of faith, takes on symbolic rather than actual meaning. Arthur A. VanderVeen argues that in *Go Down, Moses* one can see a "fear that reliable standards of value were mere arbitrary constructs" (46). This uneasiness regarding money's ability to determine absolute meaning is anticipated in *As I Lay Dying*, where money becomes a floating signifier, an unstable entity reflecting an unstable economy. Thus it is no surprise that it also carries emotional resonance and lays bare some of the twisted dynamics within the Bundren family.

Money may be a floating signifier to the reader, but it remains an absolute to the characters in the novel. It sets up the main premise of the book: the epic journey to get Addie's corpse to town for burial. When a wheel comes off the wagon carrying the wood that Darl and Jewel take to sell, the trip is delayed three days, allowing the river to rise an additional five feet. They squeeze this trip in despite Addie's impending death because, as Darl says, "It means three dollars" (17). The opportunity to earn cash dollars should not be dismissed lightly. Three dollars means a great deal in this household, including cash for the trip to Jefferson. It is not just the Bundrens who rely on real money; the reader sees the same concern over cash in Cora's disappointment at not being able to sell her cakes for two dollars apiece. Though Cora keeps repeating that they didn't really cost her anything and that the family will be able to eat them—"anybody is likely to make a miscue, but it's not all of them that can get out of it without loss, I can tell him. It's not everybody can eat their mistakes" (9)—it's clear from her insistence that losing out on the chance for cash in exchange for her cakes constitutes a major setback.

Given the scarcity of money, three dollars represents more than its cash value in a poverty-stricken household. It constitutes, according to Cora, the cost of a mother's "goodbye kiss" (22), though in true Faulknerian fashion, she misconstrues who loses out on that kiss, insisting that Darl rather than Jewel is the one to be driven away from his mother's deathbed. The scene bears considerable attention because, in fact, Darl uses the three dollars as a form of misdirection. With the meaning of money rapidly losing fixity, dollars not only change meaning but also serve as a shield for a complex network of family relations. When Dewey Dell, on being informed by Darl that Addie will die before their return, asks why he is taking Jewel with him, Darl replies, "I want him to help me load" (28). Both Darl and Dewey Dell know that Jewel is Addie's favorite; Darl's thwarting of the dying kiss to the favorite child reveals a streak of maliciousness that often gets overlooked by readers, but recognizing it is crucial in helping students understand the anger that both Jewel and Dewey Dell turn on Darl at the end. Under the guise of needing the three dollars, Darl sets in motion a complicated family drama that will eventually come back to doom him to the asylum, the committal justified by economic need. As Cash reluctantly admits, "It wasn't nothing else to do. It was either send him to Jackson, or have Gillespie sue us" (232). Darl is sent away not because he has lost hold of sanity but because he has become a financial liability. The family can no longer afford him. Having hidden his own machinations behind economic need, he now finds himself sacrificed to the economics of family survival and ends up on a train, riding "on the state's money" (254).

Money questions shadow the circumstances surrounding Addie's death. It's worth asking students what causes her death—self-determination or disease? Both have economic components. If she dies of some unspecified illness, then a lack of money probably hastens her death. Short of cash, Anse waits too long to call in medical assistance, hoping she'll improve. Peabody seems to confirm this interpretation, noting, "[I]f it had finally occurred to Anse himself that he needed one, it was already too late" (42). Anse, not surprisingly, offers contradictory comments. Once Peabody arrives, Anse grumbles, "And now I got to pay for it," whining about the expense of medical care for a dying woman (37). Yet he then turns around and denies it: "Hit aint begrudgin the money." Rather, he claims, "her mind is sot on hit" (45). Why spend the money when she's determined to die? Addie's death does appear to be largely self-willed, a decision she lays out in economic terms. Death constitutes her next action after she settles her procreative accounts by providing Anse with "three children that are his and not mine. And then I could get ready to die" (176). Addie's death wish can be acted on only after she puts her affairs in order, including paying Anse back for "the child I had robbed him of." While she may not be referring to money, she certainly views her children in economic terms; it is no accident that the two she loves are Cash and Jewel (each name invoking monetary value). Addie, who seems to define her children as either assets or liabilities, needs to settle her spreadsheet before death.

Considering the economics of Addie's death also invites discussion of Anse. He has greater depth than many students initially realize. More than any other character, Anse uses the language of economics, from his quest for the money for new teeth to his insistence on ownership (in response to multiple offers of loaned mules to take the wagon into town, he reiterates that Addie will "want to go in ourn" [185]) to his preposterously false claims that he wouldn't want to be "beholden" (117) to anyone—when, in fact, he's beholden to everyone he encounters. He's furious when he learns that Jewel has bought a horse, demanding to know, rather ludicrously, if Jewel has bought it "on my word" (135). It must be apparent to the reader by this point that Anse's word wouldn't buy a dog, let alone a horse. When informed that Jewel has bartered his labor in clearing a field for the animal, Anse is hardly appeased. "You never consulted me; you know how tight it is for us to make by, yet you bought a horse for me to feed. Taken the work from your flesh and blood and bought a horse with it" (136). Clearly, Anse expects to own his sons' labor; on other occasions he complains that conscripting Cash to help build a road has seriously weakened the family by giving Cash "carpenter notions" (36) that may enable him to make a living away from the farm and by his ensuing fall while fixing a church roof, rendering him unable to work for six months.

As far as Anse is concerned, his family, his family's labor, and his family's money belong to him. That may constitute the bulk of his assets—though Faulkner never specifies it, Anse may well be a tenant farmer rather than an owner. Anse does say that he has "a little property" (171), which constitutes one of the main reasons Addie marries him; she may be sexually frustrated, evidenced by her complaint "I thought that I could not bear it, lying in bed at night" (170), but she takes care to ascertain his financial situation: "[Y]ou've got a house and a good farm. . . . Are you going to get married?" (171). Yet Anse's claim to ownership can be interpreted in a number of ways. It was not unusual for tenant farmers to stay on land for several generations and to consider such farms as their property.[3] Both *The Hamlet* and *Go Down, Moses* make clear that the vast majority of small farmers in Yoknapatawpha County are tenants rather than owners. This is in keeping with historical reports that share tenancy was most common in "hilly, white majority areas" (Kirby 140). More than half of southern farmers during this period rented rather than owned their land, and for those who did own, mortgage debt was growing (Carlton and Coclanis 69). *The Hamlet* identifies Will Varner as owning "most of the good land in the country" and holding mortgages on "most of the rest" (6). This doesn't leave much space for independent landowners, and given what the reader knows of Anse, it's hard to imagine him as significantly more successful than his fellow farmers. Regardless of his official status, it seems clear that the family and the community are suffering from the agricultural situation, as debt squeezes out much of the distinction between tenancy and ownership, and that the conditions are part of a larger crisis in the southern economy. As long as sharecropping (a system in which farmers were basically wage laborers with no legal rights to their crops) and tenancy were so prevalent, any small farmer was treated harshly by the system.

Both tenancy and sharecropping were singled out by the 1938 report on southern economic conditions as main contributors to poverty. Since the farmer does not actually own the land, though he may own the equipment and livestock, he has little incentive to protect it for long-term productivity. Rather, he must wrest as much value as he can, because he generally has to give a quarter or a third of his crop to the landlord. This means relying on soil-exhausting crops like tobacco and cotton. Cotton, long the mainstay of southern agriculture, varied markedly in price but saw substantial decline from twenty cents a pound in 1927 to six cents in 1931 (Carlton and Coclanis 68). That spelled disaster for the numerous farmers wholly dependent on it, adding to an already sizable burden of debt, only part of which was the percentage of the total yield owed to the landlord. Usually, until the crop was harvested, the family had to live on credit from the landlord's commissary or town stores—at usurious rates—unless they had savings, which was rare among tenants and small farmers. Thus at harvest the farmer might owe a third of the crop and also have to pay off—if possible—the previous months' debt, which often left him with very little to show for a year's worth of hard labor. This illustrates why money was so hard to come by. Whatever profit a farmer might earn generally went straight to debt repayment, forcing him to rely on credit for survival. Even if Anse does actually own his land, he is still subject to similar structures of debt and credit, made clear by the obvious and deep poverty of the family.

Students need to understand this backdrop of endemic agricultural poverty. It helps explain why Anse wants to assert ownership of his family—that may be all he can lay claim to, and as the novel illustrates, he doesn't even control the family (though he does manage to appropriate Jewel's horse, Dewey Dell's ten dollars, and Cash's eight dollars). It also helps explain his insistence on some degree of independence, his need to own the mules that take them to town. Ownership becomes just as much a commodity as cash dollars. Yet it reveals Anse as more selfish than his peers, for his is clearly a community that shares, especially with Anse, according to Tull: "Like most folks around here, I done holp him so much already I cant quit now" (33). Anse, on the other hand, complains about the amount of time Cash spends helping others and about how Jewel has claimed the reward of his own labor in buying the horse. By resisting the cooperative efforts that can be crucial for surviving such economic hardships, Anse proves himself grounded in a concept of an American dream increasingly hard to sustain. He wants to have it all, not to be beholden, to see himself as a successful farmer—none of which seems possible in debt-ridden rural Mississippi. As Atkinson notes, Faulkner illustrates "the resistance to dependency" that results when desperate circumstances require a more communitarian ideology (178). Viewing Anse through a financial lens allows the reader to see a man with little to call his own, a man who desperately tries to act like the head of the household—with very limited success. A set of teeth hardly seems like an unreasonable reward. Students may not like him any better, but they should be able to understand more clearly the difficulties of Anse's situation and thus comprehend more fully how economic hardship shapes the individual and the family.

Exploring Anse's economic views can lead to fruitful discussions of family obligations and family survival: What does one owe one's family? one's community? What does one make of Jewel's insistence that the horse "wont never eat a mouthful of yours" (136)? What does this refusal to be under any obligation to Anse tell us about Jewel? What does it say about ownership? With money so tight, ownership can mean the difference between staying afloat and going bankrupt. After all, you can mortgage or sell only what you already own. The Bundrens' poverty may cast Anse in a slightly more sympathetic light; he confiscates his children's assets for a new team not just to complete the trip to Jefferson but because he can't continue to farm without one. While it's hard to excuse his robbing his own children for money for his new teeth, the fact remains that wanting teeth is not an unreasonable desire. If false teeth are considered a luxury for which one must wait ten years, the financial situation is dire indeed. Anse may not be appealing as a father and husband, but as a poor farmer he does deserve some sympathy.

It is the women, however, who are most vulnerable to the vicissitudes of poverty. Cora's concern over her cakes, despite the fact that her family will be able to eat them, reflects her anxiety over her poultry business and how meager any profit will be. She has invested in a good breed of chicken and must recoup her investment. In fact, Cora's egg business is likely helping Tull stay afloat. The poultry business was year-round, and eggs held value even as cotton fell (L. A. Jones 98–99). As she says, "We depend a lot on our chickens" (6). Losing a potential sale, then, is more than a disappointment and setback—it can actually lead to financial ruin. Cora displays some financial uneasiness regarding her role in insisting on more expensive chickens; her reiteration that the decision was based on her "say-so" (7) reflects that she must answer financially to Tull as well as to her customers. Despite her contribution to the family's economy, she has little financial independence.

Dewey Dell, with the ten dollars to buy an abortifacient, is a more tragic case. The first point to note is that the money is not hers; it was given to her by Lafe. She is both a sexual and an economic victim, utterly without the means to remedy her situation. She is dependent on Lafe's money and also on his claim that she can just walk into a drugstore and buy a miracle abortion drug for ten dollars and a promise not to tell who sold it, marking her as painfully out of touch with current abortion law and knowledge. While such drugs were widely available—and openly advertised—through the 1870s, by 1900, according to James Mohr, "virtually every jurisdiction in the United States had laws upon its books that proscribed the practice sharply and declared most abortions to be criminal offenses" (vii). What had been a flourishing abortifacient market largely disappeared, was forced underground, or was replaced with home remedies. The drugs were, of course, largely ineffectual, only occasionally initiating a miscarriage in women with a predilection to miscarry. But that did not stop their widespread distribution. The price varied widely, ranging from a dollar to twenty dollars for a box of such pills, cheaper than a surgical abortion, which could range from twenty-five dollars to a hundred dollars in the late nineteenth century (59, 96).

As the medical profession cracked down on both surgical abortion and abortifacients, the price for each apparently went up. A drug advertised as "Curing Ladies Stomach Sick and No Menses Every Month" in Chicago in 1922 was priced at twenty-five dollars (Reagan 44). Thus Dewey Dell's ten dollars would probably not be enough, even if such drugs were available. Mosely's sanctimonious advice to "go on back to Lafe and you and him take that ten dollars and get married with it" (203) subtly acknowledges this while overlooking the cost of starting out and raising a child in the Depression-era South (and Lafe, who appears to pick cotton as a wage laborer, without even a rented farm, is certainly no great financial catch). For Dewey Dell, an abortion is far more cost-effective. However, to quote MasterCard commercials, there are some things that money can't buy. Mosely makes that quite clear: "A thousand dollars wouldn't be enough in my store and ten cents wouldn't be enough" (202). Even MacGowan, the drugstore clerk in Jefferson who declares that "the hair of the dog"—sex—will cure her of her problem, makes clear that money is useless: "You see, I cant put no price on my knowledge and skill. Certainly not for no paltry sawbuck" (246). Her money is valueless, and Dewey Dell is forced to barter her body, effectively exiling her from consumer capitalism and forcing her back into a premodern form of commerce. Even she, ignorant as she is, knows that such a system offers her no hope. "It aint going to work. . . . That son of a bitch" (251). She may be naive, but she isn't stupid; she knows when she's been used and cheated. Denied access to modern medicine, she is cast as the eternal mother.

The economy of maternity operates on a different plane. The novel begins by putting a price on a dying mother's kiss and ends by ensuring that motherhood is beyond price, that no amount of money will buy one out of one's maternal obligations. This dynamic renders Addie's balancing of her maternal accounts even more important. I have found that students are often puzzled and put off by her apparent lack of affection for any of her children other than Jewel and Cash (at least when he was a baby). Students are also caught up in the cultural assumption that motherhood is the highest form of fulfillment women can achieve. Even Addie falls into that trap, deciding that Cash's birth is the "answer," that her "aloneness had been violated and then made whole again by the violation" (171, 172). But when maternity is transformed, by repetition, into "chapping" (173), Addie rebels, resenting Darl's birth as the trick that reveals her presumed calling: that of baby maker. She goes on to challenge motherhood by reformulating it in economic terms, viewing her offspring as credits and debits. As Matthews notes, "Addie mocks patriarchal economic domination in her derisive balancing of the reproductive books" ("*As I Lay*" 78).

By taking control of the family's economy, Addie usurps Anse's position; Anse may feel that he should be the owner of his children's assets, but she is the one who identifies the children as assets or liabilities. There could hardly be a more powerful statement against any sentimental piety regarding maternity. That her daughter also seeks to challenge maternity should come as no surprise, though Dewey Dell's effort comes across differently. As Katherine Henninger has observed:

> Addie apparently never considers refusing maternity through abortion, but instead develops her own system of earthly accounting in which each child is carefully registered as the fulfillment of a debt to Anse. In contrast, Dewey Dell's persistent attempts to obtain an abortion indicate an understanding of an economics wholly contained within earthly parameters. (27)

It is, however, an economy denied her. Where Addie looks to balance her maternal accounts, Dewey Dell seeks to buy her way out of them altogether. Fittingly, Dewey Dell's attempt to use money rather than language to challenge maternity fails dismally; she is forced back to her body—an ineffective form of currency. Money can do some things in this novel: it can buy bananas, new teeth, and a graphophone. What it cannot do is purchase an alternative to motherhood—at least not at a price Dewey Dell can afford.

Money does, however, have an interesting impact on religion in the novel, as the characters try desperately to read their poverty as a mark of divine favor. Anse, for all his belief in ownership, seems to imagine a communist afterlife:

> Nowhere in this sinful world can a honest, hardworking man profit. . . . I wonder why we keep at it. It's because there is a reward for us above, where they cant take their autos and such. Every man will be equal there and it will be taken from them that have and give to them that have not by the Lord. (110)

This vision of God as a kind of divine Karl Marx strikes a slightly comic note, yet it emphasizes the connection between poverty and how one views religion. The poor try desperately to believe in God's wisdom, but their living conditions make such belief a difficult sell. Cora provides a particularly interesting example. In response to Kate's complaint regarding the cake debacle ("But those rich town ladies can change their minds"), Cora muses piously, "Riches is nothing in the face of the Lord, for He can see into the heart" (7). In this case, she seems to accept with equanimity her financial loss, trusting in God for her eventual reward. But as Kate keeps harping on the injustice, Cora changes her tune: "The Lord can see into the heart. If it is His will that some folks has different ideas of honesty from other folks, it is not my place to question His decree" (8). Here she shifts to an implicit criticism of God, that God apparently allows some people greater latitude than others. By insisting that it is not her place to question, she plants the question firmly in the reader's mind: Why does God allow such inequity? Having thus challenged God's authority, she goes on to usurp it, looking at Addie and claiming, "the eternal and the everlasting salvation and grace is not on her" (8). Faulkner carefully sets up Cora's sacrilegious declaration—that she knows who gains salvation—as the end result of her gradual questioning of God's purpose, a questioning based on her increasing realization of her financial vulnerability. A God who cannot protect her assets appears to be a God who cannot be depended on to determine her neighbor's fate. Cora, better schooled in financial hardship than God, takes the job upon herself. In addition to providing an excellent exercise in close reading, these passages highlight the extent to which Faulkner recognizes the all-pervasive role of economics. It shapes family, maternity, and even religion.

Following the money allows instructors to reground the novel in the physical world. For too long, fascinated by Darl's disembodied consciousness and the narrative's complex psychology, we have overlooked the simple fact that this is also a story of the power of poverty, though much new work is now exploring the economics of the text (see, in particular, Atkinson; Lester, "As They"; and Railey). Patrick O'Donnell has rightly identified the Bundrens' trek as a journey "*toward* law and capital" ("Between the Family" 89). Anse, in particular, enters into consumer culture, buying new teeth and acquiring a wife and, indirectly, a graphophone. For this family, however, a journey into consumer capitalism is a journey into debt. They now owe Peabody for their stay in town as well as his medical services; the cultivator and seeder have been mortgaged; Jewel's horse has been sold; Dewey Dell is about to produce another mouth to feed. More important, Anse's most valuable assets—his sons—have been both reduced and damaged. The novel begins with a family that can put three healthy adult sons into the field; by the end, only one and a half remain: Darl is gone, and Cash is crippled. There seems to be scant hope for any change other than the occasional banana.

Faulkner, then, ensures that the reader not mistake the qualified success of the Bundrens' journey for any answer to the difficult conditions under which the Bundrens live. Ultimately, this is a novel about loss: loss of Addie, loss of Darl, and loss of economic standing. It is also, of course, a novel about language; money is not the only element that appears to have become unmoored. As VanderVeen puts it, both words and currency "introduce a slipperiness into the accounting of material exchanges" (53). Thus money allows the instructor to approach the ever-complex linguistic virtuosity of the book by providing a way to talk about absolute meaning versus fluid meaning. More precariously situated than ever, lacking their most articulate family members (Addie and Darl), the Bundrens remind us that living in the South is not easy. Poverty, as the southern historian Pete Daniel points out, meant more than simply being poor:

> The United States, in the minds of most people, provided opportunity, and to fail at making a living reflected not the collapse of the system or even drought; rather, it meant that they had failed as Americans. (110)

Being American proved problematic in the South in the wake of the Civil War, and failing as an American simply reinforced southern isolationism. By having students pay attention to economics, we can elicit discussions of how money can shape family values, challenge religious beliefs, and form American identity. The characters in *As I Lay Dying* are not freaks; they are constructed by the conditions under which they live, conditions that endure today, as evidenced by the poverty uncovered in the wake of Hurricane Katrina. Faulkner's South has changed less than one might have hoped or expected, and alerting students to this fact should make Faulkner seem more up-to-date, less remote. It also helps students understand that literature is not restricted to the figurative; it reflects a cultural reality that is still very much with us. Faulkner is both mythmaker and chronicler, master of the imaginative and the real. He does, as he says, "sublimate the actual into the apocryphal" ("Interview" 255), and by so doing, he reminds us all that both are integral to great fiction.

NOTES

Editors' note: See John T. Matthews and Donald M. Kartiganer in this volume for views of Anse as a landowner.

[1] Given the turbulence of the United States' economy, especially in the early twenty-first century, and the immediate impact that economic change can have on students' lives, highlighting the economic vicissitudes of the Bundren family should resonate well with students.

[2] Anse never considers mortgaging land, which may indicate either that his land—if he owns it—is already mortgaged to the full extent or that he rents rather than owns. Or it may indicate an unwillingness to take such a drastic step. But given that the issue never arises, it would appear that the land, for whatever reason, is unmortgageable. See the ensuing discussion regarding Anse's status as a renter or owner.

[3] In *Go Down, Moses* Lucas Beauchamp claims that "it was his own field, though he neither owned it nor wanted to nor even needed to" (35). While I would resist equating Lucas and Anse, given the differences in race as well as character, this example nonetheless reminds us that ownership may have a fluid meaning in Faulkner's work.

A Tale of Two Novels

Donald M. Kartiganer

Titles angling for cleverness are usually, at best, half-relevant to the subject. But over the years I have found that teaching *As I Lay Dying* often comes down to focusing on two fictional situations: on the one hand, the journey to Jefferson and the members of the Bundren family most invested in it; on the other, the characters Addie and Darl, who are not really invested at all except as passive agents, dead or indifferent, caught up in a narrative that moves independently of them. By the end of the novel, the two situations are like Addie's notion of words and deeds: "too far apart for the same person to straddle from one to the other" (173).

Of course, part of the challenge of the novel is indeed to straddle them—although not necessarily to merge or reconcile them. For numerous reasons, not least because of the interpretive difficulty of Addie and Darl, I find that the best way to begin is through the members of the family who, by virtue of certain qualities they hold in common, may be said to constitute the "Bundren family proper" and who drive the novel's narrative line. For all their uniqueness as individuals, achieved primarily through their powerful interior monologues, they each belong solidly to the family, deriving from it a core identity that they honor by their determination to carry Addie Bundren's corpse to Jefferson.

Once I propose that Anse, Cash, Jewel, Dewey Dell, and Vardaman share some common denominators, students are quick to find them, beginning with the particular image (or talisman or fetish) on which each character focuses: the teeth, the coffin, the horse, the fetus (never referred to as such—"it" is a God-given "sign when something has happened bad" [58]), and the fish. As we begin to explore what lies behind these images, how each has acquired significance, Addie emerges as a crucial source. This is more obvious with the coffin, the horse, and the fish, which ultimately become not only symbols of but virtual substitutes for the dying or deceased mother. Students can often be persuaded to consider the possibility that the fetus and the teeth have a similar origin. Dewey Dell's pregnancy is the repetition of motherhood, her exclusive link with Addie. While it is a link she hopes to break, the imagery of her outcry in this time of terrible isolation suggests her submission to a shared female force: "I feel like a wet seed wild in the hot blind earth" (64). As for Anse, the teeth, whose absence may be a sign of lost sexual potency, are also the vehicle for its revival, contingent on the replacement of Addie with a second wife (ex cathedra I divulge the wisdom that one should never go courting without one's teeth). Although more indirect than the other Bundren images, the teeth nevertheless emerge from an intimate relation with Addie that even Anse's principled superficiality cannot conceal. Most important at this point is the students' recognition of how significant the images are for the Bundren family proper and the degree to which they distinguish the family from Addie and Darl, who have no such images to substantiate or to contain their actions or interior meditations.

The next observation is also fairly obvious, and usually a student will make it once I have raised the general issue of shared Bundren attributes: namely, that Anse, Cash, Jewel, Dewey Dell, and Vardaman all have personal motives for going to Jefferson other than their desire to fulfill Addie's wish to be buried there. Here again, as with the images, some motives are stronger than others. Anse's need for teeth, Dewey Dell's hope to acquire a means of inducing a miscarriage, Cash's desire for a graphophone as well as his plan to stop at Tull's on the way back to start work on the roof, Vardaman's hope of seeing the toy train in the shop window and getting some bananas—these readings all come from the class. Jewel is the exception, since his devotion to Addie is so deep, even manic. I suggest that his plan to ride his horse into Jefferson—accompanying yet significantly separate from the family—indicates some desire apart from the need to bury Addie there. It is possibly related to the pride he takes in his horse or a sign of his urge to demonstrate his independence and maturity. Jewel is eighteen or nineteen years old, and like Dewey Dell, who takes along her Sunday clothes, he may be looking forward to an opportunity to impress the town's citizens. I point out that he has gone to Jefferson not long before to get a haircut, which, given the Bundrens' economic condition and their distance, physical and social, from town, seems excessive.

Despite the ulterior motives, the Bundrens are dedicated to completing the journey to Jefferson no matter how long it takes, no matter how much physical and psychic suffering or sheer public humiliation it demands. Jewel significantly rejoins the family after his horse has been traded—contrary to the prediction of Armstid ("And that would be the last they would see of him" [192]) but not apparently to the surprise of the Bundrens, who express no particular interest when Jewel subsequently "comes up without a word, with his pale rigid eyes in his high sullen face, and gets into the wagon" (209). The contradiction between fealty to Addie and blatant self-interest often disturbs students' sense of moral propriety and clarity, and yet part of the meaning of the novel may be that that very contradiction is necessary to the journey's completion: purity of motive and praxis always exact a toll from each other. That Faulkner himself may have seen at least a modicum of achievement in the journey is evident in his comment years later that, confronted with a difficult "fate," the Bundrens "pretty well coped with theirs" (*Lion* 254).

At about this time, in part to make up for students' possibly declining sympathy for the Bundrens, I introduce some of the novel's social, economic, and literary background. I cite the conditions of 1929 and 1930 that the novel refers to, such as the poor roads and badly maintained bridges, the depressed economic status of farmers generally (agriculture being one area that did not share in the economic boom of the 1920s), the growing attraction of commercial products out of the financial reach of these people, and the great social disparity that had opened up between urban and rural life. This is particularly apparent as the

Bundrens get nearer to Jefferson and are regarded alternately as an outrage and a subject of contempt, culminating in the callous treatment of Dewey Dell by Skeet Macgowan. Of course, the greatest textual contradiction to urban stereotypical attitudes is the novel's interior-monologue strategy, which allows us into the Bundrens' minds, where we find passions and psychic complexity that few writers before Faulkner had depicted in southern country people.

We have to be careful, however, not to overstate what are obviously serious economic conditions. Faulkner wrote the novel just after the 1929 stock market crash but before the Great Depression had set in. Moreover, and this is clearly by Faulkner's design, Anse owns his own farm (putting him in a category of thirty percent of the farm population of 1930 Mississippi), as does his neighbor Tull (Fed. Writers' Project 101).[1] Consequently, there is no reference in the novel to the harsh circumstances of tenant farming that Faulkner vividly describes in "Barn Burning" and *The Hamlet*. In short, concerning the Bundrens' financial standing, there is a complexity equal to what we find in the relation between the Bundrens' alleged purpose in undertaking the journey and their ulterior motives. The point I always try to make to students is that readers must seek meaning and moral and social implication in a literary text and that in good texts—certainly in this one—these do not reveal themselves easily or simply; that much of the readers' work and pleasure will come from the process of finding their way through to these implications; and that, when they do, they will not necessarily be in complete agreement with other readers.

By way of preparing to open discussion of Addie and Darl, I ask students to consider what kind of novel *As I Lay Dying* would be if Darl were not in it and Addie did not have the capacity for posthumous thought. The plot, built on a traditional quest motif, would scarcely change—which in itself is remarkable, given the major significance of these two characters—but our entire perspective would. The novel would become, even with its interior monologues, fairly conventional in the realist-naturalist tradition of poor rural people in the South contending with natural, social, and economic forces, trying to accommodate a mother's wish even as they also hope to gain some small urban pleasures and, in Dewey Dell's case, a significant urban privilege. As commonly happens in such fictions, the Bundrens, with the exception of Anse, are largely thwarted by the journey so far as their personal desires are concerned. To the extent that they survive the ordeal—they accomplish at least their ostensible task—it comes at considerable cost. Cash will limp for the rest of his life, Jewel has been badly burned and has lost his beloved horse, Dewey Dell will bear a child in shame, Vardaman faces the prospect of mental recovery in difficult circumstances. If, as Faulkner claimed, the Bundrens "pretty well coped with" their fate, the criteria for coping have been adjusted to the limited horizons of Mississippi hill-country farmers.

It is with the characters of Addie and Darl that Faulkner rids the novel completely of any similarity it may seem to have to stereotypical accounts of crude, uneducated, fiercely yet irrationally determined white southern farmers. He also reduces its naturalism and something of its realism: its position as a plot-controlled account of limited human possibility. It is as if Faulkner were setting a second novel within the first, contradicting its portrayal of purposeful, if at times grotesque, action, lifting it to new levels of motive and imagination. In doing so, he deprives the reader of some standard strategies and expectations for engaging the novel, forcing us into a kind of readerly groundlessness equivalent to the psychic condition of the two characters themselves. If there has been a fair degree of agreement on the Bundren family proper and the novel they make, then now disagreement will be rampant.

One question I always ask is, what are the major differences between the Bundrens and the mother and second son? The first difference should be apparent from our earlier attention to the assortment of images on which the rest of the family focuses. Neither Addie nor Darl has such an image, some obsession narrowed to a concrete object. The second difference, almost as apparent, is that at the end of the novel both Addie and Darl are unceremoniously expelled from the family. After the long, harrowing journey, Addie is dispatched in an introductory adverbial clause: "But when we got it filled and covered and drove out the gate . . ." (237), and this is followed immediately by Dewey Dell, Jewel, and Anse throwing Darl brutally to the ground and turning him over to the men who will take him to an insane asylum, where he will spend the rest of his life.

The third difference is not obvious at all, and so I generally offer it as a working hypothesis to see where it leads: that neither Addie nor Darl has ever had the slightest interest in actually going to Jefferson. The problem, of course, is not with Darl but with Addie, who requested the journey nearly thirty years earlier, following the birth of Darl. To understand Addie's request, what may be its built-in paradox and its relation to Darl, we need to go directly to her monologue.

Darl and Addie confront, from the beginning of their lives, the power of death, the limits of language, the threat of madness. Addie's freedom from the images of the Bundrens is also her lifelong struggle to gain freedom from parentage. She never mentions her mother, and she tells Anse that, as far as "living kin" are concerned, she has "never had any" (171). To put it another way, Addie claims she has had no need to construct a substitution for a sponsor from whom the outlines of identity have descended, along with the dependencies they incur. The great challenge to this claim, as Addie well knows, is her father, who exists for her as a single potentially paralyzing sentence, one she refers to three times in her monologue: "my father used to say that the reason for living was to get ready to stay dead a long time" (169). Her life will be a series of attempts to subvert the meaning of that sentence, to construe a purpose to living that the sentence claims is illusion. To that end "images" will not suffice. Addie will not be satisfied by recourse to a symptom of unspoken, possibly unknown attachment as her existential support. Instead, she seeks action wholly at one with its fully conscious goal, action that is nothing but its immediate, literal presence.

Here I introduce another text, Sigmund Freud's *Beyond the Pleasure Principle*, so I can read its most alarming sentence, which closely anticipates Addie's father: "*the goal of all life is death*" (47). Death, Freud proposes, may be an instinct more powerful and primary than the life instinct. The urge to live—eros—the instinct "towards change and development" (45), the pursuit of sexual connection, family increase, social and cultural achievement, may be no more than what Freud calls "circuitous routes to . . . death" (48), back to an original, isolated inanimate condition from which we have been disturbed and to which we wish to return.[2] Freud's circuitous routes are the equivalent of Addie's father's account of life, and Addie's resistance is her attempt to live in such a way that life is not necessarily a pointless interval in an eternity of death but can be an action of significance, the worthy complement of its opposite—indeed, an equal partner in a dynamic of dual fulfillment.

As for life as seemingly purposeful but finally inconsequential in the face of the desire to die, Addie dismisses this as a version of the corruption of language: life when it is word separated from deed, life as it is lived by those who use the signifier in unwitting ignorance of the signified—as Addie puts it, those who express "fear" but who "had never had the fear," "pride, who never had the pride": above all, those who say "love," when it is "just a shape to fill a lack" (172). The alternative is a life in which language is at one with the body of erotic desire: the desire to connect, to engage, to bind together, to expand outward. For Addie the vehicle of such connection invariably has a violent dimension, in part because of her need to rebel against a death verdict that claims to be the law of life, in part because of what she sees as the prevailing social habit of naming experience rather than existentially knowing it. As a result, her life becomes a series of aggressive acts designed to bring together words and deeds, the words "straight up in a thin line, quick and harmless," somehow at one with the deeds, the "terribly doing [that] goes along the earth" (173).[3]

To become "something" in their "secret and selfish life" (170), Addie whips her students; in love she "took" Anse (171); in her pregnancy with Cash she makes the dual discovery "that living was terrible and that this was the answer to it" (171). Paramount is her adultery with the preacher Whitfield. The intimacy of "sin" (174–75) is Addie's greatest challenge to her father's subjection of life to death. In this violation of marriage and of the relationship between minister and flock, Addie believes she has "found it": "the reason [for living] was the duty to the alive, to the terrible blood, the red bitter flood boiling through the land" (174). It is her climactic attempt to heal the breach of life and death, of living and language: "to shape and coerce the terrible blood to the forlorn echo of the dead word high in the air" (175).

Anse Bundren is for Addie the epitome of life lived entirely at the level of uprooted language. When Addie, furious with Anse over her second pregnancy, gives birth to Darl, she makes her request to be buried in Jefferson: "And when Darl was born I asked Anse to promise to take me back to Jefferson when I died" (173). No one in the family ever asks the reason for Addie's request; she divulges it only in her posthumous monologue: "my revenge would be that [Anse] would never know I was taking revenge" (173). The revenge of the journey is that Anse *should not know* its reason. In making the request, Addie has already emptied the journey of its ostensible purpose—a particular burial site—and converted it into nothing more than a circuitous route: a long march grave-ward whose primary burden is the corpse of its meaning. Unlike Anse and her children, Addie is indulging not in ulterior motive but rather in the motive of no motive: the journey for no reason whatsoever. From Addie's perspective, the journey to Jefferson—the plotline of *As I Lay Dying*—has nothing to do with *her* death but is, in its irrelevance, the seal of Anse's—confirmation that his life, in unwitting fulfillment of her father's sentence, has never been other than its long dying.

The great irony of the novel is that it is not Anse who bears the full brunt of Addie's vengeance but the second son, Darl, who is the chief victim of a sentence to detour. For many students, Darl is the most difficult character in the novel—as well as the most sympathetic, sensitive, and intelligent; he is also the most long-suffering, the one most harshly treated by the family. How to account for his "queerness" and how to grasp what that queerness consists of are not questions likely to yield consensus. Many students will see Darl as possibly the only truly sane person in the family. The greatest challenge of teaching *As I Lay Dying* is to try to understand what Darl is, his gifts and his limitations, and to help students see what the justification for his expulsion might be, even if eventually they decide it is outweighed by its cruelty.

Darl's inheritance from Addie is the same as hers from her father, except that while Addie's is a belief, a lesson to be learned (and one that she strives to reverse), Darl's is an identity not to be undone, fostered by Addie as the embodiment of her revenge. She reduces him at birth to an augury of her death and the provocation for the project of aimless action she thrusts on Anse. Like Addie's, Darl's inheritance has its benefits as well as its deficiencies. In being denied full presence by his mother at the outset, less the child of her body than the function of her resentment, Darl acquires the vision that accrues to absent sponsorship: an insight into the condition of abandonment in a world where abandonment may be the deepest truth. As a result, the images that sustain the rest of the family in the face of Addie's death are neither available nor necessary to Darl. Like his mother, he knows instinctively their limitation: that image is a compromise of conscious and unconscious motive, its solidity mocked by its illusory claim. The actions of the other Bundrens are "as if" actions: as if this coffin, this horse, this fish were Addie Bundren. The creative capacity to limn Addie's survival in the lines of meticulous carpentry or the care of a horse or the catching of a fish is the capacity, in the act of mourning, to make the motions of life. Darl knows too much to gain comfort from image, but his tragic deficiency is that, unlike Addie, he lacks sufficient conviction of his own existential presence for direct, unequivocal action: action not supported by illusion but inseparable from its known purpose, absent the deceit of "as if."[4]

One way to elicit from students a critical empathy, one that reveals something of the pathos of Darl's plight and its remoteness from ordinary human concerns and obligations, is to invite them to do a close reading of his "empty yourself for sleep" passage (80). I ask them to try to follow the logic of Darl's thought, establishing the basis of each move within that logic. There are many possibilities here, and the important thing is to encourage a kind of free-association reading, assuring students beforehand that the slipperiness of the movement in the passage is inherent to Darl's way of thinking and that it may well be that he himself never solves to his satisfaction (or to ours) the question of "what are you." As much as any passage in the novel, this one should open to a variety of readings that cannot, and need not, be reconciled.

What follows is not a "correct" reading but one that tries to respond to each move in Darl's meditation and coordinate it logically with the next.

Identity, Darl believes, becomes an issue only in a "strange room," which suggests that in familiar surroundings identity may take the shape of determinations imposed by those surroundings, the roles one has been assigned to play, the status one owns by virtue of the familiar physical and social structures in place. When secured by such external conditions, the self is not "emptied" for sleep; perhaps even in sleep—a temporary respite from consciousness—the self maintains (or is assumed to maintain) its predetermined definition. To go to sleep in a strange room, absent those conditions, is a risk, as if sleep, once the self is "emptied," were a period and place of vacancy from which one might not return. Instead of waking to the familiar and the identity structured by it, one wakes to the foreign, and identity may falter.[5]

Darl divides the process of emptying into three stages: before emptying for sleep, emptying for sleep, and filled with sleep. The first inspires the central question of the meditation, which no one need ask except in a strange room: "what are you." The second and third are flat negations: "you are not" and "you never were," providing no answer to the initial question except a claim that identity survives neither the process nor the result of emptying for sleep. In fact, once emptied for sleep, one gives up not only identity—the particular characteristics of self—but also *being*, and the implicit ramification is the question of whether one ever truly returns to it on waking, whether being, amid the familiar or the strange, is always an illusion. Darl, having proposed the loss of self in sleep, then responds to his query of "what" by raising the ante: not only does he not know before sleep what he is, he does not know if he is.

For comparison, he moves to Jewel, for whom being lies in an ignorance of the need ever to question it: "Jewel knows he is, because he does not know that he does not know whether he is or not." Having a firm but ungrounded sense of being, Jewel does not comprehend the risk of sleeping in a strange room; he "cannot empty himself for sleep," either because he recognizes no difference between the condition of self in full consciousness and in sleep or perhaps because for him there *is* no difference: his assurance of self is so great (as is manifested throughout the novel) that it survives, as illusion, the threat of its undoing. "[H]e is not what he is and he is what he is not." He is *not* what he believes himself to be, and he *is* a condition of "not knowing" that he will never realize. Consequently, Jewel is in a kind of no-man's-land, as is Darl; but unlike Darl, Jewel is protected from the knowledge of that condition by the illusion of being, by his ignorance.

Jewel avoids Addie's word-and-deed division by being all deed. This may save him from hypocrisy, from the excesses of ulteriority, but it does not save him from what Darl regards as the excesses of illusion. Jewel belongs totally to action, as if motive and meaning were inherent to it, rather than what one must constantly provide, either like Anse, by speaking them, giving them a purely verbal life, or like Addie, by ridding action of all its rationalizations—including the journey to Jefferson, which for her has neither a true nor a false reason.

Darl then turns to concrete, insentient things outside the strange room. There is a wagon carrying a load of wood. This fact is evident to Darl through the wind and rain that "shape it." The rain confirms the existence of wagon and wood by the sound it makes when it strikes them. Falling through the air, it is silent; only when it strikes the solid object does it make a sound. The wind may identify itself and the barrier that blocks it in the same way. One proof of being is the encounter with indisputable objects. But even those objects become real only as part of an interaction, an engagement: wind and rain, wagon and wood, exist to the ear as the sound of their meeting. It is possible that Darl is anticipating Addie's own version of authentic existence as meetings—in her case, violent ones. But Darl does not have faith in the validity of such meetings as Addie does.

In the process of describing meeting, Darl questions the reality of the wood by raising the issue of ownership. A thing *is* by virtue of its being possessed by someone. Perhaps he thinks this less a valid definition than a prevailing practice in the world: the "is-ness" of a thing lies in its identity as "mine." To whom does the wood belong? "[N]o longer theirs that felled and sawed it nor yet theirs that bought it and which is not ours either, lie on our wagon though it does. . . ." The wood is in a state of transition on the wagon of those transporting it; they do not own the wood; they own only the labor of transferring it to those who will own it. It is a labor in process and will never constitute ownership. The logic is little more than a trick, but perhaps it points to Darl's deepest understanding of what it is he lacks: no one "owns" him, no one sponsors him. Addie has renounced possession of him by labeling him at birth as a function, merely the occasion of revenge.

The rest of the passage moves toward a transparently invalid positive resolution. The "it" of "it is not" is the wagon, and it is not, because it is revealed only when the wind and rain stop—that is, cease their fall or flow, become "*was*" once they strike the wagon and load. And yet Darl claims the wagon "*is*" because "when the wagon is *was*, Addie Bundren will not be." The wagon will be used to transport Addie's corpse to Jefferson, so when it no longer exists, Addie will have been buried. Addie Bundren, however, "must be" (81), which is to say that the proof of Darl's existence, his mother, exists. The proof of her existence, however, rests on the flimsiest logic: "And Jewel *is*, so Addie Bundren must be." A few sentences earlier, of course, Darl has made it clear that Jewel's "is-ness" is founded on the fact that "he does not know that he does not know whether he is or not." So Addie's existence for Darl has no sound basis, and yet she is the reason "I must be." He completes in circularity the entire passage by adding that "And then I must be, or I could not empty myself for sleep in a strange room. And so if I am not emptied yet, I am *is*." Darl exists, for otherwise he could not empty himself for sleep, but he has opened the meditation by raising the question of "what are you" before sleep. He now answers it in the simple affirmative that he is, but that "is" relies on the mother proven by the brother whose own existence is as problematic as Darl's, except that he "does not know."

Although Darl thinks these thoughts in "a strange room," there is much evidence in the novel that this is increasingly his condition wherever he is. He is the opposite of Jewel, who is all deed, ignorant of the problem of coherence of word and deed, of mind and reality. Darl is always moving closer, in ways that even Addie could not conceive, to the possibility that life is "just a matter of words" (176).

This kind of speculation in Darl reveals his gifts and his curse as constant counterpoints. The attitudes toward him that this paradox raises in students are not easily resolvable. I think it is more important for students to trace the contradictions to their irresoluble end than to try to contain them at the cost of simplifying Darl's situation. Hovering always above an abyss of potential nonbeing, Darl has no access to the Bundren images, the solid counters his father and siblings use as subjective yet sustaining symbols of the deceased mother. Nor has he the privilege of ulterior motive, since he has no object of desire—the journey to Jefferson—through whose mask an ulterior motive might function. His telepathic power enables him to bypass the space and time lost to him, a world whose reality he cannot believe in. The elegant, educated, and detached prose of his magnificent descriptions are the fruit of his helpless indifference. We may be enthralled by his controlled, evenhanded depiction of Addie's death as he moves from one strikingly unique confrontation with death to another; his patient account of Cash in the rain through the long night, methodically completing the coffin for the deceased Addie; his remarkable, artful rendering of Jewel's rescue of the coffin from the fire—and yet we realize with a shock that part of our wonder is that there is not the slightest indication that the teller is the son of the deceased mother, the brother of the coffin maker, the man who started the fire. Darl contemplates the world, all of it, in Dewey Dell's words, with eyes "filled with distance beyond the land" (27).

In the classroom, discussion of Addie and Darl and the rest of the family will generate often irreconcilable valuations that tell as much about the reader as about the novel. It is an indication we have moved past text-based arguments about meaning to more personal arguments about the significance of meaning. The expulsions of Addie and Darl either condemn the members of the Bundren family proper to their imprisonment within the natural, social, and economic walls they are accomplices in building and maintaining or allow them to return to their routines of hard work, the compromises of ulterior motive, and the occasional luxuries of bananas or listening to "a new record . . . from the mail order" (261). Addie and Darl, victims of less visible forms of force, do not or cannot compromise, responding to the world with violence and violation.

Addie exploits whomever she needs—schoolchildren; Anse; and Darl, Dewey Dell, and Vardaman (the "three children who are his and not mine" [176])—in her struggle to make her life worthy of death. Darl regularly violates the sanctity of human privacy, searching out the deepest secrets of Jewel and Dewey Dell, as if glimpses of another's soul would become body in his. We wonder, is it mean calculation or life-affirming resilience that enables the Bundrens to fill Addie's designated circuitous journey with hidden purpose? Is it the Bundrens' grace or their ignorance that they share the condition of Jewel, who "knows he is, because he does not know that he does not know whether he is or not" (80)?

Faulkner, in his constant struggle for originality, tries his hand at simpler material in this novel: country lives uncluttered by an aristocratic backward look of guilt and dismay at the disappearance of misremembered values. But he then inserts two characters who, by the rules of literary decorum, do not belong there. As readers, we alternately are attracted to and step back from the dogged struggles of ordinary rural people to survive, to inhabit a rarer sphere where Addie and Darl engage directly the meaning of life and death, the real and the illusory, the world and the word.

Addie, at least, has all the lineaments of the Bundrens: the overworked, child-bearing, anchoring wife and mother who lives according to a final accounting of obligations met, of "cleaning up the house afterward" (176)—no matter whether the counters are egg money or children. But Darl, this flesh made word? Who is he?

Cash in a late monologue marking a sudden leap forward from his obsession with the coffin, the tools, the "balance," to a wider sensibility, admits that Darl is "queer," as people have been saying all along: "but that was the very reason couldn't nobody hold it personal. It was like he was outside of it too, same as you" (237).

You?

I used to think Cash was referring to the reader. But now I think he may be referring to the author, the one who writes the monologues for him and for everyone else but who is finally "outside of it." To think of an omniscient teller, moving freely from mind to mind, scene to scene, capable of a universal empathy that is not sympathy, registering the world as it is, divested of personal desire, is to think of the novelist, perhaps writing a novel about the Bundrens or about his personal representative, Darl.

Unless the class is devoted entirely to Faulkner, I generally do not say much of his passion for privacy, his aloofness, his aloneness, his impenetrability. One of his later remarks about Darl, however, has always seemed as self-revelatory as he would ever be: "Who can say how much of the good poetry in the world has come out of madness, and who can say just how much of super-perceptivity the—a—mad person might not have?" (*Faulkner* 113).

NOTES

[1] For a view of Anse as a tenant farmer, see the essay by Deborah Clarke in this volume.

[2] It is interesting to note that *Beyond the Pleasure Principle* was published in the United States in 1924 by Boni and Liveright, Sherwood Anderson's publisher and Faulkner's soon-to-be publisher. Faulkner spent the first six months of 1925 in New Orleans, where he associated closely with Anderson and numerous artists, writers, and journalists who engaged in much discussion of modernism and its theoretical background, including Freud.

[3] Freud argues in *Civilization and Its Discontents* that the inherent masochism of the death instinct can be turned outward as sadism: the death instinct "could be pressed into the service of Eros, in that the organism was destroying some other thing . . . instead of destroying its own self" (66).

[4] Even Darl's burning of Gillespie's barn, his single significant action in the novel, is reported by Darl not as his own doing but as an artfully constructed scene he witnesses.

[5] It is possible that Darl, as a World War I veteran, is the only Bundren who has ever had to take that risk on a regular basis—which is one of the few pieces of textual evidence that allow us to attach some significance to the fact that Darl has been in the war, which the novel seems to take no real account of (and an aspect surely deserving of further investigation).

As I Lay Dying: Approaching the Postcolonial

John T. Matthews

In many respects, *As I Lay Dying* is the ideal introduction to Faulkner's fiction. How Oprah Winfrey arrived at the same conclusion when she selected the novel as the first to be read in her book club's "Summer of Reading Faulkner" in 2005 lies beyond the scope of this essay, but I've successfully taught the novel for decades to non–English majors in introductory courses in American and modern literature. Typically, readers new to Faulkner respond most immediately to the novel's innovative style and structure. One reason the novel works so well as an introduction to Faulkner's way of writing—and modernist experimental technique more generally—is that its use of stream of consciousness and its perspectival organization retain traditionally realistic concerns with strong characterization and advancing narrative. Faulkner's sharp delineation of each family member's personality and goals, captured in the multitrack, voice-shifting prose, appeals to many contemporary readers. Foreign as a story of Depression-era Mississippi farm life may be at first, it becomes intriguing to students because of Faulkner's uncommon exploration of common experiences: youthful self-consciousness and isolation, family intimacy and enmity, the loss of a parent and an encounter with the mystery of mortality, the inequities of social and geographical differences, the indispensability and folly of self-importance. One feature that interests my students involves the novel's superimposition of several zones of change: of individuals, as they pass milestones of adolescence, adulthood, and death; of families and social classes, as they reorganize to meet new economic conditions; of once less developed regions like the South, as modernity transforms it; of the United States as a whole, as it promotes a sense of national economic and cultural identity; even, just detectably, of anticipations of global proletarianization in the separation of the rural poor from their land and their conversion to mobile wage laborers.

In the last decades of the nineteenth century, the rise of a few fiercely determined poor white farmers who realized they'd reached a dead end on the land—epitomized elsewhere in Faulkner by Flem Snopes—began to rearrange the social topography of the Deep South. A new bourgeoisie began to emerge, many of them drawn from the countryside to small towns, where they elbowed aside sinking remnants of the plantation gentry. Many who succeeded in these new pursuits left farming after Reconstruction policies redistributed land to freed slaves and former sources of local capitalization dried up.[1] With the decline in small family-owned subsistence farms, tenancy became the bitter fate of many who refused to leave the land. Flem arrives at the decision that there's no longer any "benefit" to farming sometime in the 1890s, when opportunities to get in on the ground floor of new commercial ventures began to multiply (*Hamlet* 25). A few decades later, southern agriculture had plunged to its nadir; farmers still trying to wring a living out of cotton, the price of which had risen during World War I shortages, now confronted a full-scale economic depression. This was years before 1929, when the collapse hit the rest of the country. Like many writers of the 1930s, Faulkner produces a sympathetic portrait of the South's white tenant farmers, who come to be the face of Depression-era poverty for the rest of the nation.[2]

All but encoffined in a dead way of life, the Bundren family struggles to understand the fatal blow they've received. If the Snopeses jump on modernity's bandwagon early, the Bundrens remain stuck, decades later, on a mule-bound hearse. Under the pretext of honoring their dead wife and mother's last wish, they haul Addie's body from their remote farm toward Jefferson, where her people are buried and also where tantalizing novelties await them. This is a long-delayed and only fleeting visit to town, but it suggests all that they're missing out on back home. Even the youngest Bundren, eight-year-old Vardaman, has metropolitan dreams: a toy train he saw displayed in a store window on an earlier expedition. When Vernon Tull helps the Bundrens cross a flooded river, he gets an odd sensation gazing across the divide at the farm behind him:

> When I looked back at my mule it was like he was one of those here spy glasses and I could look at him standing there and see all the broad land and my house sweated outen it like it was the more the sweat, the broader the land. (139)

Tull registers the fatigue and futility of a dying breed; he's sweated too much, too long, for too little. Vardaman, on the other hand, beckons as an emissary of future possibilities:

> Like he was saying about a fine place he knowed where Christmas come twice with Thanksgiving and lasts on through the winter and the spring and the summer, and if I just stayed with him I'd be all right too. (139)

Might there be a consumer utopia where laborers are freed from the bonds of seasonal fortune and the grind of production?

If there is, it's going to come too late for the adults of *As I Lay Dying*. The novel is a study in belatedness, the majority of its characters dead or mad or doomed without knowing it yet. From the title forward, the reader gets the sense that this is a book of talking corpses. According to Noel Polk and Joseph Blotner in the editors' note in the Vintage paperback edition of *As I Lay Dying*, the phrase "as I lay dying" comes from a line in the *Odyssey* in which the shade of the murdered Greek hero Agamemnon complains about the indignity of not having had his eyes closed in death (266). Here is Dewey Dell's description of the reaction of her father, Anse, to his wife's death: "He looks like right after the maul hits the steer and it no longer alive and dont yet know that it is dead" (61). Anse never expects Addie to quit on him, so he certainly registers some kind of personal loss. But her disappearance also makes palpable the profound loss that farmers like him can hardly believe: the flickering out of their land and livelihood: "His eyes look like pieces of burnt-out cinder fixed in his face, looking out over the land," says Tull (32). For Anse, Tull, and the other farmers who populate this central Mississippi hill country, a crisis threatens to destroy their world in an apocalypse equivalent to fire and flood, to make the land all but unrecognizable ("the road too had been soaked free of earth and floated upward, to leave in its spectral tracing a monument to a still more profound desolation" [143]), and to strand them from a future they may not be able to reach. Surveying the rising tide, Darl concludes that

> [i]t is as though the space between us were time: an irrevocable quality. It is as though time, no longer running straight before us in a diminishing line, now runs parallel between us like a looping string, the distance being the doubling accretion of the thread and not the interval between. (146)

Unlike the small-time farmers of *The Hamlet*, such as Mink and Ab Snopes, who have been reduced to tenancy, or Jack Houston, who has fallen into irreversible mortgage debt, the Bundrens, Tulls, and their neighbors have managed to hang on to their land,[3] perhaps because their hill country plots are among the region's least valuable and because they have figured out how to make a little money apart from farming. The bottoming out of cotton prices in the early 1920s proved catastrophic for the many southern farmers who had put every available acre into cotton production when prices had skyrocketed a few years earlier. The sorrow of grieving farmers may be heard as a constant undertone in *As I Lay Dying*. The farmers complain about nature's whims, since they are not always up to confronting the economic disadvantages that constitute their surer doom:

> *Well, I be durn if I like to see my work washed outen the ground, work I sweat over.*
>
> *It's a fact. A fellow wouldn't mind seeing it washed up if he could just turn on the rain himself.* (90–91)

> It's a hard country on man; it's hard. Eight miles of the sweat of his body washed up outen the Lord's earth, where the Lord Himself told him to put it. (110)

> Darl . . . sits at the supper table with his eyes gone further than the food and the lamp, full of the land dug out of his skull and the holes filled with distance beyond the land. (26–27)

The Bundren family's difficulty negotiating a terrain made unfamiliar by forces of nature provides a metaphor for their historical circumstances. Caught in the current of the swollen stream, they struggle to maintain "*slipping contact*" with the ground beneath: "*What had once been a flat surface was now a succession of troughs and hillocks lifting and falling about us, shoving at us, teasing at us with light lazy touches in the vain instants of solidity underfoot*" (147–48). The water mimics the very earth it savages, taunting and mocking its land-loving victims.

Farmers were often driven to self-destructive remedies in their desperate efforts to save their doomed way of life. We learn that Tull has sold much of the timber on his nonarable land to pay off a mortgage; his friends find this admirable in their exceptionally industrious neighbor, but they also joke ruefully about the general futility of their lot. "Most folks that logs in this here country, they need a durn good farm to support the sawmill. Or maybe a store," says Cash (143). It's as if the whole natural order of things has gotten reversed, and farming is a mere support for commercial activities. And it's all the more ironic that logging should subsidize farming, since it actually contributes to the natural disasters that befall the farmers, as logging companies strip bare the countryside and leave it vulnerable to flash floods. Although Anse and his neighbors suffer what they consider an act of God, they also sense the connection between taking out the trees and the land's "profound desolation" (143) as it stands covered in floodwater. Anse goes further in his analysis of the farmers' plight, grasping that the problem is fundamentally economic:

> Nowhere in this sinful world can a honest, hardworking man profit. It takes them that runs the stores in the towns, doing no sweating, living off of them that sweats. It aint the hardworking man, the farmer. Sometimes I wonder why we keep at it. It's because there is a reward for us above, where they cant take their autos and such. Every man will be equal there and it will be taken from them that have and give to them that have not by the Lord. (110)

Anse vents working-class resentment here, though he's myopic in identifying the adversary. It's not simply Jefferson bankers and merchants who exploit farmers like him, it's a national economic system that historically positioned southern agriculture as a colonized source of raw material for the northern metropolises of global industrial and commercial empire.

In *Origins of the New South, 1877–1913*, C. Vann Woodward influentially characterized the post-Reconstruction South as a colonial society, devastated by conquest and dependent on the victors' capital and entrepreneurship to construct a "New South." Woodward's assessment has proved both debatable and productive. On the one hand, it underscores a historical function of the South that continued through modern times: the region furnished unprocessed agricultural goods like cotton that were reliant on cheap labor (first in the form of chattel slavery, then in the form of tenancy and peonage) and destined for manufacturing, marketing, and transporting industries located elsewhere. Such relations resemble colonizer-colonized dyads and point to a broader history of New World domestication under European imperialism. The South's economic devastation as a result of emancipation and the loss of a war invited a reconfiguration of dependence on "foreign" capital. Articles by Susan Willis on "The Bear" and *As I Lay Dying* establish the usefulness of economic-dependency theory for understanding Faulkner's South as a colonial periphery to northern metropolis. Not only did the South become a kind of Third World, it functioned literally as a rehearsal for imperial ventures: federal reconstruction of the South gave a taste of the military administration of subjected peoples, including a large free black population. George Handley remarks that the South was the nation's first colony (20). Federal experiences with territorial occupation emboldened colonial acquisitiveness during the Spanish-American War (leading to the nation's first official colonies, in the Philippines); they also stimulated opposition to territorial acquisition across a spectrum of positions—from southern racists who warned against taking yet more people of color into the body politic to moral opponents of racial imperialism like W. E. B. DuBois and John Dewey. At the same time, any conceptualization of the South as a United States colony is complicated by the internal colonization of slaves (and later freed blacks) practiced by white southern elites. People of color in the South could also understand their dilemma on a global stage of racial anticolonialism. Recent studies of the New Negro movement as drawing together southern and worldwide anticolonial black nationalism spell out these connections. Aimé Césaire, for example, the Martinican author of the incandescently indignant *Discourse on Colonialism*, began, though never completed, a dissertation at the Sorbonne on the role of the South in Harlem Renaissance writing.[4]

As I Lay Dying is Faulkner's most probing exploration of the effects of modernization on the rural poor. The currents of change he identifies are hallmarks of modernity. Arun Appadurai in *Modernity at Large*, a study of global modernization, argues that populations in underdeveloped countries experience modernity most forcefully as a new capacity to relocate globally, spurred by new connections to mainstream hegemonic culture through electronic media. This intersection of migration and mass communication may be seen as principal components of the forces disarranging (and deranging) the Bundren family. The death of the farm wife precipitates a move to town—even a visit like theirs anticipates the flow of urbanization in the modern South. Town represents new opportunities for consumption: the toy train Vardaman wants and the false teeth Anse covets, the modern abortion medication Dewey Dell has been sent for, the graphophone Cash longs to have, even the imported bananas that substitute for less attainable goods. Some of these products are known to the Bundrens because of the mail-order catalogs that find their way down recently constructed roads. The Bundrens have been contacted by the modern world, not the least traumatic consequence of which has been Darl's being drafted into the army to join the troops fighting in France.

These subsistence farmers find themselves stumbling into a new era of cash and commodities. Cora's comic misadventures in the cake and egg market introduce the desperate farmer's naive schemes for making money: we also have the aptly named Cash falling off a roof during one of his turns as a wage laborer, Jewel working night and day to buy a teenager's dream (some souped-up horsepower of his very own—one of the infamous Snopes spotted ponies), Anse taking a gamble that Addie will last long enough for his boys to make one more wagon run because they so need the three dollars it will bring, the family holding back on summoning Dr. Peabody because Anse doesn't want to spend ten dollars until he absolutely must, the fumbling efforts of Dewey Dell to negotiate an impersonal retail transaction of the most intimate and embarrassing kind (and one that ends in her commodifying her sexuality as the only currency left to her), even Anse counting on the retention of old ways of hospitality and lending to counteract the modern town habits of constant purchase and sale. Cash stages his own resistance to commodification by lavishing his labor freely and limitlessly on the crafting of his mother's coffin. It's precisely because no one will see or care about the quality of the work that Cash is so determined to do it right, to work like a jeweler on the golden boards. To make a beautiful object intended never to pass into economic circulation constitutes the idealism of Cash's artistry, and it takes a stand against the capitalization of all labor. Anse's unfeeling robbery of his own children's money suggests the deepening monetization of personal relations, even if it also hints that the nuclear family has always been a social form keyed primarily to particular economic requirements, in this case the reproduction of a large force of "free" in-house domestic and agricultural labor. Still, whatever the economic origins of the farm family, the massive disruption and sensed disintegration are suffered by its members as a traumatic shock, a shattering of maternal nurture, sense of self, and intimacy.

The Bundrens and their neighbors have been stranded in a "primitive" rural subculture; now they're being pressured to change, and the novel acknowledges how they must strike more "advanced" moderns as only half-evolved grotesques.

Once the family gets to more civilized environs, they're made to look like aliens; a witness in one town reports:

> They came from some place out in Yoknapatawpha county, trying to get to Jefferson with [the corpse]. It must have been like a piece of rotten cheese coming into an ant-hill, in that ramshackle wagon that Albert said folks were scared would fall all to pieces before they could get it out of town, with that home-made box and another fellow with a broken leg lying on a quilt on top of it. (204)

A broken leg that they want to cast in concrete, let's not forget. The strangeness of town ways and the attitude of metropolitan superiority are not lost on these self-conscious rustics. As the cavalcade enters Jefferson, Jewel mistakenly assumes he's been insulted by a townsman and fumes, "Thinks because he's a goddamn town fellow. . . . Son of a bitch" (230).

What makes *As I Lay Dying* so unsettling is that Faulkner expertly fathoms the contradictory desires and emotions provoked by modernization. On the one hand, precious things will be lost. Dewey Dell's touching, private moment with her mother's dead body captures the genuine, if largely inarticulate, grief that the whole family, the whole community, suffers in this epitome of a disappearing way of life. The farmers' lamentation over the land is answered by the women who sing hymns at Addie's funeral: "In the thick air it's like their voices come out of the air, flowing together and on in the sad, comforting tunes. When they cease it's like they hadn't gone away" (91–92). Addie's long dying reminds Dr. Peabody of a regional fate: "That's the one trouble with this country: everything, weather, all, hangs on too long. Like our rivers, our land: opaque, slow, violent; shaping and creating the life of man in its impalpable and brooding image" (45). His remark isn't about the turning of an era, but he is mindful of how conditions are changing, elsewhere mentioning the "worry about this country being deforested someday" (42).

The transformations of modernity produce severe trauma for the rural poor. Darl, the one Bundren who has had the most experience with the modern age, ultimately suffers a mental breakdown. He has fought in the war, and his psychological torment may perhaps have some connection to the sort of trauma modern psychiatry began to diagnose as shell shock in veterans of combat. Like Virginia Woolf's Septimus Smith in *Mrs. Dalloway*, Darl is afflicted by some sort of self-alienation. He gets inside other folks' heads but hardly seems to have a home mentality of his own. He claims he doesn't have a mother. Like Quentin Compson, he possesses an ego riddled with existential doubt:

> Beyond the unlamped wall I can hear the rain shaping the wagon that is ours, the load that is no longer theirs that felled and sawed it nor yet theirs that bought it and which is not ours either, lie on our wagon though it does, since only the wind and the rain shape it only to Jewel and me,

> that are not asleep. And since sleep is is-not and rain and wind are *was*, it is not. Yet the wagon *is*, because when the wagon is *was*, Addie Bundren will not be. And Jewel *is*, so Addie Bundren must be. And then I must be, or I could not empty myself for sleep in a strange room. And so if I am not emptied yet, I am *is*. (80)

Here Darl already manifests schizophrenic tendencies that will surface more pronouncedly later, when his family arranges for his incarceration and he begins to speak of himself in the third person. Darl loses his purchase on the life he has known, his mother's death somehow letting the linchpin of identity slip. The family's centrifugal whirl toward cash mania and consumption seems to underlie Darl's addling. Notice how it is the peculiar suspended nonexistence of the load of lumber—in transit among owners and conveyers on the market—that precipitates Darl's confusion. It's as if notions of the Cartesian self as the property of consciousness, based on the simple idea of things being used and owned by those who make them, have been unmoored by the fetishistic mysteries of commodity exchange.

It's not surprising, then, that the simplest Bundren, Vardaman, instinctively finds consolation in an act of primitive fetishism. Catching his first fish the same day his mother dies prompts him to associate the two events magically. Hence the bleeding fish becomes a totem of his mother, her vanished body commemorated in the flesh of the fish "cooked and et" (67), like some homemade Eucharistic rite, her coffin a fetish object that briefly turns into a fish that has to be retrieved, Osiris-like, from the waters of the flood. Anse complains that all his troubles began when roads invaded the countryside, making bodies lurch into unnatural motion. Cora Tull edges into new marketing ventures with her cake business but is so completely befuddled by commodity logic that she fails to assign any monetary value to her own labor, accepting the mysterious abstraction of price as the only index of expense. Much like the Compsons, then, the characters of *As I Lay Dying* sustain reverses that cry out for consolation and recompense. Both *As I Lay Dying* and *The Sound and the Fury* figure social setbacks in the loss of a matrix figure, and both suggest fetishistic reflexes of denial. In *As I Lay Dying*, though, Faulkner can see more clearly how the loss of a way of life cherished by one group actually provides desperately sought-after opportunities for others. He captures the grotesque ambivalence provoked by modernity: a sense of both mourning and adventure, orphanhood and independence, self-commodification and consumer empowerment.

Not everyone in *As I Lay Dying* thinks the past is worth immortalizing. Some who have enabled southern fantasies of organic, well-ordered families and communities—many of them women—prove to be seething with rage and resentment at the sacrifices demanded of them. *As I Lay Dying* has appealed powerfully to at least two well-defined global audiences: those who read in it a sharply felt, sympathetic effort to render laboring-class poverty under broadly colonial circumstances and those who hear in it a male artist's eloquent determination to give voice to the hard lives of women. The novel has inspired numerous feminist and anticolonial literary imitations as well as trenchant critical interpretations deriving from both movements. For the moment, however, we might focus on the way Faulkner figures out the connection between the abuse of women and the abuse of agricultural laborers under global capitalism. The shock of *As I Lay Dying* lies in the sound of a dead woman talking. Addie's section opens a space for her utterance in a way that *The Sound and the Fury* does not for Caddy. Addie's complaint speaks for all those whose lives have been ruined by the lordship of others: "I could just remember how my father used to say that the reason for living was to get ready to stay dead a long time" (169). For Faulkner's women especially but also for "weak" sons like Quentin, "father says" is the kiss of death. In *Absalom, Absalom!* Rosa Coldfield is another father-haunted ghost. Addie's fury at all the men in her life originates in their repeated efforts to use her for their own purposes. Anse professes love but turns out to practice it as a hard reproductive regimen. When Addie tries to call a halt to her relentless self-division child by child ("I was three now," she thinks when she learns she's pregnant with her second), Anse crudely corrects her: "you an me aint nigh done chapping yet, with just two" (173). What Addie wants is to recover a sense of her own self; in her affair with Reverend Whitfield she exults in the prospect that "I would be I" while her husband has been "negatived" as "not-Anse" (174), made "dead" by her betrayal (173).

Addie understands that a discourse of masculine power long precedes her existence and is responsible for insisting that she yield to its authority. When she tries to recall the "shape of my body where I used to be a virgin," all that occurs to her is that it "is in the shape of a   and I couldn't think *Anse*, couldn't remember *Anse*" (173). That Addie's most intimate space should in effect be colonized by male command evokes again the connection between female bodies and the land. Addie underscores the syndrome by naming her child Dewey Dell, and it's worth remembering that the word *colony* comes from "*colon*," a Latin word for *farmer*. Faulkner senses the deep identity between masculine conquests of foreign spaces and domestic places, the prerogatives that seize lands and also women's bodies as territorial possessions. In this context, *As I Lay Dying* can be seen as a successor to Joseph Conrad's *Heart of Darkness*, in which the confidence of an expansionist British empire and the reassertion of endangered Victorian masculinity coincide in the figures of a domestic fiancée and a bride of the jungle (see J. Smith). I've often taught *To the Lighthouse* with these two novels, a combination that for me has helped explain the preoccupation with domination that irradiates Woolf's great novel of modernity. Mrs. Ramsay explicitly links her regard for Victorian female propriety with a reverence for imperial command (think of her recollection of her infatuation with a colonial administrator and of Leonard Woolf's own background as an emissary of the crown in India). At the same time, Woolf allows the ambivalence of domestic and foreign ruling mentality to fissure her text. It's Mr. Ramsay's pitiful mouthings of British military failure (from Tennyson's "The Charge of the Light Brigade," about a mishap in the Crimean War) that underscore his weakness as the male head of house; both kinds of failure indict the masculinist fantasies subtending English Victorian culture. If Addie at least turns her dying into a form of belated revenge, she's perpetrating a kind of silent anticolonial terrorism, striking at the will of oedipal power. Gilles Deleuze and Félix Guattari observe that the anticolonialist should be anti-oedipalism's best friend.[5] As many subsequent subaltern and so-called Third World readers have sensed, *As I Lay Dying* illuminates the alignment of western colonialisms: domestic, of the female body; regional, of the rural South; global, of the laboring world's producing classes.[6] In the disruptions caused by modern transformations, protests against colonial domination erupt, and confusing but instructive contradictions become visible, such as the double position of men like Anse Bundren, who are exploited by town merchants while treating their wives like mules.

Dewey Dell attempts the next stage of female defiance of oedipal law by seeking to terminate her pregnancy. Though she is blocked by men like Moseley, who advises her to entrust her problem to "your pa or your brothers if you have any or the first man you come to in the road" (202), she goes as far as she dares, even trading her body for pills she knows won't really emancipate her. Still, her determination outlines a course of action for women unwilling to reproduce their confinement without at least some effort to resist. Likewise, Jewel rebels against Anse's authority, compensating himself for the way fathers monopolize mothers by finding a substitute source of gratification. Even Cash chafes at Anse's meddling, but this quiet son's need for balance helps him adjust to the reengineering of life under modernity and the renovation of oedipal order: "Meet Mrs Bundren" (261). Seduced by what he hears as the entirely lifelike reproduction of music by the phonograph, Cash accepts the costs of updating. He accommodates himself to Darl's committal to the asylum and gets rewarded when Anse's new wife brings as part of her dowry exactly the sort of graphophone he coveted before his father stole his cash for "them teeth" (111).

Faulkner imagines the numerous individual styles by which people engage the conflicting components of an event as complex as modernization. His earlier experimentation with perspectival narrative and first-person discourse in *The Sound and the Fury* gives him a flexible instrument for rendering diverse, often ambivalent states of mind. In one respect, Faulkner achieves an unprecedented range of identification with different personalities and temperaments. He partners his language with the sensibilities of an inarticulate hill farmer, a depressed wife, a cheerful Protestant saint, an illiterate eight-year-old, an overwhelmed pregnant teenager, a furious bastard son, a clairvoyant schizophrenic, and so on. Each narrative creates the impression of a distinct human voice belonging to a real person who otherwise might mean nothing to cultivated readers beyond being an abstract illustration of rural poverty. At the same time, each section also sounds like Faulkner's own voice, a highly stylized, emphatically literary rendering of sensibilities too culturally impoverished to command such aesthetic resources. Dewey Dell compares the big-bellied Dr. Peabody to her own heaviness: "He is his guts and I am my guts. And I am Lafe's guts. That's it" (60). But also, she thinks, "The cow breathes upon my hips and back, her breath warm, sweet, stertorous, moaning. The sky lies flat down the slope, upon the secret clumps" (63). In one sense, Faulkner indemnifies these subaltern subjects by giving them access to the richest language he possesses. On the other, he veers toward speaking for them, which puts him in the position cautioned against by Gayatri Chakravorty Spivak, who points out the inauthenticity, however well motivated, of representing those whom colonialism has silenced and whose vernacular identities and languages it has refused to recognize.[7] Here we can appreciate Faulkner for staging such complexities so uncompromisingly.

In much the same way, we can see the perspectival narrative structure as both replicating and trying to overcome the centrifugal tendencies of family and even the individual self. The Bundrens are rapidly degenerating into a clump of isolated wage-earning consumers, each pursuing his or her own interest, cooperating only as far as their selfish objectives may be advanced. On the other hand, Faulkner takes these modern monadic individuals and manages to incorporate them around their central lack, putting them into communication with one another and folding them into a single narrative that they execute as a united entity. The novel imagines a much more sustained merging of individuals than, for example, the fleeting moments Woolf salvages from the flux in *To the Lighthouse*. It is this kind of endurance *despite itself* that distinguishes the Bundrens as a kind of heroic family, or at least one capable of pulling off a comic denouement. As the Bundrens gamely recover their balance at the end of *As I Lay Dying*, we realize that the characters who survive have always been all about gratifying desire rather than mourning loss and about the future, however belatedly arrived at, rather than the past. Even Addie understands this, making the burial of her corpse the matter of a protracted journey down the road ahead. Once we get to town, the novel shows its hand: we never get to the presumptive climax of an actual burial scene but instead witness a frenzy of acquisition, the most notable success being Anse's unexplained procurement of a new Mrs. Bundren to replace the one he wore out. Like many other members of the modern workforce in the 1910s and 1920s, southern farmers were being converted from producers into wage laborers, their salaries expected to fuel an emergent consumer culture. The personal disorientation and social disintegration sustained by newly mobile, mass media–shaped, nationally conscious populations were balanced by a new sense of enfranchisement ("I reckon we can stop to buy something same as airy other man," Anse declares [204]) as well as new sources of consolation ("But now I can get them teeth. That will be a comfort. It will" [111]). The novel shrewdly observes how modernity goes about trying to fill the holes it has itself dug.

In 1930 Faulkner foresees that while the family was once primarily a unit of labor production, the modern family will be an engine of consumption. It's instructive to follow *As I Lay Dying* with a novel like *White Noise*, by Don DeLillo, a book that's proved to be the ultimate word on the postwar culture of consumption. A family like the Gladneys seems engineered for nothing except acquisition. From the brilliant depiction of "the day of station wagons" (5) at the beginning of the College-on-the-Hill's fall semester—with its glut of consumables spewing out of crammed family vehicles—through the torrent of compulsive consumption, DeLillo records the American way of buying, and the novel's families represent a stage of evolution beyond the Bundrens. Reassembled units of discarded parents and offspring team to forage shopping malls, inflating themselves with fleeting self-importance and gratification, only to retreat to furtive acts of eating, watching, dreaming, in altered states of consumer enchantment, as unappeasable feelings of futility attack. There's no filling the vacancies that spell death to these monads of denial, and DeLillo sets the challenge of rediscovering where the sources of mystery, nature, and faith might be hiding, and how one might not be able to use a credit card to get them.

The next time I teach *As I Lay Dying,* I plan to carry the question of the postmodern family as an apparatus of late capitalist consumption into a consideration of the present era's greatest mass media fiction: *The Sopranos*. As a study of the contemporary culture of consumption, *The Sopranos* picks up where *White Noise* (a book by our foremost Italian American novelist, after all) leaves off. I'm not sure there's ever been a work of drama in which characters speak more lines with their mouths full: every show exhibits the orgy of consumption that American affluence has become. Characters do little but lurch from table to table, seemingly putting on pounds as you watch, the upper end of the scales held down by the obese wife and daughter of Johnny "Sack" Sacramoni. Tony Soprano's so hungry, he doesn't even wait to get dressed in the morning before groping his way to the fridge, a bathrobed zombie at first light, and he ends the day a disheveled "snack shovel" drifting off into the TV-lit night. As the families gorge, attempts to resist prove feeble: Christopher Moltisanti, who fails repeatedly to keep his orifices shut until Tony finally cures his overindulgence once and for all; Anthony, Jr., whose disgust with the imperatives to eat, to buy, to make money, to brutalize everything on the planet—and the planet too—at first makes him heartsick, then pathologizes him, and finally evaporates into cooptation when the next best thing comes along (a film job and a BMW). Massive consumption of this sort inscribes a logic of massive waste—the depredation of the soul inseparable from the desecration of the environment, emblematized in the show as industrial New Jersey. Tony doesn't see that waste is the other end of consumption, even though he makes his living managing it, an occupation DeLillo freights with far more insistent significance in *Underworld*, which is the thematic sequel to *White Noise*.

The underworld Tony Soprano represents seems to be a criminalized version of the American dream, *The Sopranos* taking its place in the subgenre of Mafia fiction that works the insubstantial line between legitimate and illegal realizations of national success. But for all the early preoccupation among viewers with the ethnic realism of David Chase's depiction of northeastern mafioso subculture, the sociological interests of the show were always elsewhere. No more than

Faulkner's Bundrens are exclusively Mississippian farmers, Chase's Sopranos are hardly just Italian mobsters. The conceit of the show reverses the direction of a stale analogy: it's not that Italian American mobs function like extended suburban families but that extended suburban families function like mobs. Tony is a hard-driving businessman; Carmela, a frustrated, terrified dependent; their offspring, conscience-stricken "aristo-kids." Who wouldn't be depressed? Left desolate by the death of his own married-to-the-mob mother, Tony characteristically tries to fill the void with things, instructing his family what it means to go after what you want, fight to the death to get it and keep it, torture your enemies till they cry uncle. The Soprano family isn't America's criminal element writ large; it's all the rest of us writ large. We've become them—as might be suggested by the spectacle of plutocractic oil dynasties that dispatch soldiers to dispose of rival clans, that declare war on those deranged by the fear of our depthless greed and materialism, or that try to talk sense into a public that sometimes gets disturbed by reports of massive human suffering just beyond the mansion gates. As in the closing scene of *As I Lay Dying*, *The Sopranos* ends with the reunion of the family after all (a Meadow for a Dewey Dell), still tense with anxiety about the unknown future but at least poised to resume the pleasurable amnesia of consumption.

NOTES

Portions of this essay appeared in the author's *William Faulkner: Seeing through the South*. They are used with the permission of the publisher.

[1] For an account of declining farm conditions and the growth of towns in Lafayette County, Mississippi, see Doyle, especially chapters 9–10, "Rednecks" and "The Town."

[2] See Stott for an account of how the depiction of poor whites was a strategic choice by the directors of the federal Works Project Administration, who intended to make it easier for better-off whites to sympathize with those who were suffering. *As I Lay Dying* anticipates the eventual photodocumentary tradition that includes works like Erskine Caldwell's novels *Tobacco Road* (1932) and *God's Little Acre* (1933); Caldwell's volume with the photographer Margaret Bourke White, *You Have Seen Their Faces* (1937); and James Agee and Walker Evans's *Let Us Now Praise Famous Men* (1941). Faulkner's solution to the problem of representing mentalities and sensibilities so different from his own proved idiosyncratic. Caldwell tended to foreground the objectification of the poor in the national imaginary, while Agee and Evans longed to represent the subjectivities of the poor by drawing them into dialogues real and imagined with agents of representation like themselves.

[3] *Editors' note*: For a view of the Bundrens as tenant farmers, see the essay by Deborah Clarke in this volume.

[4] See Edwards. Numerous essays in the collection *Look Away! The U.S. South in New World Studies* (Smith and Cohn) take up postcolonial analyses of southern writers. Hosam Aboul-Ela's *Other South* argues for the greater suitability of indigenous Third World postcolonial theory to an understanding of Faulkner.

[5] Speaking of Frantz Fanon, Deleuze and Guattari remark, "The revolutionary is the first to have the right to say: 'Oedipus? Never heard of it'" (96). For a reading of the novel through Deleuzian anti-oedipalism, see O'Donnell, "Spectral Road."

[6] In his novel *The Ship*, Jabra I. Jabra organizes a perspectival narrative around a set of diasporic Arab passengers on a cruise vessel to convey the keen sense of loss suffered by Palestinians for their homeland. Toni Morrison replicates Addie's stream-of-consciousness lament for her lost life when she imagines the unlived life of Sethe's dead infant: at the middle of *Beloved*, as at the heart of *As I Lay Dying*, there appears a hypothetical posthumous memoir: for Morrison, of Beloved's passage from Africa, her mothering by Sethe, her sisterhood with Denver, in unison as a family terribly separated. Suzan-Lori Parks forges a virtual pastiche of *As I Lay Dying* in her first novel, *Getting Mother's Body*, but "postmodernizes" its themes by emphasizing the recovery of the buried mother's body and an attendant rehabilitation of once prohibited female desires, particularly, in this instance, same-sex love. (*Editors' note*: See Cedric Gael Bryant in this volume for further discussion of the intertextual relationship between *As I Lay Dying* and Parks's *Getting Mother's Body*.)

[7] Spivak's main point goes beyond the question of how subjected people may represent their own lives. Even the respectful request that such populations represent themselves (to an interested but typically hegemonic audience) replicates the dynamics of colonial power. Spivak's essay "Can the Subaltern Speak?" was first read at a conference in 1988; it has been revised several times, and an expanded form appears in her *A Critique of Postcolonial Reason*, ch. 3, "History" (198–311).

"Inspiriting Influences": Textual Performance in William Faulkner's *As I Lay Dying* and Suzan-Lori Parks's *Getting Mother's Body*

Cedric Gael Bryant

> To write is to blacken whiteness, to fill in gaps, to dress wounds. All texts aspire to the compactness of living bodies. But here the body is dismembered, the text bursts asunder, the discourse falters and gapes, as if to remind us of the lure and lability of all writing and to let us glimpse, in the interstices between words, where nothing can be seen, what words can neither say nor give up saying—to make us see what they fail to make us hear. . . . (Bleikasten, *Ink* 159)

> Don't the Great Wheel keep rolling along
> Don't the Great Wheel keep rolling along
> I stopped in yr town this morning,
> But tonight, this gal, she's gotta be gone.
> Don't the Great Wheel keep rolling right along. (Parks 255)

The felicitous trope, "inspiriting influences," coined by Michael Awkward to describe the creative, intergenerational kinship among African American women writers, applies with equal felicity across gender and race to reading and teaching William Faulkner's *As I Lay Dying* and Suzan-Lori Parks's seriocomic riff on it, *Getting Mother's Body.*[1] The two novels provoke the reader to perform multiple roles by constantly shifting among different bodies as the voices and structure expand. What develops is a phenomenology between the reader and the text bound up with questions about the relation between "saying something" and "doing something"[2] that inform both action and thought. The dramatic positioning and reversals in these novels multiply interpretative possibilities and engage readers in acts of repetition and revision as different ways of seeing evolve. My approach to teaching *As I Lay Dying* and *Getting Mother's Body* stresses the signifying and inspiriting intertexualities in verbal constructions (symbol, metaphor) and theme (social and moral critique) inferable from the interplay of beginnings and endings in each novel.

Edward Said contends that making meaning is bound up with beginnings that "indicate, clarify, or define a *later* time, place, or action" in discursive forms such as novels (5). His assertion links the "idea of precedence and/or priority" (4–5) to the inevitability of endings or closure—the later time and ultimately final place or action in a novel's structure. "The beginning is the first point (in time, space, or action) of an accomplishment or process that has duration and meaning. *The beginning, then, is the first step in the intentional production of meaning*" (5). However, the inverse of what Said calls "a common sense understanding about 'beginnings'" (4) is equally tenable because the production of meaning is also invested in a novel's "closural strategies" (Torgovnick 12–13); the "sense making" requirements of fiction and myth (Kermode 39); and "the process of anticipation and retrospection" (Iser 290), which are all dependent upon a narrative's end and its dynamic relation to its middle and beginning. Such patterns, Wolfgang Iser suggests, constantly compel the reader to read backward, phenomenologically making meaning of the gaps or indeterminancies formed by the anticipatory function of beginnings and the retrospective function of endings. Switching "texts" for a moment, the reader who is also an avid filmgoer will recognize these strategies in M. Night Shyamalan's third film, *The Sixth Sense.* In the final dramatic minutes, Shyamalan and the cinematographer Tak Fujimoto flash back to scenes, dialogue, and images in the middle and beginning—for example, the color red and the sudden sensation of cold—to make explicit what is implied throughout the film but what the audience may have missed: the character from whose point of view the action is presented is dead. This crucial fact becomes shockingly clear to many viewers only through retrospection, the process of expanding interpretive possibilities, or filling the gaps, that seeing the film backward creates. Faulkner's and Parks's novels perform these intertextual possibilities in inspiriting ways that foreground their thematic and structural affinities and differences, which are expressed in how and what words and actions signify.

This relation between saying and doing—between words and actions—is performed by Anse Bundren, the feckless patriarch of *As I Lay Dying*. The promise he gives to Addie to bury her body in Jefferson is contractual, but its successful execution depends on both the physical and mental actions and the words of others inside and outside the Bundren family. The "I" that precedes Anse's promise and such constructions as "me and the boys" are grammatical misdirections leading away from the truth about Anse's ability to complete any action solely on personal initiative or energy. This underscores the unreliability of saying and words alone: "I promised my word me and the boys would get her there quick as mules could walk it, so she could rest quiet. . . . No man ever misliked it more" (19). Anse's speech is full of irreconcilable binaries, such as doing the act quickly while walking and the declaratory, contractual "I" that makes promises dependent on the performance of others.

Saying and doing has an important corollary in a dramatically different, nonverbal performativity that resides in the gaps or, in Bleikasten's words, "the interstices between words, where nothing can be seen, what words can neither say nor give up saying—to make us see what they fail to make us hear . . . " (*Ink* 159). Interstitial spaces give *As I Lay Dying* its subtle and dramatic form in the opening scene:

> Jewel and I come up from the field, following the path in single file. Although I am fifteen feet ahead of him, anyone watching us from the cottonhouse can see Jewel's frayed and broken straw hat a full head above my own. . . .
>
> When we reach [the cottonhouse] I turn and follow the path which circles the house. Jewel, fifteen feet behind me, looking straight ahead, steps in a single stride through the window. Still staring straight ahead, his pale eyes like wood set into his wooden face, he crosses the floor in four strides with the rigid gravity of a cigar store Indian dressed in patched overalls and endued with life from the hips down, and steps in a single stride through the opposite window and into the path again just as I come around the corner. In single file and five feet apart and Jewel now in front, we go on up the path toward the foot of the bluff. (3–4)

This scene is performative for the ways the visual geometry of Jewel and Darl walking single-file reveals each brother's essential nature and temperament. Darl's intuitive sensitivity to the phenomenal world directs him *around* the cottonhouse, while Jewel's aggressive resoluteness and impetuosity propel him *through* the cottonhouse. The novel begins with a dramatic but silent performance of character, which is inextricably bound up with fate and gives the motion and positioning of bodies a profoundly prescient effect.

Similar to a medieval dumb show, the narrative form of address at the beginning of *As I Lay Dying* and at pivotal places throughout it is pantomimic. Like Darl, Jewel is a mime who silently dramatizes his character, especially his intractability and aggressive single-mindedness, wherein action is always a straight line between two fixed points, the shortest, most practical distance. Cleanth Brooks calls Jewel "the high-strung man of action, impatient, ardent, flamboyant, and heroic" (*Yoknapatawpha Country* 145). Viewing the outbuilding that stands in his path as a nonnegotiable object seems not to enter Jewel's consciousness. He simply moves through it "staring straight ahead, his pale eyes like wood set into his wooden face" (4). Darl, who is called "queer" by Cora Tull (24) and also by Vernon Tull, has a sensitivity to the natural world and seems to see and know more than others. Tull says:

> [Darl] is looking at me. He dont say nothing; just looks at me with them queer eyes of hisn that makes folks talk. I always say it aint never been what he done so much or said or anything so much as how he looks at you. It's like he had got into the inside of you, someway. Like somehow you was looking at yourself and your doings outen his eyes. (125)

In the opening scene, Darl's motion around the cottonhouse makes a spatial allowance for things outside his own being; Darl acts in ways that acknowledge diversity and mystery in the world. He seems, initially, incapable of ignoring the physical presence of any person or object he encounters, even a simple cottonhouse.

This is also a scene that constructs and simultaneously deconstructs character, that compels the reader to interpret and then, based on the paradoxical symmetry and asymmetry this visual geometry creates, revise what seems to be revealed about Darl's and Jewel's temperament and nature. In the classroom, where the experience of ideas is bound up with the paradox of saying something and doing something, this dynamic can be produced by posing questions that invite students to step beyond comfortable, seemingly unassailable readings of the text. Here are a few statements and questions to consider: Isn't transforming a literal window into a figurative door, as Jewel does, more creative than simply making a half circle around the cottonhouse? Darl's choice to make the half circle may be a more sensitive recognition of the reality of things beyond his own existence and ego. If so, what value or advantage does Darl's way of being in the world have in the novel? Jewel's "plumb-line" straight movement and "rigid gravity" (3, 4) are, perhaps, no less poetic for the imaginative way they transform windows into doors. Moreover, Jewel's actions may be more efficient, economical, and practical than Darl's, as the role reversal and spacing when their single line re-forms after the cottonhouse suggests: "In single file and five feet apart and Jewel now in front, we go on up the path toward the foot of the bluff." Doesn't Jewel's unyielding straight line bring him to his objective in less time and, possibly, with less energy expended than Darl's indirection? If so, what value or advantage does Jewel's way of being in the world have in the novel?

Perhaps more than any other novel by Faulkner, *As I Lay Dying* makes visualization the medium of action, and the reader becomes both observer and participant. Seeing is intimately bound up with doing for characters and readers, and when the latter are also students, the classroom can become a dynamic space in which to perform the text. It is easy to miss the subtleties of character revealed about Jewel and Darl unless the opening scene is visualized as performance. Two students can represent Darl and Jewel, a desk can be the cottonhouse, another desk can represent Tull's wagon farther away, and one more desk, farther still, can stand for the Bundren house, where the sound of Cash's saw and the "Chuck. Chuck. Chuck. of the adze" can be heard, as Cash builds Addie's coffin outside her window (5). Performance helps the students—who have not yet read enough to comprehend the plot or know the personalities—see how this seemingly simple beginning introduces the character traits that will produce and resolve conflict throughout the novel.

As I Lay Dying deploys a second model of deconstructive thinking that challenges the reader's subject-object interpretation of characters predicated on the dramatic display, or absence, of powerful feelings—that is, on words and actions. Like the first scene, the second one, which objectifies Cora Tull's thoughts about Darl and Jewel, is directed toward the reader of the text, who possesses greater information than Cora does. Surmising that Darl can't bear to be separated from Addie or doesn't want to go on the errand to deliver wood for three dollars for fear of her dying before he returns, Cora misinterprets reality:

> It was the sweetest thing I ever saw. It was like [Darl] knew he would never see [Addie] again, that Anse Bundren was driving him from his mother's death bed, never to see her in this world again. I always said Darl was different from those others. I always said he was the only one of them that had his mother's nature, had any natural affection. (21)

Cora is equally mistaken about Jewel.

> Not that Jewel. . . . Not him to come and tell her goodbye. Not him to miss a chance to make that extra three dollars at the price of his mother's goodbye kiss. A Bundren through and through, loving nobody, caring for nothing except how to get something with the least amount of work. (21–22)

What Jewel really wants for himself and his mother is to retreat to some solitary place away from the loud noise of death and dying and away from public scrutiny, like Quentin Compson in *The Sound and the Fury*. For Quentin, retreat is a clean, quiet corner of Hell where his disgraced sister, Caddy, and he can be together; for Jewel, it's a "high hill," with Addie protected from people who stare at her coffin as he rolls "rocks down the hill at their faces, picking them up and throwing them down the hill faces and teeth and all by God until she was quiet and not that goddamn adze going One lick less. One lick less and we could be quiet" (15). These misconstructions of reality are gaps in the text created by complex personalities who instinctively distrust words and privilege action because, as Addie opines, "words go straight up in a thin line, quick and harmless" (173); for her, words are "no good; . . . dont ever fit even what they are trying to say at" (171) and are "just a shape to fill a lack" (172). The paradox implicit throughout *As I Lay Dying* is that action may be just as subject to misreading as language is.

Brooks has expressed the possibility of reversing the binary opposition that informs Cora's biases:

> Darl represents . . . the detachment and even callousness which we sometimes associate with the artist. Darl is pure perception. . . . In general, in spite of his poetry, he is a rationalizing and deflating force—the antiheroic intelligence. (*Yoknapatawpha Country* 145)

Then Brooks, as though he were reading the text as a Derridean rather than as an American formalist critic writing in the early 1960s, reverses the terms of the opposition by centering Jewel:

> Indeed, though we are disposed to think of Darl as being the poet of the group, it might be argued that Jewel represents more truly the poetic

> temperament, though his is the poetry associated with high-heartedness and the heroic gesture—the poetry of action rather than that of contemplation. (146)

At a critical moment in the novel, this "high-heartedness," "heroic gesture," and economy of energy enable Jewel to dive repeatedly into the rushing river after the coffin-bearing wagon is broadsided by a log and attempt to recover Cash's valuable tools. Jewel does this while his siblings and father look on helplessly and safely from the shore.

As I Lay Dying and *Getting Mother's Body* exemplify what Awkward calls "a paradigmatic system of explicit or implied repetition of, or allusion to, signs, codes, or figures within a cultural form such as the novel" (5). Although both texts are novels, each is intertexually linked to drama as a cultural form, like the award-winning stage productions Suzan-Lori Parks has written and directed.[3] Moreover, the signs, codes, or figures the novels share have stage properties, especially as dramatic monologues conflating soliloquy, staging, and comic effect.

Beyond the questions these two novels raise about perception and language, *Getting Mother's Body* makes race central to Faulkner's cautionary modernist tale about the fragmentation and bonding of family. Faulkner paired race with class struggle dramatically in *The Sound and the Fury* but elected to marginalize it in favor of class and caste themes in *As I Lay Dying*. Reading *Getting Mother's Body* and *As I Lay Dying* together affirms the difference that race, class, gender, and caste make to what Wallace Stevens, in "Of Modern Poetry," calls "finding / What will suffice" to survive in the twentieth century. Moreover, while Parks's novel repeats Faulkner's by affirming the possibilities of language to both reveal and conceal meaning through the multiple first-person voices that narrate *As I Lay Dying*, it revises the relation between gender and language by assigning the principal responsibilities for narrating to Billy Beede, whose voice and consciousness inform the lives of the other black characters by mediating, summarizing, conjecturing. Addie Bundren, like Caddy Compson in *The Sound and the Fury*, is narratively mediated through the consciousness of others—mostly men—and she does not enter the novel dramatically and in the first person until the final third. Reading *Getting Mother's Body* as a repetition and revision of the gender politics both novels are invested in enlarges this shared subject by adding race and exploring it in a late, rather than early, modernist moment.

Getting Mother's Body begins with a performative act that, like *As I Lay Dying*'s opening scene, is gestural and not spoken by Billy Beede and her boyfriend, Snipes; however, unlike Faulkner's opening scene, it is graphically sexual. Arriving too late to watch Billy Beede and Snipes "going at it" in the front seat of his car, Laz Jackson is filled with regret: "I wished I coulda caught them doing it. If I coulda caught them doing it, then my anger woulda come up and I woulda tolt Snipes that Billy Beede belongs to me and I woulda been so mad I mighta maybe kilt him" (13). A few pages later, Laz embodies the first construction of "as I lay dying," as he lies in the middle of the road waiting for Billy Beede, whom he is pining for, to walk past. "Whut the hell you laying there for?" Billy says. "I'm dead," Laz replies (14). Laz also demonstrates a version of the visual geometry in *As I Lay Dying*'s opening scene: "I sit up, rising from the dead. If I had me a car and was sitting in it, the way I'm sitting would be towards Midland" (14). Laz is lying supine in the road and on a north-south plane with his feet pointed toward Billy Beede (and Midland) as she approaches him. Billy stops as she reaches Laz's head. At this point, the line of sight changes from horizontal to vertical, which forces Billy to pull her housecoat tight so Laz can't invade her privacy. This seriocomic scene performs the oppositions, contrasts, distance, and tensions between Billy and Laz that, at the end of the novel, dissolve happily into their marriage. The beginning here, as in *As I Lay Dying*, anticipates—and in an important sense determines—the "closural" shape of the novel by performing the character traits (erotic desire, an indefatigable sense of hope, Laz's self-sacrificial willlingness to do anything to secure Billy's affections, and Billy's stubborn determination to make a life for herself) that will, again as in *As I Lay Dying*, create and resolve conflict.

Billy and Laz's relationship is also, in Awkward's terms, a repetition and revision of Dewey Dell and Lafe's affair in *As I Lay Dying*, which only approximates the marital closure that Parks's comically Shakespearean plot richly fulfills. In doing so, *Getting Mother's Body* uses parody to revise *As I Lay Dying* by removing its ambivalence about love and its ambiguity about marriage. Parks's novel is ultimately an unironic celebration of love, marriage, and loyalty that critiques Addie's pessimistic worldview as well as the precipitous courting of the new "Mrs Bundren" before Addie has been properly interred or a respectful interval of grieving has concluded. Unlike the uncertainties surrounding Dewey Dell and Lafe's relationship, there is no ambiguity about Laz's desire to marry Billy, no breach of the decorum Anse commits, no question about Laz's assuming parental care of another man's child or his ability to meet Billy's high ideals of family. *Getting Mother's Body* radically revises the dominant, patriarchal distribution of marital authority in *As I Lay Dying* by substituting the more equitable and harmonious partnership Billy Beede and Laz Jackson forge.

Both *As I Lay Dying* and *Getting Mother's Body* have a Shakespearean "all's well that ends well" closural strategy that restores order over chaos and affirms love, life, family, and marriage. Notably, the restoration of family values is codified in two types of blood kinship—one based on family, the other on race. The Bundrens stick together, despite grave dysfunctional differences, *because* they are Bundrens, whose shared familial identity is their principal defense against their collective misfortunes and the burden of Anse, the "luckless" head of the family (18, 42). The Beedes bond together less from familial identity than from the recognition that race and racism are shared, experiential corollaries to survival that make collective action essential. This is unmistakably the lesson that the naive and headstrong Homer Beede Rochfoucault learns after he and his uncle Roosevelt are stopped for speeding in Tryler, Texas—and then are arrested and detained for "DWB," driving while black. Being a Beede is almost never seen as a positive trait by either the outside world or the Beedes themselves, who at best take solace in knowing, like Roosevelt Beede, that it means "being able to bear the unbearable" and at worst realize, like Estelle "Star" Beede Rochfoucault, that it means "they will always be grubbing in the dirt" (107, 137). Race and racism, then, are crucial signifying differences in Parks's novel; they threaten but do not negate the comic Shakespearean vision in which chaos is ultimately trumped by the restoration of order and harmony.

By contrast, race and the metaphorical construction of blackness in *As I Lay Dying* are generally a sideshow, minimalist props that serve, for example, to capture emotionally the grotesque arrival of Addie's decaying body in Jefferson: "When we pass the negroes their heads turn suddenly with that expression of shock and instinctive outrage. 'Great God' one says; 'what they got in that wagon?'" (229). In some places in the text, racial blackness is reduced to the simple epithet "nigger," evoked to mark a putative difference that, for the Bundrens, is inherent in nature. The most interesting and significant constructions of race in *As I Lay Dying* are expressed by Vardaman, the youngest child, who uses racial blackness to make an abstract, incomprehensible world more comprehensible. The blackness that circles Addie's coffin, for example, is the metonymic way Vardaman identifies and keeps count of the vultures he fears will "light on her" and on his injured brother, Cash (195). As the number of the vultures fluctuates from four to seven to five, the "little tall black circles" (194) represent Vardaman's childlike challenge to the inevitability of decay and death: "'Do you know what I would do if he tries to light on the wagon again? . . . I wouldn't let him light on her. . . . I wouldn't let him light on Cash, either'" (194–95). Such bravado, however, gives way to fear and astonishment as Vardaman associates both Cash's broken leg and Jewel's burned back with the alienating blackness of "niggers":

> "Does it hurt, Jewel?" I said. "Your back looks like a nigger's, Jewel." I said. Cash's foot and leg looked like a nigger's. Then they broke [the cement cast] off. Cash's leg bled. (224)

Each text answers the rhetorical question Willa Mae Beede poses in her blues composition quoted at the beginning of this essay: "Don't the Great Wheel keep rolling right along[?]" Despite the presence of the politics of race in *Getting Mother's Body* and its virtual absence in *As I Lay Dying*, the answer in both is emphatically yes. The tragicomic worldviews of the novels stress the resilience of family and its irreducible importance to both personal and collective identity, no matter how dysfunctional the relationships or flawed the individuals. "Everybody's got a Hole," Willa Mae announces in "Big Hole Blues," all kinds of them. "Ain't nobody ever lived who don't got a Hole in them somewheres" (30) that needs something particular to fill or to satisfy it: "if a person's got a Hole in they *heart* and you offer them knowledge, you won't be able to sway them none. A Hole-in-the-heart person craves company and kindness, not no book" (31).

As I Lay Dying and *Getting Mother's Body* are full of characters with this kind of hole—what Addie Bundren calls a "lack," which is what words like "love" and "fidelity" are: "just a shape to fill a lack." Addie is precisely this kind of "hole-in-the-heart" person who craves company and kindness when she is courted by Anse. She marries him only to discover "that living was terrible" and "that words are no good; that words dont ever fit even what they are trying to say at."

Addie's is essentially a Derridean view of language, which emphasizes its perpetual ruptures and devolution from meaning. Addie's views about love and happiness are, significantly, a revision, not a repetition, of Willa Mae Beede's blues-informed compositions that say yes emphatically to life and embrace the totality of its emotional and experiential scales. However, the textual place and emotional space where Addie and Willa Mae are most kindred and Willa Mae's "hole" blues meets Addie's conviction that "the reason for living was to get ready to stay dead a long time" (169) are expressed in another of Willa Mae's compositions about loneliness, absence, and holes:

> Deep down in this hole
> I got to thinking
> About the promises I made but ain't been keeping.
> Deep down in this hole
> I got to drinking
> I got drunk and I done cried myself to sleep.
> Deep down in this hole
> It's a cold cold lonesome hole
> I made my bed
> Now I'm laying in it all alone. (218)

Contrary to Ida Cox's confident assertion that "wild women don't worry, wild women don't have the blues" (Barlow 151), Willa Mae does—in death if defiantly not in life—worry, regret, miss, and mourn what has been lost by her choosing to be a wild blues woman. That choice left little space for conventional kinds of female bonding between mother and daughter or unconventional same-sex relationships that Willa Mae's erstwhile lover, Dill Smiles, reluctantly admits to missing.

For the characters in both *As I Lay Dying* and *Getting Mother's Body*, missing—which is a form of mourning—is located in absence-presence and passive-aggressive emotionality. In one of June Flowers Beede's internal monologues, Billy Beede, her niece, asks, "You miss your family?" June's respose is "Yes and no" (173). Billy replies:

> I know whatchu mean. . . . Sometimes I miss Willa Mae. Sometimes I don't. I mean I miss that she ain't alive but I don't wish she was here. If she was here, me and her'd be in the jailhouse and I'd be listening to

> her either cuss that Deputy out or sweet-talk him into bringing her some Lucky Strikes. (173)

Without missing-mourning, which pushes the individual through the both-and of emotional extremes, neither the Beedes nor the Bundrens can emerge on the other side of death into life-affirming patterns that repeat and revise what has been lost and also, as Bleikasten stresses, ensures "the continuance of family beyond the demise" (175) of the one missing. In *As I Lay Dying*, this signifying by repetition and revision is evident in the closural shape of the novel that abruptly introduces the new Mrs. Bundren shortly after Addie Bundren has been laid to rest.

The appearance of Anse's new wife compels the reader to read backward to find the subtle hints of Anse's intentions that may have been missed, such as the protracted time it takes to borrow the tools needed to bury Addie, the ten dollars Anse wheedles out of Dewey Dell, his trip to the barbershop to get a shave, and his mysterious errand—"some business to tend to" (259)—on the morning of the family's return journey home. Interestingly, it is Cash who may have more insight into Anse's intentions than either his family or the reader when he remarks, "I wouldn't mind hearing a little more of that music myself" (259), referring to the phonograph music they all heard the previous day coming from the house where Anse has gone to get the shovels.

As I Lay Dying and *Getting Mother's Body* are centered on the tensions inherent in loss and recovery, absence and presence, and on the inevitability of change. Constancy and the recognition that life depends on stability, especially in the perpetuation of marriage and family, are also articles of faith in both novels. These are among the irreducible truths the Great Wheel reveals about life in its tragicomic extremities and in the banalities of simple existence. The closural design, or sense of an ending, opens up in both novels spaces for these transcendent truths. In doing so, *Getting Mother's Body* and *As I Lay Dying* circle back to the quotations at the beginning of this essay that, to recall Said's thesis about beginnings, mark "*the first step in the international production of meaning*." What Faulkner's and Parks's narratives do, through repetition and revision, mourning and recovery, is "fill in gaps . . . dress wounds" (Bleikasten 159), which are the "holes" where so much that is essential to survival and communal family is missing. For Roosevelt Beede, for example, his lost church and his ability to preach return with the power to say grace and his newfound respect for his wife. For Dill Smiles, who, as Billy rightly says, "got a Hole in her heart" (248) that neither grief nor anger toward Willa Mae can fill, only time can possibly recover her loss. For June Flowers Beede, whose missing leg is a lesser loss than the "face" her husband had when they were young and full of promise, it is "the face I married" (233) that is recovered. "To fill in gaps, to dress wounds" like the hole Billy, Laz, and Dill collectively dig that unearths Willa Mae's dry bones and *undresses* all their wounds, exposes them, as Laz says, to "what's really there:

just a bunch of brownish-colored bones dressed in rotten scraps of a red dress, wrapped in quilt tatters and laying in a cheap pine box" (252).

The act of stripping away, of laying bare what lies beneath the earth and in the innermost recesses of the human heart, makes possible the poignant, comic closural design of *As I Lay Dying* and the cathartic ending of *Getting Mother's Body*. Much of the poignancy at the end of Faulkner's novel is embodied in Darl's pathetic fate. Because Darl is too full of words that Cash and Jewel, for example, do not possess, Darl's sensitive nature—his "queerness," or what Brooks calls his "antiheroic intelligence" (*Yoknapatawpha Country*)—cannot be ordered or sublimated, nor can it be projected on to objects ouside himself. (By contrast, Cash has carpentry and Jewel has his horse.) Darl's failed effort to end the journey to Jefferson, which he believes is an insult to Addie's memory, by burning the barn where her coffin lies, makes his madness and his being sent to Jackson where the state mental hospital is located inevitable. Ironically and seriocomically (because it takes one to know one), it is Vardaman, who believes his mother is a fish, who gives Darl his ultimate identity: *"My brother he went crazy and he went to Jackson too. Jackson is further away than crazy"* (252). That Jackson is "further away" emotionally than any normative construction of time and space makes Darl hopelessly crazy and Vardaman's loss comprehensible.

Like Parks's novel, Faulkner's is characterized by various kinds of loss, absence, and holes that are corollaries to mourning, burial, and resurrection. Through these three symbols, each novel addresses the inescapable fact of human suffering and, no less emphatically, affirms that life continues despite if not because of it. Darl's madness is a form of loss, for example, that cannot be redeemed or recovered or, in a sense, cashed in as the other Bundrens (and the Beedes) do. Whether the journey is to inter or to disinter the mother's body, the corpse is a host and the familial relation to it is transubstantial. Only Darl and Dill Smiles—a brother-son in one text and a lover-friend in the other—are unable to transform the host body to their material advantage. Addie's transubstantiated body becomes a new wife and new teeth for Anse; a phonograph for Cash; possibly a baby and possibly marriage for Dewey Dell; and, for Vardaman, a new mother. For all the Bundrens except Darl, grief and loss are *redressed* by the continuation of family, the tie that binds most, and the "Great Wheel [that] keep[s] rolling right along."

Undressing Willa Mae Beede's body reveals the diamond ring sewn into the tattered hem of her skirt (for safekeeping). Together, Willa Mae's body and her diamond ring are a symbol of transubstantiation worth "sixteen hundred and twenty three dollars and fifty-nine cents" (256) that helps fill the holes or dresses the wounds caused by each person's desires. However, this implication of the mother's body-diamond is a lesser part of the communion-communal idea that provides the "all's well that ends well" closure. Like the final section of *As I Lay Dying*, the last section of *Getting Mother's Body*, "Billy Beede," is very short. It is situated among three locales in time and space: the drive back from La Junta with Willa Mae's body and the diamond ring; the time shortly after returning to Lincoln, Texas; and a flash-forward to five years later. The simple themes that hold this Faulknerian play with chronology together are that "[f]olks take after they folks" and "there's lots of things between now [life, living] and them bones [death]" (257).

Finally, as the novel closes, Parks places an unmistakable Faulknerian construction about "was" on to Billy's final assessment of what her journey means. Billy is thinking of the nameless life inside her that she, like Dewey Dell, once thought of aborting, and she knows that she can now name her unborn child: "Not pick out a name though, just let one come to me without thinking. Like it had a name already, and if it had a name already then it already was. And if it already was then it was always gonna be" (257). Billy accepts the inevitability of time and events, which echoes an idea that Faulkner articulated in an interview in *Lion in the Garden*: "There is no such thing as was—only *is*. If *was* existed there would be no grief or sorrow" (255).

NOTES

[1] Awkward's book appropriates Harold Bloom's argument about oedipal struggles between literary fathers and sons, which stresses an "anxiety of influence" and resistance to repetition. The African American literary tradition, Awkward argues, in contradistinction to anxiety, is marked by "inspiriting influences"—signified by the familial, maternal tropes and shared themes in black women's writings—that differentiate African American expressive culture from the tradition of white male writers. He further argues that "the textual affinities" in black women's works occur because of the "conscious acts of refiguration and revision" of premodern texts by black female and male writers (4).

[2] The intertwined questions Andrew Parker and Eve Kosofsky Sedgwick pose in their introduction to *Performativity and Performance* that resonate profoundly in both Faulkner's and Parks's novels are: When is saying something doing something? How is saying something doing something?

[3] Parks is also the author of *The American Play* and won the Pulitzer Prize in 2002 for her play *Topdog/Underdog*. To date, the work of only three other African American women playwrights has been performed successfully on Broadway: Lorraine Hansberry, Anna Deavere Smith, and Ntozake Shange.

Teaching *As I Lay Dying* in Cross-Cultural Contexts

Mark Frisch

In the several generations that have passed since William Faulkner wrote his strongest works, his "postage stamp of native soil" ("Interview" 255) has extended well beyond the boundaries of his native Mississippi. His fictions reach across borders with facility, drawing from the past, gazing into the future, and providing insights into other cultures and perspectives. In particular, *As I Lay Dying* resonates in a variety of cultural contexts. I have used it in my world literature class, Modernism, the Postmodern Turn, in which we read a number of Latin American, United States, and European literary works. In the classroom discussions, *As I Lay Dying* lends itself to comparisons with T. S. Eliot's *The Waste Land* and Juan Rulfo's *Pedro Páramo* as well as works like Franz Kafka's *Metamorphosis* and Albert Camus's *The Stranger.* In intertextual readings, I underscore *As I Lay Dying*'s critique of modern, materialistic culture; its emphasis on community; the characters' struggles with solitude; the masterly manipulation of narrative voice and how that speaks to a pluralistic vision; the confrontation with the absurdity of existence; the focus on the hypocrisy of organized religion; and the treatment of the death of the mother. My purpose is to help students see how other works develop similar themes and employ common methods. In its problematic, ambivalent way, *As I Lay Dying* proves helpful in the discussion of both modernism and postmodernism. Comparing it with other novels highlights the remarkable reach of Faulkner's methods in other hands, lands, and contexts and reveals its openness to rereadings.

As I Lay Dying and *The Metamorphosis*

In my world literature class, we study the works in more or less chronological order. In discussing modernism and postmodernism, I draw on Matei Calinescu's *The Five Faces of Modernity*, Jean François Lyotard's *The Postmodern Condition,* Ihab Hassan's *The Postmodern Turn,* and Octavio Paz's *Los hijos del limo* (*Children of the Mire*). Early in the course we read *The Metamorphosis*, since numerous themes of Kafka's appear in *As I Lay Dying* and other works. In discussing *The Metamorphosis,* I highlight Gregor Samsa's isolation and alienation from his culture. Near the beginning of the book, Gregor describes how the life of a salesman has taken a toll on him:

> "Oh God," he thought, "what a grueling job I've picked! Day in, day out—on the road. The upset of doing business is much worse than the actual business in the home office, and besides, I've got the torture of traveling, worrying about changing trains, eating miserable food at all

> hours, constantly seeing new faces, no relationships that last or get more intimate. To the devil with it all!" (4)

In his complaints about his daily routine, Gregor rages against modern culture—the mass migration to large cities, where the jobs are; the fast pace of life; the mobility that comes with the life of the salesman in this new, technological society. Immediately after this, he becomes aware of the metamorphosis of his body:

> He felt a slight itching up on top of his belly; shoved himself slowly on his back closer to the bedpost, so as to be able to lift his head better; found the itchy spot, studded with small white dots, which he had no idea what to make of; and wanted to touch the spot with one of his legs but immediately pulled it back, for the contact sent a cold shiver through him. (4)

The anxiety of the modern, industrialized workplace and the demands of mobile, urban life contribute to Gregor's dehumanization and transformation. The office manager's visit to his home underscores his distress:

> Gregor only had to hear the visitor's first word of greeting to know who it was—the office manager himself. Why was only Gregor condemned to work for a firm where at the slightest omission they immediately suspected the worst? Were all employees louts without exception, wasn't there a single loyal, dedicated worker among them who, when he had not fully utilized a few hours of the morning for the firm, was driven half-mad by pangs of conscience and was actually unable to get out of bed? (8–9)

The image of Gregor transforming into a bug proves particularly effective for leading my students to see the link between modern culture and alienation. Initially, I ask what alienation is. The responses vary, but usually they emphasize being isolated or alone. Then I ask if a person feels like a bug, how is he or she feeling in relation to other people? Someone usually mentions feeling depressed and dehumanized. The excerpts above and others that are similar allow me to link Gregor's condition to the workplace, the Industrial Revolution, and the sociological and Marxist concepts of alienation.

As Gregor loses his voice and his language, the issue of communication becomes central in the story. On the one hand, when he cannot make himself understood, his alienation and feelings of dehumanization increase: "That was the voice of an animal" the office manager declares (13). However, his parents' initial response calms Gregor down and draws him in. They believe something is physically wrong with him. They want to get a locksmith to unlock the door and a doctor to help cure him—one trained to fix the mechanical problems of the modern culture; the other, the physical problems. "The assurance and confidence with which the first measures had been taken did him good. He felt integrated into human society once again and hoped for marvelous, amazing feats from both the doctor and the locksmith" (13).

Gregor is reluctant to relinquish all his human qualities and clings desperately and aggressively to them, as the episode of the removal of his furniture and his defense of his sister's music make clear. He discovers how tied he is to the things in his room:

> Had he really wanted to have his warm room, comfortably fitted with furniture that had always been in the family, changed into a cave, in which, of course he would be able to crawl around unhampered in all directions but at the cost of simultaneously, rapidly and totally forgetting his human past? (33)

When his mother and sister begin removing his furniture, Gregor makes an effort to defend this aspect of his humanity. He crawls onto a picture of a lady in furs and embraces her by affixing himself to the picture. However, his actions and the sight of him turn his family against him. When his mother faints, Gregor, in an attempt to help, leaves his room but then encounters his father, who bombards him with apples, wounding him and forcing him back into the room.

Gregor's metamorphosis into a bug speaks to his dehumanization, but his embracing of the picture and his attachment to his belongings show Gregor defending his humanity. Since the picture is of a beautiful woman, it carries aesthetic and erotic overtones. I ask the students what Gregor's attaching himself to the picture represents. For me, it suggests that family, past, love, and art are indelible qualities of being human. Students usually pick up on the family, family history, and love-sexuality themes, but they tend to overlook the picture as a symbol of art and artistic creation. Gregor's family fails to understand his defense of his humanity and feels threatened by his breaking out. The physical wounds that his father inflicts cut ever deeper into his emotional sense of self and being.

Gregor's defense of his sister's music has similar overtones. When the boorish roomers do not appreciate his sister's violin playing, Gregor feels compelled to come to her defense. The issues of art, family, sexuality, eroticism, and love merge here as Gregor once again affirms his humanity. This time, the students more readily connect Gregor's defense of his humanity and his appreciation of music because it is more explicitly expressed:

> Was he an animal that music could move him so? He felt as if the way to the unknown nourishment he longed for were coming to light. He was determined to force himself on until he reached his sister, to pluck at her skirt, and to let her know in this way that she should bring her violin into his room, for no one here appreciated her playing the way he would appreciate it. He would never again let her out of his room—at least not for as long as he lived. (49)

Kafka raises the issues of the nature of humanity here, perhaps in response to Darwin's theory of evolution, Freudian psychology, and other positivistic approaches that assume that we are no different from other animals. Of course, Gregor's appearance drives the roomers out and turns Greta and his parents against him further, leading to their recognition that they cannot live with him and provide for him any longer. This rejection ultimately causes his death. Cut off from love and a caring, supportive family, he loses his sense of humanity and his will to live.

When we turn to *As I Lay Dying*, I point out that Faulkner's novel touches on many of the same modernist themes. Isolation and alienation are major issues. Faulkner's narrative method, deploying a variety of voices to tell the tale, suggests that each character is enclosed in his or her own isolated world.

Anse sets the tone for the isolation of the family with his extended diatribe against and denunciation of the road that runs by his house (35–38). The road symbolizes his link to the outside world, his communication with others, and his way to get to town. But it also represents movement, motion, travel, and change—in short, the modern world he does not want to join. He wants no part of it because it will cost him money. He prefers to remain apart, out of touch, isolated from the town and the community in general.

The contrast and the clash between town and country, urban and rural, are in play throughout the novel. I find that students usually need help in drawing out this tension. While the monologues highlight the individual characters, the community's vision and values are harder to discern. Anse emphasizes the conflict between town and country in his monologue:

> Nowhere in this sinful world can a honest, hardworking man profit. It takes them that runs the stores in the towns doing no sweating, living off of them that sweats. It aint the hardworking man, the farmer. Sometimes I wonder why we keep at it. It's because there is a reward for us above, where they cant take their autos and such. Every man will be equal there and it will be taken from them that have and give to them that have not by the Lord. (110)

Moseley captures this tension from the perspective of the town dweller in his incredulity and outrage at Dewey Dell's attempt to buy an abortion pill and at the family's treatment of Addie's body and Cash's leg. MacGowan's monologue also emphasizes the conflict when the Bundrens arrive in Jefferson. His assistant, Jody, initially describes Dewey Dell as a "country woman" (241). When MacGowan asks if she is young, Jody replies, "She looks like a pretty hot mamma, for a country girl" (242). MacGowan says to himself, "Them country people. Half the time they dont know what they want, and the balance of the time they cant tell it to you" (243). His deprecating attitude also comes through when he thinks about her not being married: "I never saw no ring. But like as not, they aint heard yet out there that they use rings" (243–44). And of course he exhibits this attitude most fully in the way he deceives and takes sexual advantage of her.

Jewel feels compelled to fight to defend his honor over this tension. Only Darl's restraining him prevents it from getting out of hand: "'Thinks because he's a goddam town fellow,' Jewel says, panting, wrenching at me. 'Son of a bitch,' he says" (230). Interestingly, when this incident occurs, three African Americans walk by the coffin, sniff the air, and question what is in it. Jewel, however, picks a fight with the white man out front.

Certainly, class conflict plays out in the country-city dichotomy. But other subtle tensions are at work here. Modern culture privileges the city—urban life—despite all its problems. The city is the hub of progress and the foundation of sophistication as well as the center of commerce and economic development. The Bundrens feel like second-class citizens, outsiders, unequal, estranged from the larger society. On another level, the Bundrens are us. They are everyman and everywoman seeking his or her place in a larger world.

Several of the Bundrens have other issues that contribute to the isolation, loneliness, and alienation that each of them feels. Dewey Dell's unwanted pregnancy and Vardaman's difficulty reconciling his mother's death and the dead fish are two examples. Curiously, the characters who are most self-conscious, Addie and Darl, feel the most estranged and alienated. Clearly, Addie is unhappy with her marital-family situation and with life in general. She never should have become a mother or a teacher, as she hates children (169–70). She relishes whipping her students and drawing blood to make them aware of her. Her father's advice—"the reason for living was to get ready to stay dead a long time" (169)—suggests that life has little meaning. The births of Cash and her other children violate her "aloneness," her solitude (172). Addie emphasizes how Anse, Cora, Tull, and the others are dead in life, a reference to *The Waste Land,* which we also read and discuss in class.

The limits of language and the breakdown of communication figure in Faulkner's work as well as in Kafka's. The narrative structure of *As I Lay Dying*, with individual, isolated monologues, brings this theme to the fore. Addie highlights it when she discusses words and deeds. Love and motherhood have little meaning for her. She asserts that words are empty and dead and that life comes from action.

> And so when Cora Tull would tell me I was not a true mother, I would think how words go straight up in a thin line, quick and harmless, and how terribly doing goes along the earth, clinging to it so that after a while the two lines are too far apart for the same person to straddle from one to the other; and that sin and love and fear are just sounds that people who never sinned nor loved nor feared have for what they never had and cannot have until they forget the words. (173–74)

After we read the monologue, I ask students their opinion of Addie. They often tend to be harsh and judgmental with her. No doubt she deserves such an opinion, at least in part. However, they do not always recognize that she is a strong, independent woman who feels severely confined by the limits placed on women of her day. If a student does not highlight this, I do, after which I sense a shift toward a more sympathetic attitude. It provides a link to other works we read with strong female characters: Henrik Ibsen's *A Doll's House,* Toni Morrison's *Beloved* or *Song of Solomon,* and Wendy Wasserstein's *The Heidi Chronicles*.

Darl is the most complex, self-conscious, and alienated figure in *As I Lay Dying*. His character lends itself to comparisons with Gregor and Camus's Meursault. Darl's alienation peaks (as does Gregor's) when the family turns on him. In Addie's definition, he is a man of words, not deeds. In contrast to Cash's and Jewel's heroic efforts to save the coffin, Darl jumps from the wagon when he sees the folly of trying to cross the river. Although he appears to communicate little with the others, he is the most verbal, poetic, sensitive, and intelligent member of the family, and his narrations carry the story, often providing details and filling in gaps. He highlights his own fluid sense of self early in the novel when he ruminates on his sense of being and the line between sleeping and waking:

> In a strange room you must empty yourself for sleep. And before you are emptied for sleep, what are you. And when you are emptied for sleep, you are not. And when you are filled with sleep, you never were. I dont know what I am. I dont know if I am or not. Jewel knows he is, because he does not know that he does not know whether he is or not. (80)

Darl's clairvoyance and his ability to see the folly of his family's actions separate him from the others and often make him seem weird, even to his family. Anse underscores Darl's status as the strange outcast:

> [W]e hadn't no more than passed Tull's lane when Darl begun to laugh. Setting back there on the plank seat with Cash, with his dead ma laying in her coffin at his feet, laughing. How many times I told him it's doing such things as that that makes folks talk about him, I dont know. (105)

Tull, as a community voice, echoes these sentiments. After warning about the folly of trying to cross the river, he asks Darl's opinion. While he awaits Darl's answer, he thinks:

> He is looking at me. He don't say nothing; just looks at me with them queer eyes of hisn that makes folks talk. I always say it aint never been what he done or said or anything so much as how he looks at you. It's like he had got into the inside of you, someway. Like somehow you was looking at yourself and your doings outen his eyes. (125)

Toward the end of our class discussions, I ask the students how Darl's character and breakdown reflect the themes of the novel. I point to his last narrative, where alienation, the family's rejection, and the divide between self and other push him over the edge and where he speaks of himself in the third person:

> Darl has gone to Jackson. They put him on the train, laughing, down the long car laughing, the heads turning like the heads of owls when he passed. "What are you laughing at?" I said.
>
> "Yes yes yes yes yes." (253)

I usually get a variety of responses to this. Most students sympathize with Darl and see the family as selfish, cruel, and insensitive; some argue that it was the family that drove him mad. Some suggest that Darl is the only sane one—yet ironically he is committed to an institution. I acknowledge these perspectives and try to use the scene to touch on other works we have read or will be reading by asserting that Darl is like us. Darl is laughing at Darl, at himself. Like Darl, we laugh at the absurdity of the journey, the foolhardiness of the undertaking and the motives, and at Darl. But we are Darl. We are the family. We are Gregor Samsa. We are Meursault. We are misunderstood. We laugh at ourselves. We suffer alienation, isolation, and pain.

As I Lay Dying and *The Waste Land*

We read T. S. Eliot's *The Waste Land* before we read *As I Lay Dying*. Eliot's poem reaches out to world literature in a way that very few works of Western art do. *As I Lay Dying* draws on and speaks to it. In helping the students understand and piece together this poem, I take Jewel Spears Brooker's suggestion in *Approaches to Teaching Eliot's Poetry and Plays*. At first, I emphasize "when love fails, a waste land develops" as a unifying theme, and then I move to more complex literary and cultural issues (103). This gives the students an entry into the work and provides the groundwork for a link to *As I Lay Dying* later. I also draw on Cleanth Brooks's analysis of the poem in *Modern Poetry*. I emphasize Eliot's scathing critique of modernist culture and stress that *The Waste Land* presents an image of a severely fragmented culture and tradition. Humanity has lost the knowledge of good and evil. Conflicts between memory and desire, the past and the future, the religious and the secular, and the spiritual and the material permeate the poem. Symbolic images of life and death, death in life, and death and rebirth run through it. Eliot links water with life and drought and dryness with death. Empty love, sexual passion devoid of love, and life devoid of meaning produce a wasteland. There is the recurring symbol of fire, representing passion and sexuality. But much of the passion has been lost. Humankind lives a directionless existence filled with fear, unwilling to commit and afraid of transformation. However, sacrifice, even sacrificial death, may be life-giving. I underscore how questioning the meaning of certain symbols can remove the curse of the Fisher King on the land, and I emphasize that the work sees the possibility of hope and renewal.

As I Lay Dying intertextually engages Eliot's poem on many levels. Making the connections helps students better understand both works. For instance, I point out how Eliot acknowledges the breakdown of communication:

> "My nerves are bad to-night. Yes, bad. Stay with me.
> Speak to me. Why do you never speak. Speak.
> What are you thinking of? What thinking? What?
> I never know what you are thinking. Think." (lines 111–14)

Eliot links the problems associated with communication to the overarching themes of death in life, fear, and the emptiness and meaninglessness of existence. This becomes clear when the male voice responds to the woman's plea to think:

> I think we are in rats' alley
> Where the dead men lost their bones
> "What is that noise?"
> The wind under the door
> "What is the noise now? What is the wind doing?"
> Nothing again nothing.
> "Do
> You know nothing? Do you see nothing? Do you remember
> Nothing?" (lines 115–23)

The death-in-life theme runs through Addie's only monologue as well. Addie repeatedly refers to life and death in symbolic terms: "He did not know that he was dead, then" (173); "And then he died. He did not know he was dead" (174). The references here are to Anse, but I point out that Addie's division between words and deeds has implications for life and death for numerous characters, the people of action being the living, the vital, the movers. Although Cora emphasizes sin, she is empty and dead because she has never experienced it.

Faulkner includes numerous intertextual references to Eliot's poem that suggest that he wanted to comment on, expand on, and rework Eliot's message. The most direct instance occurs when Peabody arrives and Addie rejects his help and clings to Anse. Peabody states, "That's what they mean by the love that passeth understanding" (45–46). I ask the students where they have heard something similar before, and usually someone makes the connection. While the reference may have biblical overtones (Phil. 4.7), it also speaks to the last line of Eliot's poem: "Shantih shantih shantih" (line 434). Eliot tells us in the notes that it is a formal ending to a Upanishad and means "The Peace which passeth understanding" (note to line 434). In *As I Lay Dying*, Peabody gives it a different twist from what Eliot or Scripture had in mind. He is an appropriate person to make that reference—as a member of the middle to upper-middle class of the community, he may very well have been familiar with both references.

There are other explicit references in *As I Lay Dying* that students sometimes succeed in linking to *The Waste Land.* Dewey Dell's pregnancy and desired abortion parallel Lil's abortion in part 2 of the poem and suggest Eliot's theme of failed love (lines 139–73). While several family members have ulterior motives in taking Addie to Jefferson for burial, one of Anse's motivations is his desire for new teeth—again a reference to the Lil section, where her husband gave her money for new teeth and she used it for the abortion. Here we have the reversal of the T. S. Eliot reference, as the money for the abortion goes for the teeth. Both authors suggest that an individual or a society that resorts to an abortion or values shiny teeth is marked by decadence and superficiality. That Anse finds a new wife within hours of burying Addie also speaks to the theme of failed love in *The Waste Land.* The new Mrs. Bundren owns a gramophone, a reference to the empty love-sex scene that Tiresias watches, where the woman puts a record on the gramophone when the sexual encounter is over (lines 218–56). The association serves to criticize our technological culture in both works. Furthermore, in part 5, "What the Thunder Said," Eliot draws on a Upanishad in his emphasis on self-control and self-sacrifice in lifting the curse of the Waste Land: "'Datta, dayadhvam, damyata' [Give, sympathize, control]" (note to line 402). In *As I Lay Dying,* the two most heroic and selfless family members, Jewel and especially Cash, exhibit these qualities. In his devotion to the family project, the burial of his mother in Jefferson, Jewel proves to be unwavering. Although at times he has trouble controlling his temper, he acquiesces and sacrifices his horse so the journey to Jefferson can continue. Cash displays a self-control that Jewel lacks and also willingly sacrifices something even more wrenching for the family project: his legs.

In referencing Eliot's work the way he does, Faulkner, like Eliot, criticizes the superficiality of modernist society. He portrays a duplicitous, self-serving world bordering on the absurd. But he distances himself from Eliot in certain respects, including religion. With a bit of a nudge, students can usually define some religious differences. In *The Waste Land,* Eliot affirms the religious vision and suggests that if we returned to a cultural past in which religious values played a more central role in our lives, the curse of the Waste Land could be lifted. Faulkner, in contrast, criticizes the hypocrisy of religious practice. Cora Tull and Reverend Whitfield symbolize organized religion, and hypocrisy and hollowness dominate their characters. Cora, who has a much easier time seeing others' faults than her own, blatantly misjudges people. Cora suggests that Darl, not Jewel, loved Addie most and tells Addie that she, Addie, does not really understand sin, whereas the opposite is the case (24). Similarly, Reverend Whitfield commits adultery with Addie, and since she dies without telling Anse, Whitfield convinces himself that the Lord has forgiven him and made it possible for him not to confess to Anse either.

Faulkner makes an affirmation of life and the human effort to do something purposeful in a way that Eliot does not. While part 5 of Eliot's poem, "What the Thunder Said," suggests an affirmation, Faulkner's approach is different. The

Bundrens are comic bunglers. Their motives are often suspect and less than honorable. Their actions are reprehensible, and their project, their journey, borders on the absurd. Yet they are us, and they ultimately muddle through. Their struggle is ours: to achieve something meaningful and worthwhile. While this struggle may not be easy or pretty, Faulkner suggests that it may just be possible.

As I Lay Dying and *The Stranger*

The themes of meaning and chaos, absurdity and purpose lead nicely into Camus's *The Stranger*. While not a postmodern novel, the work highlights qualities of postmodernism and thus provides an opportunity to discuss postmodern theory.

Initially, we discuss existentialism and the implications of believing the world is absurd. Early on, I comment on the colonial and racist landscape in Algeria at the time the story takes place, and I raise two questions: Is the killing of the Arab murder—a criminal act—or an accident? Are Meursault's conviction and death sentence justified or a travesty of justice? I usually get a mixture of responses, with some disagreement. We discuss further the ambiguity and indeterminacy of the work. The opening paragraphs call attention to the indeterminacy of time and place: "Mamon died today. Or yesterday, maybe. I don't know" (3). Meursault's mother is in Marengo, about eighty kilometers from Algiers, but Meursault does not indicate in which direction, as Raymond Gay-Crosier points out (71). I offer several different readings of the novel (philosophical, psychological, social political, feminist, etc.) and suggest how each reader is an interpreter. I then turn to Meursault's outburst against the certainty of the priest.

> He seemed so certain about everything, didn't he? And yet none of his certainties was worth one hair of a woman's head. He wasn't even sure he was alive, because he was living like a dead man. Whereas it looked as if I was the one who'd come up empty handed. But I was sure about me, about everything, surer than he could ever be, sure of my life and sure of the death I had waiting for me. (120)

The passage provides an opportunity to discuss uncertainty and the crisis of knowledge as characteristics of the postmodern turn. I do not consider Meursault a postmodern character. Postmodernism, as I define it, is not atheistic. Atheism is as monistic as theism in its affirmation of God's nonexistence. Postmodernism, in its pluralism, in problematizing, and in talking about the limits of knowledge, is agnostic in attitude. Nonetheless, Camus's existentialism lays the groundwork for postmodernism.

The reference to the priest living like a dead man opens a window into Addie's monologue in *As I Lay Dying* and the relation between the two works. I point out that Camus wrote a stage adaptation of Faulkner's *Requiem for a Nun*. I also point out that in the translator's note to the edition we use, Matthew Ward states that Camus acknowledged employing an "American method" in writing *The Stranger*. Ward mentions Faulkner as one of the precursors of Camus's style (v). I mention here the automation woman whom Meursault meets in Celeste's and who attends his trial and his critique of the mechanical guillotine. Both highlight Camus's criticism of industrial, technological society.

We also discuss similarities and differences between Darl and Meursault. Both are outsiders, strangers, alienated figures and have recently lost their mothers. Both are misunderstood outcasts who are tuned to the absurdity of existence and who suffer an injustice at the hands of their family, society, state, and the law. While Darl's crime, the destruction of a man's property and livelihood—his barn—is quite serious, Meursault's killing of an Arab is more severe. In contrast to Meursault's motives, Darl's may be commendable.

We discuss the role of the absurd in the two novels as well. Camus and Meursault assume that life is absurd. Faulkner, as I read him, plays with that notion here but steps back from a clear acceptance of it. We are the Bundrens. We are all bunglers, yet our goals are achievable. Of course, other critics read Faulkner's statement on the human condition differently. Edmond Volpe states that "this short novel presents human existence as an absurd joke" (126). Brooks reads the Bundrens' actions ultimately as heroic (*Yoknapatawpha Country* 141–66). For Olga Vickery, the interplay between interior monologue and exterior action creates ambivalent, often contradictory, and unresolved tensions between the grotesque and comedy, between tragedy and farce, between hilarity and despair ("Dimensions" 246–47). Whatever your readings, the two works lend themselves to dynamic comparisons around this theme.

As I Lay Dying and *Pedro Páramo*

After a discussion of some of Jorge Luis Borges's short stories, Samuel Beckett's *Waiting for Godot*, and postmodern theory, we turn to Juan Rulfo's novel *Pedro Páramo*. Like *As I Lay Dying*, this novel portrays a son dealing with the death of a parent in the context of a community. The narrative voice and methods also show similarities with *As I Lay Dying*. However, a shift occurs in the representation of the world, and as a class we draw out some of those distinctions.

I begin the class discussion by pointing out the reason for Juan Preciado's trip to Comala, the mythic search for the father, much like Telemachus searching for Odysseus, and the fulfillment of his promise to his dying mother. The conversation quickly shifts to how death dominates the book. I ask for images of death in this novel and for a comparison of death in the two works. The students mention most of them: the death of Juan's mother, as in *As I Lay Dying*; Miguel's death; the death-murder of Toribio Aldrete; the death of all the characters in the village; Juan's death; and Pedro's death. They agree that death is more prevalent here than in *As I Lay Dying*. While Addie's death certainly plays a central role, death in *Pedro Páramo* permeates every aspect of the novel. The whole village of Comala is dead, physically, emotionally, morally, and spiritually.

This is a wasteland, and Rulfo plays on that image much as Faulkner does. To illustrate that Rulfo was probably aware of Eliot's poem, I ask the Spanish students in my class what "*páramo*" means. One of the advanced students or a native speaker usually will say "barren plain" or "wasteland." I point out that Eliot's poem was translated into Spanish in 1930 by Enrique Mungía as *El Páramo* in the Mexican magazine *Contemporaneos* (Wilson 233). The weather further suggests that this is a wasteland. As Abundio leads Juan Preciado to Comala in the beginning, Juan senses the heat as they descend toward the village:

> We had left the hot wind behind and were sinking into pure, airless heat. The stillness seemed to be waiting for something.
>
> "It's hot here," I said.
>
> "You might say. But this is nothing," my companion replied. "Try to take it easy. You'll feel it even more when we get to Comala. That town sits on the coals of the earth, at the very mouth of hell. They say that when people from there die and go to hell, they come back for a blanket." (5–6)

Paradoxically, it is always hot and dry, and it is always raining.

It is a land where nothing seems to grow. While Father Rentería and the priest from Contla are walking, the latter points out that everything that grows on the land is bitter. Father Rentería replies:

> I've tried to grow grapes over in Comala. They don't bear. Only guavas and oranges; bitter oranges and bitter guavas. I've forgotten the taste of sweet fruit. Do you remember the China guavas we had in the seminary? The peaches? The tangerines that shed their skin at a touch? I brought seeds here. A few, just a small pouch. Afterwards I felt it would have been better to leave them where they were, since I only brought them here to die. (72)

Juan regularly remembers his mother's description of Comala as green and plush. However, Pedro Páramo has allowed the land to fall into ruin because of his disillusionment and anger over his lost love (80). Nonetheless, the bitterness of the land occurred before Susana San Juan's death. The priest's suggestion is that Pedro's manipulative, greedy abuse of power sours the land. It seems that everyone who comes in contact with the land or the community suffers from and carries the curse. Even Juan Preciado dies when he sleeps with Donis's sister, who is involved in an incestuous relationship with her brother. Rulfo also draws on the Catholic religious symbols of purgatory and hell to underscore the moral corruption of the community. As Jason Wilson asserts, the outer geography reflects the inner mentality of the characters, who are between worlds, in a no-man's-land. They have been unable to integrate into modern, progressive, postrevolutionary Mexico; official history has bypassed Comala. There is "no land reform, no social justice, no socialist equality, just the powerful 'macho' Pedro Páramo, with his obedient priest, the Padre Rentería. No one knows what the revolution stands for" (Wilson 235). While Faulkner and Eliot employ wasteland symbols to critique modernist culture, Rulfo uses these images for two purposes of his own. One is to criticize Mexican culture and a historical tradition that turned a blind eye to corruption and abuse and subverted the ideals of the Mexican Revolution of 1910. The other is to subtly question modernism itself.

Faulkner and Rulfo express similar attitudes toward organized religion. Rulfo highlights its shortcomings and hypocrisy and its failure to prevent political bosses like Pedro Páramo from dominating and abusing the community. Father Rentería is a helpless, tragic figure who is too weak to effectively challenge the rape of his young niece by Miguel, Pedro's son. He is even less able to prevent Pedro's exploitation of other women in the community, let alone the murders that Pedro arranges to consolidate his power and wealth. In despair, the priest ultimately flees the village and joins the revolutionaries. However, Pedro's manipulation of the revolutionary groups for his own ends suggests that the transformation and justice that Father Rentería and the other revolutionaries desire will not be achieved. Yet much like Faulkner in a number of his works, Rulfo uses religious symbols to suggest an affinity with the general religious vision while criticizing its present organized, bureaucratic expression. After our discussion of religion in *As I Lay Dying*, students usually succeed in defining this similarity once I call attention to it.

Rulfo's narrative methods are similar to Faulkner's in both *As I Lay Dying* and *The Sound and the Fury*. The Mexican novelist's work opens with Juan Preciado's narration of his arrival in Comala. The voices of the other characters quickly chime in, sketching out the rise and fall of Pedro Páramo. As in *As I Lay Dying*, where different members of the family and the community narrate the travails of the death and burial of Addie, here members of the village, including Pedro himself, relate personal and communal histories. While *As I Lay Dying* indicates which character is speaking, in *Pedro Páramo* the reader is not told, but certain cues imply who the narrator or subject is in each section. The students recognize this difference and usually feel that Rulfo's work is more challenging because of it. At times, Rulfo's methods resemble the stream-of-consciousness technique of *The Sound and the Fury*. They create the effect of voices moving onto a stage to present their scene or story. Juan Preciado and the reader become witnesses as well as audience as the ghosts walking the earth repeat their tales. Also, the community offers its communal perspectives. From time to time, unnamed individuals will give a wide-angle explanation of what is happening, often with value judgments. The method affirms the pluralism of the world and the value of differing perspectives.

Rulfo handles the second-to-last narrative in a masterly fashion. The narrator views the events initially through the eyes of Doña Inés, a member of the community and the owner of a store, as Abundio announces the death of his wife and asks to buy some alcohol in an attempt to bury the pain. There are overtones here of Faulkner's short story "Pantaloon in Black" from *Go Down, Moses.* Then the narrative perspective shifts to looking at the world through the eyes of Abundio, as he unwittingly murders Pedro, his father. It is clear that Abundio is so drunk that he does not really know what he is doing, as he begs Pedro to give him money to bury his wife. It is only through the reactions of the others around him and the details provided in the last narrative segment that the reader deciphers what has occurred.

This piecing together of the narrative occurs throughout, as it does in *As I Lay Dying*. Coupled with the voices of the ghosts who tell the tale, it critiques the monism and realism of modernism and raises issues about the nature of representation and reality. It would seem to fit with Carlos Alonso's claim that Latin American writers have been ambivalent about the modernist agenda because it has done little to improve the material and political well-being of Latin America. Pedro's consolidation of power through murder, corruption, manipulation, and extortion parallels the centralization of control and power in many governments in Latin America and Europe during the modernist period. The destruction of Comala suggests the dissolution and failures of the modernist communal and social visions. The Mexican Revolution, the product of modernism's vision and values, falls short of its goals, at least in places like Comala. This novel is a critique of rural Mexico but even more a critique of the revolution and of modernism itself.

At the same time, however, Rulfo presents us with a different sense of reality. I ask the students how this sense of reality is different from Ibsen's and Faulkner's, and they emphasize the supernatural, the ghosts. We discuss magic realism and Alejo Carpentier's "real marvelous"—the sense that everyday reality is a mixture of various legends, myths, and visions of different cultures. According to Carpentier, reality is so stark, cruel, incredible, *and* ordinary that in the Latin American consciousness the fantastic and the ordinary merge, blend, and become indistinguishable. This depiction of the "real" suggests a turn toward a new way of representing the world—toward postmodernism.

Then I ask the class to reconsider the character of Darl. I ask what his clairvoyance and extrasensory perception suggest about Faulkner's sense of reality in relation to Rulfo's. The students usually say that while the two are similar, they are generally different. I point out that Darl's vision of the world challenges the limits of our sensory knowledge. It crosses the border between positivism and fantasy; between dream, myth, and magic and naturalism; between objectivity and subjectivity. Just as many in Rulfo's Mexico may accept spirits walking the earth as part of their reality, so too do many in Faulkner's Mississippi find Darl's visionary powers believable. Like most of Faulkner's works, *As I Lay*

Dying is a product of and is grounded in the modernist vision of the world. Yet Darl's character, coupled with the multiplicity of narrative perspectives, decenters the work and enables it to move between certainty and ambiguity, between naturalism and magic realism, and between the modern and the postmodern. In so doing, Faulkner's novel and its fluid nature reach out across cultures and to other literary works.

NOTES ON CONTRIBUTORS

Cedric Gael Bryant is the Lee Family Professor of English and American Literature at Colby College, where he teaches nineteenth- and twentieth-century American and African American literature. His book in progress includes a discussion of Lucille Clifton's "Shapeshifter" poems and the African American Gothic imagination. He has published on Toni Morrison, Charles Frazier, and William Faulkner and was named Professor of the Year for the state of Maine by the Carnegie Center for the Advancement of Teaching.

Deborah Clarke is professor of English at Arizona State University. Her books include *Driving Women: Fiction and Automobile Culture in Twentieth-Century America* and *Robbing the Mother: Women in Faulkner*. She has published articles on Faulkner and twentieth-century American fiction; her current project focuses on credit and debt in twentieth-century American fiction.

Mark Frisch is associate professor of modern languages and literatures at Duquesne University. He has published *You Might Be Able to Get There from Here: Reconsidering Borges and the Postmodern*; *William Faulkner, su influencia en la literatura hispanoamericana: Mallea, Rojas, Yáñez y García Marquez*; and articles on United States and Latin American literature, with a special emphasis on Faulkner and Borges.

Donald M. Kartiganer is Howry Professor of Faulkner Studies Emeritus at the University of Mississippi and director of the annual Faulkner and Yoknapatawpha Conference. He is the author of *The Fragile Thread: The Meaning of Form in Faulkner's Novels* and coeditor of *Theories of American Literature* and seven volumes of Faulkner criticism.

Barbara Ladd is professor of English at Emory University. She is the author of *Resisting History: Gender, Modernity, and Authorship in William Faulkner, Zora Neale Hurston, and Eudora Welty* and *Nationalism and the Color Line in George W. Cable, Mark Twain, and William Faulkner*. Her current project is a book on transatlantic currents and southern writing.

Cheryl Lester is associate professor of English at the University of Kansas. She has published articles in *Modern Fiction Studies*, the *Faulkner Journal*, *The Blackwell Companion to Faulkner*, and *Faulkner and Postmodernism*. She is the cotranslator (with Philip Barnard) of Philippe Lacoue-Labarthe and Jean-Luc Nancy's *The Literary Absolute: The Theory of Literature in German Romanticism* and the coauthor (with Alice Lieberman) of *Social Work Practice with a Difference: A Literary Approach*.

John T. Matthews is professor of English at Boston University. He is the founding coeditor and associate editor of the *Faulkner Journal* and the author of *The Play of Faulkner's Language*, The Sound and the Fury*: Faulkner and the Lost Cause*, and *William Faulkner: Seeing through the South*. He is the editor of *The Blackwell Companion to the Modern American Novel, 1900–1950* and is working on a book entitled *Look Away, Look Awry: The Problem of the South in the American Imagination*.

E. L. McCallum is associate professor of English at Michigan State University. She is the author of *Object Lessons: How to Do Things with Fetishism* and articles in *Differences, Camera Obscura, and Poetics Today*. *Queer Times, Queer Becomings*, edited with

Mikko Tuhkanen, is forthcoming. She is writing a book on aesthetic theory and Gertrude Stein's *The Making of Americans*.

Sean McCann is professor of English at Wesleyan University. He is the author of *A Pinnacle of Feeling: American Literature and Presidential Government* and *Gumshoe America: Hard-Boiled Crime Fiction and the Rise and Fall of New Deal Liberalism*.

Patrick O'Donnell is professor of English at Michigan State University. He is the author of *John Hawkes*; *Passionate Doubts: Designs of Interpretation in Contemporary American Fiction*; *Echo Chambers: Figuring Voice in Modern Narrative*; *Latent Destinies: Cultural Paranoia in Contemporary U.S. Fiction*; and *The American Novel Now: Reading Contemporary American Fiction since 1980*. He is the editor of *New Essays on* The Crying of Lot 49, the coeditor of *Intertextuality and Contemporary American Fiction*, and an associate editor of *The Columbia History of the American Novel*. He is currently working on a book about Henry James and contemporary cinema.

Lisa K. Perdigao is associate professor of English at the Florida Institute of Technology. She is the author of *From Modernist Entombment to Postmodernist Exhumation: Dead Bodies in Twentieth-Century American Fiction* and the coeditor, with Mark Pizzato, of *Death in American Texts and Performances: Corpses, Ghosts, and the Reanimated Dead*. She has published articles in book collections on Adrienne Rich's poetry, Toni Morrison's fiction and prose, Caribbean women's writing, and children's and adolescent literature.

Homer B. Pettey is associate professor of film and television studies at the University of Arizona. He is the author of "Cannibalism, Slavery, and Self-Consumption in *Moby-Dick*" in Harold Bloom's *Modern Critical Interpretations* and "Perception and the Destruction of Being in *As I Lay Dying*" in the *Faulkner Journal*. He was script consultant for the six-part ABC miniseries *Empire*; his current project is a book on the aesthetics of film noir.

Annette Wannamaker is associate professor at Eastern Michigan University. She is the author of *Boys in Children's Literature and Popular Culture: Masculinity, Abjection, and the Fictional Child* and the editor of *Mediated Boyhoods: Boys, Teens and Young Men in Popular Media and Culture*.

Michael Zeitlin is associate professor in the Department of English at the University of British Columbia. He is the editor of *Méconnaissance, Race, and the Real in Faulkner's Fiction*. He has published essays on postmodern American literature, psychoanalytic theory, and the wars in Vietnam, the Gulf, and Iraq.

Heide Ziegler is professor and chair of the Program in American Studies at the University of Stuttgart; she is a former president of the university. She has published in German and English on Faulkner and on modernist and postmodernist American literature as well as in the areas of knowledge management and educational politics in Germany. She is the author of *John Barth* and the editor of *Facing Texts: Encounters between Contemporary Writers and Critics*. Her current project is a book on private and public universities in Germany, with reference to the university system in the United States.

Lynda Zwinger is associate professor of English at the University of Arizona. She is the author of *Daughters, Fathers, and the Novel: The Sentimental Romance of Heterosexuality* and of essays on Dickens, Henry James, queer theory, world literature, and popular film.

WORKS CITED

Aboul-Ela, Hosam. *Other South: Faulkner, Coloniality, and the Mariátegui Tradition*. Pittsburgh: U of Pittsburgh P, 2007. Print.

Adams, Richard P. *Faulkner: Myth and Motion*. Princeton: Princeton UP, 1968. Print.

Aiken, Conrad. "William Faulkner: The Novel as Form." *Atlantic Monthly* Nov. 1939: 650–54. Print.

Allen, William Rodney. "The Imagist and Symbolist Views of the Function of Language: Addie and Darl Bundren in *As I Lay Dying*." *Studies in American Fiction* 10.2 (1982): 185–96. Print.

Alonso, Carlos. "The Mourning After: García Márquez, Fuentes and the Meaning of Postmodernity in Spanish America." *MLN* 109.2 (1994): 252–67. Print.

Andrew, Dudley, ed. *The Image in Dispute: Art and Cinema in the Age of Photography*. Austin: U of Texas P, 1997. Print.

À nous la liberté. Dir. René Clair. 1931. Criterion, 2002. DVD.

Appadurai, Arun. *Modernity at Large: Cultural Dimensions of Globalization*. Minneapolis: U of Minnesota P, 1996. Print.

Aristotle. *Poetics*. Ed. and trans. Stephen Halliwell. Cambridge: Harvard UP, 1995. Print.

Armstrong, Tim. *Modernism, Technology, and the Body: A Cultural Study*. Cambridge: Cambridge UP, 2008. Print.

Arnason, H. H., and Marla F. Prather. *History of Modern Art: Painting, Sculpture, Architecture, Photography*. New York: Abrams, 1998. Print.

As I Lay Dying. By Frank Galati. Dir. Galati. Steppenwolf Theatre Company. Steppenwolf Theatre, Chicago. 30 April 1995. Performance.

As I Lay Dying: Song Cycle. Perf. Tom House, Tommy Goldsmith, David Olney, Karen Pell. Opera Memphis. 2002. Performance.

Atkinson, Ted. *Faulkner and the Great Depression: Aesthetics, Ideology, and Cultural Politics*. Athens: U of Georgia P, 2006. Print.

Awkward, Michael. *Inspiriting Influences: Tradition, Revision, and Afro-American Women's Novels*. New York: Columbia UP, 1989. Print.

Bailey, Ilena. "A Study of the Management of the Farm Home." *Journal of Home Economics* 7 (1915): 348–53. Print.

Baldassari, Anne. "Picasso, 1901–1906; Painting in the Mirror of the Photograph." *The Artist and the Camera: Degas to Picasso*. Ed. Dorothy Kosinski. New Haven: Yale UP, 1999. 286–309. Print.

Barenblat, Neal. "Biography of Faulkner." *YouTube*. YouTube, Dec. 2007. Web. 13 Nov. 2009.

Barker-Benfield, Ben. *The Horrors of the Half-Known Life: Male Attitudes to Women and Sexuality in Nineteenth-Century America*. 2nd ed. New York: Routledge, 2000. Print.

Barlow, William. *Looking Up at Down: The Emergence of Blues Culture*. Philadelphia: Temple UP, 1989. Print.

Benjamin, Hazel C. "Lobbying for Birth Control." *Public Opinion Quarterly* 2.1 (1938): 48–60. Print.

Benjamin, Walter. "The Work of Art in an Age of Mechanical Reproduction." *Illuminations: Essays and Reflections*. Ed. Hannah Arendt. Trans. Harry Zohn. New York: Schocken, 1968. 217–51. Print.

Blaine, Diana York. "The Abjection of Addie and Other Myths of the Maternal in *As I Lay Dying.*" *William Faulkner: Six Decades of Criticism*. Ed. Linda Wagner-Martin. East Lansing: Michigan State UP, 2002. 83–103. Print.

Bleikasten, André. *Faulkner's* As I Lay Dying. Trans. Roger Little. Rev. ed. Bloomington: Indiana UP, 1973. Print.

———. *The Ink of Melancholy: Faulkner's Novels from* The Sound and the Fury *to* Light in August. Bloomington: Indiana UP, 1990. Print.

Blotner, Joseph. *Faulkner: A Biography*. 1974. New York: Random, 1984. Print.

Booth, Wayne. *The Rhetoric of Fiction*. 2nd ed. Chicago: U of Chicago P, 1983. Print.

Bourdieu, Pierre. *Distinction: A Social Critique of the Judgement of Taste*. Trans. Richard Nice. Cambridge: Harvard UP, 1984. Print.

Bragaglia, Anton Giulio. "Futurist Photodynamism 1911." *Futurist Manifestos*. Ed. Umbro Apollonio. Boston: Museum of Fine Arts, 2001. Print.

Breunig, L. C. "Vicente Huidobro." *The Cubist Poets in Paris: An Anthology*. Ed. Breunig. Lincoln: U of Nebraska P, 1995. 195–97. Print.

Brodie, Janet Farrell. *Contraception and Abortion in Nineteenth-Century America*. Ithaca: Cornell UP, 1994. Print.

Bronfen, Elisabeth. *Over Her Dead Body: Death, Femininity, and the Aesthetic*. New York: Routledge, 1992. Print.

Brooker, Jewel Spears. "When Love Fails: Reading *The Waste Land* with Undergraduates." *Approaches to Teaching Eliot's Poetry and Poems.* New York: MLA, 1988. 103–08. Print.

Brooks, Cleanth. *Modern Poetry and the Tradition.* 1939. Chapel Hill: U of North Carolina P, 1965. Print.

———. *William Faulkner: First Encounters*. New Haven: Yale UP, 1983. Print.

———. *William Faulkner: The Yoknapatawpha Country*. New Haven: Yale UP, 1963. Print.

Broughton, Panthea Reid. *William Faulkner: The Abstract and the Actual*. Baton Rouge: Louisiana State UP, 1974. Print.

Brylowski, Walter. *Faulkner's Olympian Laugh: Myth in the Novels*. Detroit: Wayne State UP, 1968. Print.

Calinescu, Matei. *The Five Faces of Modernity: Modernism, Avant Garde, Decadence, Kitsch, Postmodernism.* 2nd ed. Durham: Duke UP, 1987. Print.

Camus, Albert. *The Stranger.* Trans. Matthew Ward. New York: Vintage, 1989. Print.

Capps, Jack L. As I Lay Dying*: A Concordance to the Novel*. Ann Arbor: Univ. Microfilms, 1977. Microform.

Carey, John. *Intellectuals and the Masses: Pride and Prejudice among the Literary Intelligentsia, 1880–1939*. London: Faber, 1992. Print.

Carlton, David L., and Peter A. Coclanis, eds. *Confronting Southern Poverty in the Great Depression: The Report on Economic Conditions of the South with Related Documents*. Boston: St. Martin's, 1996. Print.

Carpentier, Alejo. *El reino de este mundo* [*The Kingdom of This World*]. Montevideo: Arca, 1969. Print.

Césaire, Aimé. *Discourse on Colonialism*. Trans. Joan Pinkham. New York: Monthly Rev., 1972. Print.

Cézanne, Paul. "To Emile Bernard, Aix, 26 May 1904." Chipp 19–20.

Chatman, Seymour. *Story and Discourse: Narrative Structure in Fiction and Film*. Bloomington: Indiana UP, 1978. Print.

Chipp, Herschel B., ed. *Theories of Modern Art: A Source Book by Artists and Critics*. Berkeley: U of California P, 1996. Print.

Cixous, Hélène. "Sorties: Out and Out: Attacks/Ways Out/Forays." *The Feminist Reader: Essays in Gender and the Politics of Literary Criticism.* Ed. Catherine Belsey. New York: Blackwell, 1989. 91–103. Print.

Clarke, Deborah. *Robbing the Mother: Women in Faulkner*. Jackson: UP of Mississippi, 1994. Print.

Cohn, Dorrit. *Transparent Minds: Narrative Modes for Presenting Consciousness in Fiction*. Princeton: Princeton UP, 1978. Print.

Cosslett, Tess. *Women Writing Childbirth: Modern Discourses of Motherhood*. Manchester: Manchester UP, 1994. Print.

Cowley, Malcolm, ed. *The Portable Faulkner*. New York: Viking, 1946. Print.

Culler, Jonathan. "Omniscience." *Narrative* 12.1 (2004): 22–34. Print.

Daniel, Pete. *Standing at the Crossroads: Southern Life since 1900*. New York: Hill, 1986. Print.

Davis, Thadious M. *Faulkner's "Negro": Art and the Southern Context*. Baton Rouge: Louisiana State UP, 1983. Print.

Degler, Carl. *At Odds: Women and the Family in America from the Revolution to the Present*. New York: Oxford UP, 1981. Print.

Deleuze, Gilles, and Félix Guattari. *Anti-Oedipus: Capitalism and Schizophrenia*. Trans. Robert Hurley, Mark Seem, and Helen R. Lane. New York: Viking, 1977. Print.

DeLillo, Don. *Mao II*. New York: Penguin, 1991. Print.

———. *White Noise*. New York: Penguin, 1995. Print.

Derrida, Jacques. "Structure, Sign, and Play in the Discourse of the Human Sciences." *The Critical Tradition*. Ed. David H. Richter. 3rd ed. Boston: Bedford, 2005. 915–26. Print.

Douglas, Mary. Foreword. Mauss ix–xxii.

Doyle, Don H. *Faulkner's County: The Historical Roots of Yoknapatawpha*. Chapel Hill: U of North Carolina P, 2001. Print.

DuBois, W. E. B. *The Souls of Black Folk*. 1903. New York: Penguin, 1989. Print.

Duvall, John N. *Faulkner's Marginal Couple: Invisible, Outlaw, and Unspeakable Communities*. Austin: U of Texas P, 1990. Print.

Duvall, John N., and Ann J. Abadie, eds. *Faulkner and Postmodernism: Faulkner and Yoknapatawpha, 1999*. Jackson: UP of Mississippi, 2002. Print.

Edwards, Brent Hayes. *The Practice of Diaspora: Literature, Translation, and the Rise of Black Internationalism*. Cambridge: Harvard UP, 2003. Print.

Eisenstein, Sergei. *Film Form: Essays in Film Theory*. Ed. and trans. Jay Leyda. San Diego: Harvest, 1977. Print.

Eliot, T. S. The Waste Land *and Other Poems*. New York: Harcourt, 1962. Print.

Falkner, Murry C. *The Falkners of Mississippi: A Memoir*. Baton Rouge: Louisiana State UP, 1967. Print.

Faulkner, Jim. *Across the Creek: Faulkner Family Stories*. Jackson: UP of Mississippi, 1986. Print.

Faulkner, John. *My Brother Bill: An Affectionate Reminiscence*. New York: Trident, 1963. Print.

Faulkner, William. *Absalom, Absalom!* 1936. New York: Vintage, 1990. Print.

———. *As I Lay Dying*. 1930. New York: Mod. Lib., 2000. Print.

———. *As I Lay Dying*. 1930. Corrected text ed. New York: Vintage, 1990. Print.

———. "Barn Burning." *Collected Stories of William Faulkner*. New York: Random, 1950. 3–25. Print.

———. *Essays, Speeches, and Public Letters*. Ed. James B. Meriwether. New York: Mod. Lib., 2004. Print.

———. *Faulkner in the University*. Ed. Frederick L. Gwynn and Joseph L. Blotner. Charlottesville: U of Virginia P, 1995. Print.

———. *Go Down, Moses*. 1942. New York: Vintage, 1990. Print.

———. *The Hamlet*. 1939. New York: Vintage, 1991. Print.

———. "Interview with Jean Stein Vanden Heuvel." Faulkner, *Lion* 237–55.

———. *Light in August*. 1932. New York: Vintage, 1991. Print.

———. *Lion in the Garden: Interviews with William Faulkner, 1926–1962*. Ed. James B. Meriwether and Michael Millgate. New York: Random, 1968. Print.

———. *Requiem for a Nun*. New York: Random, 1951. Print.

———. *Sanctuary*. 1931. New York: Vintage, 1993. Print.

———. *Sartoris*. 1929. New York: Random, 1956. Print.

———. *The Sound and the Fury*. 1929. New York: Vintage, 1990. Print.

Federal Writers' Project of the Works Progress Administration. *Mississippi: The WPA Guide to the Magnolia State*. 1938. Jackson: UP of Mississippi, 1988. Print.

Ford, Margaret Patricia, and Suzanne Kincaid. *Who's Who in Faulkner*. Baton Rouge: Louisiana State UP, 1963. Print.

Fowler, Doreen. *Faulkner: The Return of the Repressed*. Charlottesville: UP of Virginia, 1997. Print.

Fowler, Doreen, and Ann J. Abadie, eds. *Faulkner and Race*. Jackson: UP of Mississippi, 1987. Print.

Franklin, R. W. "Narrative Management in *As I Lay Dying*." *Modern Fiction Studies* 13 (1967): 57–65. Print.

Freedman, Estelle. "The New Woman: Changing Views of Women in the 1920s." *Journal of American History* 64 (1974): 398–411. Print.

Freud, Sigmund. *Beyond the Pleasure Principle*. 1920. Trans. C. J. M. Hubback. New York: Boni, 1924. Print.

———. *Civilization and Its Discontents*. 1930. Trans. James Strachey. New York: Norton, 1961. Print.

———. *The Interpretation of Dreams*. 1900. Freud, *Standard Edition,* vols. 4–5.

———. "Negation." 1923. Freud, *Standard Edition* 19: 233–39.

———. *The Standard Edition of the Complete Psychological Works of Sigmund Freud*. Ed. and trans. James Strachey, with Anna Freud. 24 vols. London: Hogarth, 1953–74. Print.

———. *Totem and Taboo*. 1912–13. Freud, *Standard Edition* 13: 1–161.

Garland, Hamlin. "Lucrezia Burns." *Other Main-Travelled Roads*. New York: Harper, 1910. 81–115. Print.

Garnier, Caroline. "Women and Trauma in William Faulkner's Fiction." Diss. Emory U, 2002. Print.

Gay-Crosier, Raymond. The Stranger. Detroit: Gale, 2002. Print.

Genette, Gerard. *Narrative Discourse: An Essay on Method*. Trans. Jane E. Lewin. Ithaca: Cornell UP, 1980. Print.

Glissant, Édouard. *Faulkner, Mississippi*. New York: Farrar, 1999. Print.

Godden, Richard. *Fictions of Labor: William Faulkner and the South's Long Revolution*. New York: Cambridge UP, 1997. Print.

———. *William Faulkner: An Economy of Complex Words*. Princeton: Princeton UP, 2007. Print.

Gordon, Linda. "Voluntary Motherhood: The Beginnings of Feminist Birth Control Ideas in the United States." *Feminist Studies* 1.3–4 (1973): 5–22. Print.

———. *Woman's Body, Woman's Right: A Social History of Birth Control in America*. New York: Penguin, 1976. Print.

Gray, Richard J. *The Life of William Faulkner: A Critical Biography*. Oxford: Blackwell, 1994. Print.

Gregory, James N. *The Southern Diaspora: How the Great Migrations of Black and White Southerners Transformed America*. Chapel Hill: U of North Carolina P, 1997. Print.

Gresset, Michel. *Fascination: Faulkner's Fiction, 1919–1936*. Durham: Duke UP, 1989. Print.

———. *A Faulkner Chronology*. Jackson: UP of Mississippi, 1985. Print.

Guerard, Albert J. "Faulkner the Innovator." *The Maker and the Myth: Faulkner and Yoknapatawpha, 1977*. Ed. Evans Harrington and Ann J. Abadie. Jackson: UP of Mississippi, 1978. 71–88. Print.

Gunning, Tom. *D. W. Griffith and the Origins of American Narrative Film: The Early Years at Biograph*. Urbana: U of Illinois P, 1991. Print.

Gutting, Gabriele. *Yoknapatawpha: The Function of Geographical and Historical Facts in William Faulkner's Fictional Picture of the Deep South*. New York: Lang, 1992. Print.

Gwin, Minrose C. *The Feminine and Faulkner: Reading (beyond) Sexual Difference.* Knoxville: U of Tennessee P, 1990. Print.

Hagood, Margaret Jarman. *Mothers of the South: Portraiture of the White Tenant Farm Woman*. Charlottesville: UP of Virginia, 1996. Print.

Hale, Dorothy. "*As I Lay Dying*'s Heterogeneous Discourse." *Novel* 23.1 (1989): 5–23. Print.

Hamblin, Robert W., and Charles A. Peek, eds. *A William Faulkner Encyclopedia*. Westport: Greenwood, 1999. Print.

Hampsten, Elizabeth. *Read This Only to Yourself: The Private Writings of Midwestern Women, 1880–1910*. Bloomington: Indiana UP, 1982. Print.

Handley, George. *Postslavery Literatures in the Americas: Family Portraits in Black and White*. Charlottesville: UP of Virginia, 2000. Print.

Harrison, Charles, Francis Frascina, and Gill Perry. *Primitivism, Cubism, Abstraction: The Early Twentieth Century*. New Haven: Yale UP, 1993. Print.

Hassan, Ihab. *The Postmodern Turn: Essays in Postmodern Theory and Culture.* Columbus: Ohio State UP, 1987. Print.

Hegel, G. W. F. *The Phenomenology of Mind*. Trans. J. B. Bailie. London: Allen, 1955. Print.

Henninger, Katherine. "'It's a Outrage': Pregnancy and Abortion in Faulkner's Fiction of the Thirties." *Faulkner Journal* 12.1 (1996): 23–41. Print.

Hewson, Marc. "'My Children Were of Me Alone': Maternal Influence in Faulkner's *As I Lay Dying*." *Mississippi Quarterly* 53.4 (2000): 551–67. Print.

Hoffert, Sylvia. *Private Matters: American Attitudes toward Childbearing and Infant Nurture in the Urban North, 1800–1860*. Urbana: U of Illinois P, 1989. Print.

Hollingworth, Leta S. "Social Devices for Impelling Women to Bear and Raise Children." *American Journal of Sociology* 22.1 (1916): 19–29. Print.

Howe, Irving. *William Faulkner: A Critical Study*. 2nd ed. New York: Vintage, 1962. Print.

Hughes, Robert. *The Shock of the New: The Hundred-Year History of Modern Art*. New York: Knopf, 1980. Print.

Hustis, Harriet. "The Tangled Webs We Weave: Faulkner Scholarship and the Significance of Addie Bundren's Monologue." *Faulkner Journal* 12.1 (1996): 3–21. Print.

Huyssen, Andreas. *After the Great Divide: Modernism, Mass Culture, Postmodernism.* Bloomington: Indiana UP, 1986. Print.

I'll Take My Stand: The South and the Agrarian Tradition. 1930. New York: Harper, 1962. Print.

In a Strange Room. By Michael Gardner. Dir. Gardner. Brick Theater, Brooklyn. 2004. Performance.

"Intention." *New Princeton Encyclopedia of Poetry and Poetics*. Ed. Alex Preminger and T. V. F. Brogan. Princeton: Princeton UP, 1993. Print.

Irigaray, Luce. *Speculum of the Other Woman.* Trans. Gillian C. Gill. Ithaca: Cornell UP, 1985. Print.

Irwin, John T. *Doubling and Incest / Repetition and Revenge: A Speculative Reading of Faulkner*. Baltimore: Johns Hopkins UP, 1975. Print.

Iser, Wolfgang. "The Reading Process: A Phenomenological Approach." *The Implied Reader: Patterns of Communication in Prose Fiction from Bunyan to Beckett.* Baltimore: Johns Hopkins UP, 1974. 274–94. Print.

Jabra, Jabra I. *The Ship*. Trans. Adnan Haydar and Roger Allen. Washington: Three Continents, 1985. Print.

Jameson, Fredric. *Postmodernism; or, The Cultural Logic of Late Capitalism*. Durham: Duke UP, 1991. Print.

Jaspers, Karl. *The Origin and Goal of History*. Trans. Michael Bullock. New Haven: Yale UP, 1953. Print.

Jastrow, Joseph. *Character and Temperament*. New York: Appleton, 1915. Print.

Jehlen, Myra. *Class and Character in Faulkner's South*. New York: Columbia UP, 1976. Print.

Jenkins, Andrea Powell. "'The Last . . . Thing One Needed to Know': Kristeva's 'Herethics' in Evelyn Scott's *Escapade* and *The Narrow House*." *Journal of Modern Literature* 29.3 (2006): 78–102. Print.

Jones, Lu Ann. *Mama Learned Us to Work: Farm Women in the New South*. Chapel Hill: U of North Carolina P, 2002. Print.

Jones, Paul C. "Becoming [M]other: The Anxiety of Maternity in Evelyn Scott's *Escapade*." *Evelyn Scott: Recovering a Lost Modernist*. Ed. Dorothy M. Scura and Jones. Knoxville: U of Tennessee P, 2001. 37–52. Print.

Joyce, James. *Ulysses*. 1922. New York: Mod. Lib., 1961. Print.

Kafka, Franz. *The Metamorphosis.* Ed. and trans. Stanley Corngold. New York: Bantam, 1986. Print.

Kartiganer, Donald M. "The Farm and the Journey: Ways of Mourning and Meaning in *As I Lay Dying*." *Mississippi Quarterly* 43.3 (1990): 281–303. Print.

———. *The Fragile Thread: The Meaning of Form in Faulkner's Novels*. Amherst: U of Massachusetts P, 1979. Print.

Kartiganer, Donald M., and Ann J. Abadie, eds. *Faulkner and Psychology*. Jackson: UP of Mississippi, 1994. Print.

———, eds. *Faulkner in Cultural Context*. Jackson: UP of Mississippi, 1997. Print.

Kawin, Bruce. "The Montage Elements in Faulkner's Fiction." *Faulkner, Modernism, and Film: Faulkner and Yoknapatawpha, 1978*. Ed. Evans Harrington and Ann J. Abadie. Jackson: UP of Mississippi, 1978. 103–26. Print.

Kelly, Sean K. "A Reading of *As I Lay Dying*: Another Proposal for Thinking Faulkner's Aesthetics/Politics of Failure." *Arizona Quarterly* 59.1 (2003): 117–35. Print.

Kermode, Frank. *The Sense of an Ending: Studies in the Theory of Fiction*. 1967. New York: Oxford UP, 2000. Print.

Kerr, Elizabeth M. *Yoknapatawpha: Faulkner's "Little Postage Stamp of Native Soil."* New York: Fordham UP, 1969. Print.

Kincaid, Nanci. "As Me and Addie Lay Dying." *Southern Review* 30.3 (1994): n. pag. *Free Library*. Web. 16 Feb. 2011.

Kinney, Arthur F. *Faulkner's Narrative Poetics: Style as Vision*. Amherst: U of Massachusetts P, 1978. Print.

Kirby, Jack Temple. *Rural Worlds Lost: The American South, 1920–1960*. Baton Rouge: Louisiana State UP, 1987. Print.

Klaus, Alisa C. *Every Child a Lion: The Origins of Maternal and Infant Health Policy in the United States and France, 1890–1920*. Ithaca: Cornell UP, 1993. Print.

Kolmerten, Carol A., Stephen M. Ross, and Judith Bryant Wittenberg, eds. *Unflinching Gaze: Morrison and Faulkner Re-envisioned*. Jackson: UP of Mississippi, 1997. Print.

Kristeva, Julia. *Powers of Horror: An Essay on Abjection*. Trans. Leon S. Roudiez. New York: Columbia UP, 1982. Print.

Kyriakoudes, Louis M. *The Social Origins of the Urban South: Race, Gender, and Migration in Nashville and Middle Tennessee, 1890–1930*. Chapel Hill: U of North Carolina P, 2003. Print.

Lacan, Jacques. *The Seminar of Jacques Lacan: Book II: The Ego in Freud's Theory and in the Technique of Psychoanalysis, 1954–1955*. Ed. Jacques-Alain Miller. Trans. Sylvana Tomaselli, with notes by John Forrester. New York: Norton, 1991. Print.

Ladd, Barbara. *Nationalism and the Color Line in George W. Cable, Mark Twain, and William Faulkner*. Baton Rouge: Louisiana State UP, 1996. Print.

———. *Resisting History: Gender, Modernity, and Authorship in William Faulkner, Zora Neale Hurston, and Eudora Welty*. Baton Rouge: Louisiana State UP, 2007. Print.

Laidlaw, James. "A Free Gift Makes No Friends." *Journal of the Royal Anthropological Institute* 6.4 (2000): 617–34. Print.

Lautréamont, comte de [Isidore-Lucien Ducasse]. *Œuvres complètes*. Ed. Hubert Juin. Paris: Gallimard, 1973. Print.

Lawrence, D. H. *Studies in Classic American Literature*. New York: Seltzer, 1923. Print.

Leavitt, Judith, and Whitney Walton. "'Down to Death's Door': Women's Perceptions of Childbirth in America." *Women and Health in America: Historical Readings*. Ed. Leavitt. Madison: U of Wisconsin P, 1984. 155–65. Print.

Léger, Fernand. "A New Realism—the Object." 1926. Chipp 279.

Lemahieu, D. L. *A Culture for Democracy: Mass Communication and the Cultivated Mind in Britain between the Wars*. Oxford: Clarendon, 1988. Print.

Lester, Cheryl. "As They Lay Dying: Rural Depopulation and Social Dislocation as a Structure of Feeling." *Faulkner Journal* 21.1–2 (2005–06): 28–50. Print.

———. "Racial Awareness and Arrested Development: *The Sound and the Fury* and the Great Migration (1915–1928)." Weinstein, *Cambridge Companion* 123–45.

Levenson, Michael. Introduction. *The Cambridge Companion to Modernism*. Ed. Levenson. Cambridge: Cambridge UP, 1999. 1–8. Print.

Leyda, Julia. "Shifting Sands: The Myths of Class Mobility." *A Companion to William Faulkner*. Ed. Richard C. Moreland. Malden: Blackwell, 2007. 165–79. Print.

Liddell Hart, B. H. "'Woman Wanders—the World Wavers' or 'Woman and the World-Quake.'" *English Review* 59.3 (1934): 310–25. Print.

Link, William A. *The Paradox of Southern Progressivism, 1880–1930*. Chapel Hill: U of North Carolina P, 1992. Print.

Lockyer, Judith. "Language and the Process of Narration in Faulkner's *As I Lay Dying*." *Arizona Quarterly* 43.2 (1987): 165–77. Print.

Luce, Dianne C. *As I Lay Dying*. New York: Garland, 1990. Print. Garland Faulkner Annotation Ser.

Lucenti, Lisa Marie. "Willa Cather's *The Professor's House*: Sleeping with the Dead." *Texas Studies in Literature and Language* 41.3 (1999): 236–61. Print.

Lurie, Peter. *Vision's Immanence: Faulkner, Film, and the Popular Imagination*. Baltimore: Johns Hopkins UP, 2004. Print.

Lyotard, Jean François. *The Postmodern Condition: A Report on Knowledge*. Trans. Geoff Bennington and Brian Massuni. Minneapolis: U of Minnesota P, 1984. Print.

Lytle, Andrew Nelson. "The Hind Tit." *I'll Take* 201–45.

Malin, Jo. *The Voice of the Mother: Embedded Maternal Narratives in Twentieth-Century Women's Autobiographies*. Carbondale: Southern Illinois UP, 2000. Print.

Man with a Movie Camera. Dir. Dziga Vertov. 1929. Image Entertainment, 1998. DVD.

Marti, Donald B. *Women of the Grange: Mutuality and Sisterhood in Rural America, 1866–1920*. New York: Greenwood, 1991. Print.

Marx, Karl, and Friedrich Engels. *The Communist Manifesto*. 1848. New York: Penguin, 1985. Print.

Matsuoka, Shinya. "Cut and Montage: Genetic Processes of Faulknerian Counterpoint." *Studies in American Literature* 38 (2002): 75–90. Print.

Matthews, John T. "*As I Lay Dying* in the Machine Age." *Boundary 2* 19.1 (1992): 69–94. Print.

———. "Intertextuality and Originality: Hawthorne, Faulkner, Updike." *Intertextuality in Faulkner*. Ed. Michel Gresset and Noel Polk. Jackson: UP of Mississippi, 1985. 144–57. Print.

———. *The Play of Faulkner's Language*. Ithaca: Cornell UP, 1982. Print.

———. *William Faulkner: Seeing through the South*. Malden: Wiley-Blackwell, 2009. Print.

Matthews, Nancy Mowll, and Charles Musser, eds. *Moving Pictures: American Art and Early Film, 1880–1910*. Manchester: Hudson Hills, 2005. Print.

Mauss, Marcel. *The Gift: The Form and Reason for Exchange in Archaic Societies*. 1924. Trans. W. D. Halls. London: Routledge, 1990. Print.

Maxwell, Catherine. *The Female Sublime from Milton to Swinburne: Bearing Blindness*. Manchester: Manchester UP, 2001. Print.

Maxwell, W. B. "The Sort of Woman a Man Likes: A Symposium of the Opinions of Well Known Novelists." *Strand* 45 (1913): 646–52. Print.

McCann, Barry R. "Faulkner's *As I Lay Dying*: The Coffin Pictogram and the Function of Form." *University of Mississippi Studies in English* 11–12 (1993–95): 272–81. Print.

McGovern, James. "The American Woman's Pre–World War I Freedom in Manners and Morals." *Journal of American History* 58 (1968): 315–33. Print.

McKee, Patricia. *Producing American Races: Henry James, William Faulkner, Toni Morrison*. Durham: Duke UP, 1999. Print.

McMillen, Sally G. *Motherhood in the Old South: Pregnancy, Childbirth, and Infant Rearing*. Baton Rouge: Louisiana State UP, 1990. Print.

Mellard, James M. "Realism, Naturalism, Modernism: Residual, Dominant, and Emergent Ideologies in *As I Lay Dying*." *Faulkner and Ideology*. Ed. Donald M. Kartiganer and Ann J. Abadie. Jackson: UP of Mississippi, 1995. 217–37. Print.

Michaelson, Bruce. *Printer's Devil: Mark Twain and the American Publishing Revolution*. Berkeley: U of California P, 2006. Print.

Miller, William Ian. "Requiting the Unwanted Gift." *Humiliation: And Other Essays on Honor, Social Discomfort, and Violence.* Ithaca: Cornell UP, 1993. 15–52. Print.

Millgate, Michael. *The Achievement of William Faulkner*. Lincoln: U of Nebraska P, 1978. Print.

Minter, David. *A Cultural History of the American Novel: Henry James to William Faulkner*. Cambridge: Cambridge UP, 1954. Print.

———. *William Faulkner: His Life and Work*. Baltimore: Johns Hopkins UP, 1980. Print.

Mohr, James C. *Abortion in America: The Origins and Evolution of National Policy, 1800–1900.* New York: Oxford UP, 1978. Print.

Moreland, Richard C. *Faulkner and Modernism: Rereading and Rewriting*. Madison: U of Wisconsin P, 1990. Print.

———. "Faulkner and Modernism." Weinstein, *Cambridge Companion* 17–30.

Morris, Wesley, and Barbara Alverson Morris. *Reading Faulkner*. Madison: U of Wisconsin P, 1989. Print.

Mortimer, Gail L. *Faulkner's Rhetoric of Loss: A Study in Perception and Meaning*. Austin: U of Texas P, 1983. Print.

Obama, Barack. "Obama Race Speech: Read the Full Text." *The Huffington Post*. HuffingtonPost.com, 18 Mar. 2008. Web. 13 Nov. 2009.

O'Donnell, Patrick. "Between the Family and the State: Nomadism and Authority in *As I Lay Dying*." *Faulkner Journal* 7.1–2 (1991–92): 83–94. Print.

———. "Faulkner and Postmodernism." Weinstein, *Cambridge Companion* 31–50.

———. "The Spectral Road: Metaphors of Transference in Faulkner's *As I Lay Dying*." *Papers on Language and Literature* 20.1 (1984): 60–79. Print.

Padgett, John B. *William Faulkner on the Web*. U of Mississippi, 2009. Web. 13 Nov. 2009.

Page, Walter Hines. *The Rebuilding of Old Commonwealths: Being Essays towards the Training of the Forgotten Man in the Southern States*. 1902. New York: AMS, 1970. Print.

Parini, Jay. *One Matchless Time: A Life of William Faulkner*. New York: Harper, 2004. Print.

Parker, Andrew, and Eve Kosofsky Sedgwick, eds. *Performativity and Performance*. New York: Routledge, 1995. Print.

Parker, Robert Dale. *Faulkner and the Novelistic Imagination*. Urbana: U of Illinois P, 1985. Print.

———. "Sex and Gender, Feminine and Masculine: Faulkner and the Polymorphous Exchange of Cultural Binaries." *Faulkner and Gender: Faulkner and Yoknapa-*

tawpha, 1994. Ed. Donald M. Kartiganer and Ann J. Abadie. Jackson: UP of Mississippi, 1996. 73–96. Print.

Parks, Suzan-Lori. *Getting Mother's Body*. New York: Random, 2003. Print.

Parry, Jonathan. "The Gift, the Indian Gift, and the 'Indian Gift.'" *Man* 21.3 (1986): 453–73. Print.

Paz, Octavio. *Children of the Mire: Modern Poetry from Romanticism to the Avant-Garde*. Trans. Rachel Phillips. Cambridge: Harvard UP, 1974. Print.

Pitavy, François L. "Through Darl's Eyes Darkly: The Vision of the Poet in *As I Lay Dying*." *William Faulkner: Materials, Studies, and Criticism* 4 (1982): 37–62. Print.

Porter, Carolyn. *Seeing and Being: The Plight of the Participant Observer in Emerson, James, Adams, and Faulkner*. Middletown: Wesleyan UP, 1981. Print.

———. "Symbolic Fathers and Dead Mothers: A Feminist Approach to Faulkner." Kartiganer and Abadie, *Faulkner and Psychology* 78–121.

Putzel, Max. *Genius of Place: William Faulkner's Triumphant Beginnings*. Baton Rouge: Louisiana State UP, 1985. Print.

Railey, Kevin T. *Natural Aristocracy: History, Ideology, and the Production of William Faulkner*. Tuscaloosa: U of Alabama P, 1999. Print.

Ransom, John Crowe. "Reconstructed but Unregenerate." *I'll Take* 1–27.

Reagan, Leslie J. *When Abortion Was a Crime: Women, Medicine, and Law in the United States, 1867–1973*. Berkeley: U of California P, 1997. Print.

Rich, Adrienne. *Of Woman Born: Motherhood as Experience and Institution*. New York: Norton, 1976. Print.

Rippetoe, Rita. "Unstained Shirt, Stained Character: Anse Bundren Reread." *Mississippi Quarterly* 54 (2001): 313–25. Print.

Roberts, Diane. *Faulkner and Southern Womanhood*. Athens: U of Georgia P, 1994. Print.

Roberts, Elizabeth Madox. *The Time of Man*. 1926. Lexington: UP of Kentucky, 2000. Print.

Rosenblum, Robert. *Cubism and Twentieth-Century Art*. New York: Abrams, 2001. Print.

Ross, Stephen M. *Faulkner's Inexhaustible Voice: Speech and Writing in Faulkner*. Athens: U of Georgia P, 1989. Print.

———. "Shapes of Time and Consciousness in *As I Lay Dying*." *Texas Studies in Literature and Language* 16.4 (1975): 723–37. Print.

Rousseau, Jean-Jacques. *Politics and the Arts: A Letter to M. D'Alembert on the Theatre*. Trans. A. Bloom. Ithaca: Cornell UP, 1968. Print.

Rulfo, Juan. *Pedro Páramo*. Trans. Margaret Sayers Peden. New York: Grove, 1994. Print.

Said, Edward W. *Beginnings: Intention and Method*. New York: Columbia UP, 1975. Print.

Saussure, Ferdinand de. "From *Course in General Linguistics*." *Critical Theory since 1965*. Ed. Hazard Adams and Leroy Searle. Tallahassee: Florida State UP, 1986. 646–56. Print.

Schleifer, Ronald. *Rhetoric and Death: The Language of Modernism and Postmodern Discourse Theory*. Urbana: U of Illinois P, 1990. Print.

Schwartz, Lawrence H. *Creating Faulkner's Reputation: The Politics of Modern Literary Criticism*. Knoxville: U of Tennessee P, 1988. Print.

Scott, Evelyn. *Escapade*. 1923. Charlottesville: UP of Virginia, 1995. Print.

Sebold, Alice. *The Lovely Bones*. 2002. New York: Back Bay, 2004. Print.

Sernett, Milton C. *Bound for the Promised Land: African American Religion and the Great Migration*. Durham: Duke UP, 1997. Print.

Shapiro, Henry D. *Appalachia on Our Mind: The Southern Mountains and Mountaineers in American Consciousness, 1870–1920*. Chapel Hill: U of North Carolina P, 1978. Print.

Singal, Daniel Joseph. *William Faulkner: The Making of a Modernist*. Chapel Hill: U of North Carolina P, 1997. Print.

Smith, Johanna M. "'Too Beautiful Altogether': Ideologies of Gender and Empire in *Heart of Darkness*." Heart of Darkness*: Complete, Authoritative Text with Biographical and Historical Contexts, Critical History, and Essays from Five Contemporary Critical Perspectives*. Ed. Ross C. Murfin. Boston: Bedford, 1996. 169–84. Print.

Smith, Jon, and Deborah Cohn, eds. *Look Away! The U.S. South in New World Studies*. Durham: Duke UP, 2004. Print.

Snead, James A. *Figures of Division: William Faulkner's Major Novels*. New York: Methuen, 1986. Print.

Snell, Susan. *Phil Stone of Oxford: A Vicarious Life*. Athens: U of Georgia P, 1991. Print.

The Sopranos. Exec. prod. David Chase. HBO with Brillstein Grey Entertainment. 1999–2007. Television.

Spivak, Gayatri Chakravorty. *A Critique of Postcolonial Reason: Toward a History of the Vanishing Present*. Cambridge: Harvard UP, 1999. Print.

Stonum, Gary Lee. *Faulkner's Career: An Internal Literary History*. Ithaca: Cornell UP, 1979. Print.

Stott, William. *Documentary Expression and Thirties America*. 1974. Chicago: U of Chicago P, 1986. Print.

Sundquist, Eric J. *Faulkner: The House Divided*. Baltimore: Johns Hopkins UP, 1983. Print.

Swiggart, Peter. *The Art of Faulkner's Novels*. Austin: U of Texas P, 1962. Print.

Teaching Faulkner. Center for Faulkner Studies. Southeast Missouri U, 8 Oct. 2009. Web. 13 Nov. 2009.

Tebbetts, Terrell. "*Sanctuary*, Marriage, and the Status of Women in 1920s America." *Faulkner Journal* 19.1 (2003): 47–60. Print.

Tindall, George B. *The Emergence of the New South: 1913–1945*. Baton Rouge: Louisiana State UP, 1967. Print.

Torgovnick, Marianna. *Closure in the Novel*. Princeton: Princeton UP, 1981. Print.

Towner, Theresa M. *Faulkner on the Color Line: The Later Novels*. Jackson: UP of Mississippi, 2000. Print.

Vacche, Angela Dalle, ed. *The Visual Turn: Classical Film Theory and Art History*. New Brunswick: Rutgers UP, 2003. Print.

VanderVeen, Arthur A. "Faulkner, the Interwar Gold Standard, and Discourses of Value in the 1930s." *Faulkner Journal* 12.1 (1996): 43–62. Print.

Vertov, Dziga. *Kino-Eye: The Writings of Dziga Vertov*. Ed. Annette Michaelson. Trans. Kevin O'Brien. Berkeley: U of California P, 1984. Print.

Viatte, Germain, ed. *Peinture, cinéma, peinture*. Paris: Hazan, 1989. Print.

Vickery, Olga W. "The Dimensions of Consciousness: *As I Lay Dying*." *William Faulkner: Three Decades of Criticism*. Ed. Frederick J. Hoffman and Vickery. New York: Harcourt, 1963. 232–47. Print.

———. *The Novels of William Faulkner: A Critical Interpretation*. Rev. ed. Baton Rouge: Louisiana State UP, 1964. Print.

Volpe, Edmond. *A Reader's Guide to William Faulkner.* New York: Farrar, 1964. Print.

Vonnegut, Kurt. *Slaughterhouse-Five*. 1969. New York: Laurel, 1991. Print.

Wadlington, Warwick. As I Lay Dying*: Stories out of Stories*. New York: Twayne, 1992. Print.

———. *Reading Faulknerian Tragedy*. Ithaca: Cornell UP, 1983. Print.

Ward, Matthew. Translator's Note. Camus v–vii.

Wasson, Ben. *Count No 'Count: Flashbacks to Faulkner*. Jackson: UP of Mississippi, 1983. Print.

Weinstein, Philip M. *Becoming Faulkner: The Art and Life of William Faulkner*. New York: Oxford, 2010. Print.

———, ed. *The Cambridge Companion to William Faulkner*. Cambridge: Cambridge UP, 1995. Print.

———. *Faulkner's Subject: A Cosmos No One Owns*. New York: Cambridge UP, 1992. Print.

———. *What Else but Love? The Ordeal of Race in Faulkner and Morrison*. New York: Columbia UP, 1996. Print.

Weisgerber, Jean. *Faulkner and Dostoevsky: Influence and Confluence*. Trans. Dean McWilliams. Athens: Ohio UP, 1974. Print.

Wertz, Richard W., and Dorothy C. Wertz. *Lying-In: A History of Childbirth in America.* New York: Free, 1977. Print.

Wilde, Meta Carpenter, and Orin Borsten. *A Loving Gentleman: The Love Story of William Faulkner and Meta Carpenter.* New York: Simon, 1976. Print.

Williams, David. *Faulkner's Women: The Myth and the Muse.* Montreal: McGill-Queens UP, 1977. Print.

Williamson, Joel. *William Faulkner and Southern History*. New York: Oxford UP, 1993. Print.

Willis, Susan. "Aesthetics of the Rural Slum: Contradictions and Dependency in 'The Bear.'" *Social Text* 2 (1979): 82–103. Print.

———. "Learning from the Banana." *American Quarterly* 39.4 (1987): 586–600. Print.

Wilson, Charles Reagan, and William Ferris, eds. *Encyclopedia of Southern Culture*. Chapel Hill: U of North Carolina P, 1989. Print.

Wilson, Jason. "*Pedro Páramo* by Juan Rulfo." *The Cambridge Companion to the Latin American Novel.* Ed. Kristal Efrain. Cambridge: Cambridge UP, 2005. 232–44. Print.

Wittenberg, Judith Bryant. *Faulkner: The Transfiguration of Biography*. Lincoln: U of Nebraska P, 1979. Print.

Woodward, C. Vann. *Origins of the New South, 1877–1913*. Rev. ed. Baton Rouge: Louisiana State UP, 1971. Print.

Wright, Austin M. *Recalcitrance, Faulkner, and the Professors: A Critical Fiction*. Iowa City: U of Iowa P, 1990. Print.

Yeats, W. B. "The Second Coming." *Dial* 69.5 (1920): 466. Print.

Zender, Karl F. *The Crossing of the Ways: William Faulkner, the South, and the Modern World*. New Brunswick: Rutgers UP, 1989. Print.

INDEX

Modern Language Association of America

Approaches to Teaching World Literature

Achebe's Things Fall Apart. Ed. Bernth Lindfors. 1991.
Arthurian Tradition. Ed. Maureen Fries and Jeanie Watson. 1992.
Atwood's The Handmaid's Tale *and Other Works*. Ed. Sharon R. Wilson, Thomas B. Friedman, and Shannon Hengen. 1996.
Austen's Emma. Ed. Marcia McClintock Folsom. 2004.
Austen's Pride and Prejudice. Ed. Marcia McClintock Folsom. 1993.
Balzac's Old Goriot. Ed. Michal Peled Ginsburg. 2000.
Baudelaire's Flowers of Evil. Ed. Laurence M. Porter. 2000.
Beckett's Waiting for Godot. Ed. June Schlueter and Enoch Brater. 1991.
Beowulf. Ed. Jess B. Bessinger, Jr., and Robert F. Yeager. 1984.
Blake's Songs of Innocence and of Experience. Ed. Robert F. Gleckner and Mark L. Greenberg. 1989.
Boccaccio's Decameron. Ed. James H. McGregor. 2000.
British Women Poets of the Romantic Period. Ed. Stephen C. Behrendt and Harriet Kramer Linkin. 1997.
Charlotte Brontë's Jane Eyre. Ed. Diane Long Hoeveler and Beth Lau. 1993.
Emily Brontë's Wuthering Heights. Ed. Sue Lonoff and Terri A. Hasseler. 2006.
Byron's Poetry. Ed. Frederick W. Shilstone. 1991.
Camus's The Plague. Ed. Steven G. Kellman. 1985.
Writings of Bartolomé de Las Casas. Ed. Santa Arias and Eyda M. Merediz. 2008.
Cather's My Ántonia. Ed. Susan J. Rosowski. 1989.
Cervantes' Don Quixote. Ed. Richard Bjornson. 1984.
Chaucer's Canterbury Tales. Ed. Joseph Gibaldi. 1980.
Chaucer's Troilus and Criseyde *and the Shorter Poems*. Ed. Tison Pugh and Angela Jane Weisl. 2006.
Chopin's The Awakening. Ed. Bernard Koloski. 1988.
Coleridge's Poetry and Prose. Ed. Richard E. Matlak. 1991.
Collodi's Pinocchio *and Its Adaptations*. Ed. Michael Sherberg. 2006.
Conrad's "Heart of Darkness" and "The Secret Sharer." Ed. Hunt Hawkins and Brian W. Shaffer. 2002.
Dante's Divine Comedy. Ed. Carole Slade. 1982.
Defoe's Robinson Crusoe. Ed. Maximillian E. Novak and Carl Fisher. 2005.
DeLillo's White Noise. Ed. Tim Engles and John N. Duvall. 2006.
Dickens's Bleak House. Ed. John O. Jordan and Gordon Bigelow. 2009.
Dickens's David Copperfield. Ed. Richard J. Dunn. 1984.
Dickinson's Poetry. Ed. Robin Riley Fast and Christine Mack Gordon. 1989.
Narrative of the Life of Frederick Douglass. Ed. James C. Hall. 1999.
Duras's Ourika. Ed. Mary Ellen Birkett and Christopher Rivers. 2009.
Early Modern Spanish Drama. Ed. Laura R. Bass and Margaret R. Greer. 2006.

Eliot's Middlemarch. Ed. Kathleen Blake. 1990.
Eliot's Poetry and Plays. Ed. Jewel Spears Brooker. 1988.
Shorter Elizabethan Poetry. Ed. Patrick Cheney and Anne Lake Prescott. 2000.
Ellison's Invisible Man. Ed. Susan Resneck Parr and Pancho Savery. 1989.
English Renaissance Drama. Ed. Karen Bamford and Alexander Leggatt. 2002.
Works of Louise Erdrich. Ed. Gregg Sarris, Connie A. Jacobs, and James R. Giles. 2004.
Dramas of Euripides. Ed. Robin Mitchell-Boyask. 2002.
Faulkner's As I Lay Dying. Ed. Patrick O'Donnell and Lynda Zwinger. 2011.
Faulkner's The Sound and the Fury. Ed. Stephen Hahn and Arthur F. Kinney. 1996.
Fitzgerald's The Great Gatsby. Ed. Jackson R. Bryer and Nancy P. VanArsdale. 2009.
Flaubert's Madame Bovary. Ed. Laurence M. Porter and Eugene F. Gray. 1995.
García Márquez's One Hundred Years of Solitude. Ed. María Elena de Valdés and Mario J. Valdés. 1990.
Gilman's "The Yellow Wall-Paper" and Herland. Ed. Denise D. Knight and Cynthia J. Davis. 2003.
Goethe's Faust. Ed. Douglas J. McMillan. 1987.
Gothic Fiction: The British and American Traditions. Ed. Diane Long Hoeveler and Tamar Heller. 2003.
Grass's The Tin Drum. Ed. Monika Shafi. 2008.
Hebrew Bible as Literature in Translation. Ed. Barry N. Olshen and Yael S. Feldman. 1989.
Homer's Iliad *and* Odyssey. Ed. Kostas Myrsiades. 1987.
Hurston's Their Eyes Were Watching God *and Other Works*. Ed. John Lowe. 2009.
Ibsen's A Doll House. Ed. Yvonne Shafer. 1985.
Henry James's Daisy Miller *and* The Turn of the Screw. Ed. Kimberly C. Reed and Peter G. Beidler. 2005.
Works of Samuel Johnson. Ed. David R. Anderson and Gwin J. Kolb. 1993.
Joyce's Ulysses. Ed. Kathleen McCormick and Erwin R. Steinberg. 1993.
Works of Sor Juana Inés de la Cruz. Ed. Emilie L. Bergmann and Stacey Schlau. 2007.
Kafka's Short Fiction. Ed. Richard T. Gray. 1995.
Keats's Poetry. Ed. Walter H. Evert and Jack W. Rhodes. 1991.
Kingston's The Woman Warrior. Ed. Shirley Geok-lin Lim. 1991.
Lafayette's The Princess of Clèves. Ed. Faith E. Beasley and Katharine Ann Jensen. 1998.
Works of D. H. Lawrence. Ed. M. Elizabeth Sargent and Garry Watson. 2001.
Lazarillo de Tormes *and the Picaresque Tradition*. Ed. Anne J. Cruz. 2009.
Lessing's The Golden Notebook. Ed. Carey Kaplan and Ellen Cronan Rose. 1989.
Mann's Death in Venice *and Other Short Fiction*. Ed. Jeffrey B. Berlin. 1992.
Marguerite de Navarre's Heptameron. Ed. Colette H. Winn. 2007.
Medieval English Drama. Ed. Richard K. Emmerson. 1990.
Melville's Moby-Dick. Ed. Martin Bickman. 1985.
Metaphysical Poets. Ed. Sidney Gottlieb. 1990.

Miller's Death of a Salesman. Ed. Matthew C. Roudané. 1995.
Milton's Paradise Lost. Ed. Galbraith M. Crump. 1986.
Milton's Shorter Poetry and Prose. Ed. Peter C. Herman. 2007.
Molière's Tartuffe *and Other Plays*. Ed. James F. Gaines and Michael S. Koppisch. 1995.
Momaday's The Way to Rainy Mountain. Ed. Kenneth M. Roemer. 1988.
Montaigne's Essays. Ed. Patrick Henry. 1994.
Novels of Toni Morrison. Ed. Nellie Y. McKay and Kathryn Earle. 1997.
Murasaki Shikibu's The Tale of Genji. Ed. Edward Kamens. 1993.
Nabokov's Lolita. Ed. Zoran Kuzmanovich and Galya Diment. 2008.
Works of Tim O'Brien. Ed. Alex Vernon and Catherine Calloway. 2010.
Works of Ovid and the Ovidian Tradition. Ed. Barbara Weiden Boyd and Cora Fox. 2010.
Poe's Prose and Poetry. Ed. Jeffrey Andrew Weinstock and Tony Magistrale. 2008.
Pope's Poetry. Ed. Wallace Jackson and R. Paul Yoder. 1993.
Proust's Fiction and Criticism. Ed. Elyane Dezon-Jones and Inge Crosman Wimmers. 2003.
Puig's Kiss of the Spider Woman. Ed. Daniel Balderston and Francine Masiello. 2007.
Pynchon's The Crying of Lot 49 *and Other Works.* Ed. Thomas H. Schaub. 2008.
Novels of Samuel Richardson. Ed. Lisa Zunshine and Jocelyn Harris. 2006.
Rousseau's Confessions *and* Reveries of the Solitary Walker. Ed. John C. O'Neal and Ourida Mostefai. 2003.
Scott's Waverley Novels. Ed. Evan Gottlieb and Ian Duncan. 2009.
Shakespeare's Hamlet. Ed. Bernice W. Kliman. 2001.
Shakespeare's King Lear. Ed. Robert H. Ray. 1986.
Shakespeare's Othello. Ed. Peter Erickson and Maurice Hunt. 2005.
Shakespeare's Romeo and Juliet. Ed. Maurice Hunt. 2000.
Shakespeare's The Tempest *and Other Late Romances.* Ed. Maurice Hunt. 1992.
Shelley's Frankenstein. Ed. Stephen C. Behrendt. 1990.
Shelley's Poetry. Ed. Spencer Hall. 1990.
Sir Gawain and the Green Knight. Ed. Miriam Youngerman Miller and Jane Chance. 1986.
Song of Roland. Ed. William W. Kibler and Leslie Zarker Morgan. 2006.
Spenser's Faerie Queene. Ed. David Lee Miller and Alexander Dunlop. 1994.
Stendhal's The Red and the Black. Ed. Dean de la Motte and Stirling Haig. 1999.
Sterne's Tristram Shandy. Ed. Melvyn New. 1989.
Stowe's Uncle Tom's Cabin. Ed. Elizabeth Ammons and Susan Belasco. 2000.
Swift's Gulliver's Travels. Ed. Edward J. Rielly. 1988.
Teresa of Ávila and the Spanish Mystics. Ed. Alison Weber. 2009.
Thoreau's Walden *and Other Works*. Ed. Richard J. Schneider. 1996.
Tolstoy's Anna Karenina. Ed. Liza Knapp and Amy Mandelker. 2003.
Vergil's Aeneid. Ed. William S. Anderson and Lorina N. Quartarone. 2002.
Voltaire's Candide. Ed. Renée Waldinger. 1987.

Whitman's Leaves of Grass. Ed. Donald D. Kummings. 1990.
Wiesel's Night. Ed. Alan Rosen. 2007.
Works of Oscar Wilde. Ed. Philip E. Smith II. 2008.
Woolf's Mrs. Dalloway. Ed. Eileen Barrett and Ruth O. Saxton. 2009.
Woolf's To the Lighthouse. Ed. Beth Rigel Daugherty and Mary Beth Pringle. 2001.
Wordsworth's Poetry. Ed. Spencer Hall, with Jonathan Ramsey. 1986.
Wright's Native Son. Ed. James A. Miller. 1997.